About this book

Perceptual, cognitive, and linguistic development is a direct reprint of Part II of *Developmental psychology: An Advanced Textbook*. Therefore, the chapter and page numbers correspond with that edition. The Subject Index is reproduced in its entirety from *Developmental psychology* as this was felt to be a help rather than a hindrance to the reader.

LEA

Contents

Preface

Developmental psychology is a unique, comprehensive, and important aspect of psychology for at least three reasons. First, developmental psychologists adopt a vital perspective on psychological theory and research. When psychologists conduct experiments in perception, investigate language, or study personality, they usually concentrate on perception, language, or personality in individuals of a particular age, be they children, college students, or the elderly. In so doing they may gain important knowledge about perception, language, or personality. To study psychological phenomena at only one point in the life cycle, however, is to limit knowledge about those phenomena by failing to consider the continuity or change in psychological phenomena that are the province of developmental psychology. Indeed, it could be argued that when we undertake the psychological study of any phenomenon, we must—wittingly or unwittingly—do so in a developmental context. The chapters in this volume on substantive areas of psychology, like perception, cognition, and language, by Bornstein, Kuhn, Sternberg, and Glietman and Wanner, and those on personality and social psychology by Lamb, Eisenberg, Hoffman, Ruble, and Achenbach, all demonstrate that the developmental perspective transcends and enriches any focus on particular points in the life span. One purpose of this volume, then, is to provide the inescapable and valuable developmental perspective on all substantive areas in psychology.

Second, developmental psychology is also a major subdiscipline in its own right. It has its own history and systems, as Dixon and Lerner point out; its own methodologies, as Seitz shows; its own tradition of measurement and analysis, as Hartmann demonstrates; and its own perspectives, as each of the authors illustrate. If studying psychology comprehensively involves attending to developmental psychology, then, there are systems, methodologies, and perspectives to be learned, and a second purpose of this volume is to clarify those systems, methodologies, and perspectives for the would-be student of psychology.

Third, the many aspects of developmental psychology have obvious and immediate relevance in applied issues and problems. Each of the chapters in this book illustrates the relevance of developmental psychology through reviews of the history, theory, and substance of the subdiscipline. In addition, questions about application are specifically emphasized in the chapter by Zigler and Finn-Stevenson.

In summary, developmental psychology provides a perspective that bears on all substantive phenomena in psychology, that applies across the life span, that has its own internal value, and that has manifest relevance to everyday life. It is for these reasons that we, the editors, have taken up the study of developmental psychology and have organized this introduction to developmental psychology for the advanced student of psychology.

This volume meets a need for texts in this area that can be used at the advanced undergraduate and introductory graduate levels. We knew of no other work available to the instructors of such courses when the first edition was prepared. Sadly, it is not possible today for any one or two individuals to convey, with proper sensitivity, the breadth of contemporary developmental psychology at this level. For that reason we invited several experts to prepare original, comprehensive, and topical treatments of the major areas of developmental psychology. We then organized and edited these chapters, with their cooperation and good will, into a single coherent volume. The success of this first edition encouraged us to prepare an updated second edition to which we have added chapters on measurement and statistics, and information processing, while expanding the purview of several other chapters.

Developmental Psychology has many purposes. We hope that readers will obtain a new perspective on psychology, a greater appreciation of the varied phenomena that constitute psychology, and a fundamental grounding in developmental psychology itself.

Work on this book was conducted in our private capacities, largely before we joined the NICHD staff. Our institutional affiliation is listed for informational purposes only, and no official support is implied or intended.

January 1988

Marc H. Bornstein
Michael E. Lamb
Bethesda, Maryland

4 Perceptual Development Across the Life Cycle

Marc H. Bornstein
New York University
and The National Institute of Child Health and Human Behavior

> all that a mammal does is fundamentally dependent on . . . perception,
> past or present.
>
> —D. O. Hebb (1953, p. 44)

INTRODUCTION

Perception constitutes a necessary "first step" in experiencing and interpreting the world, and for this reason philosophers, psychologists, physiologists, and physicists have been motivated to study it. Our everyday experiences provoke many challenging questions about perception. Some are quite general: How similar to our perceptions of them are properties or objects or events in the real world? How different? How is a stable world perceived amidst continuous environmental fluctuation? How are perceptual aspects of the world invested with meaning? Other questions which perceptual experience provokes are specific: How does the quality of *bitter* differ from the quality of *red?* How is a three-dimensional world seen when visual processing begins with only a two-dimensional image in the eye? How are the individual features of things synthesized into wholes?

Another reason for studying perception is epistemological and derives from questions about the origins and nature of human knowledge. Extreme views have been put forward by *empiricists,* who have asserted that all knowledge derives from the senses and grows by way of experience; and by *nativists,* who have reasoned that some kinds of knowledge could not possibly rely on experience and thus that humans enter the world with a sensory apparatus equipped at the very least to order and organize rudimentary knowledge.[1] These positions define the classic *nature–nurture* debate.

Philosophy focused attention especially on the development of perception near the beginning of life, since this was the period at which epistemologically meaningful issues, related to the origins of knowledge, could be most directly addressed. Thus, the study of perceptual development originally captured the philosopher's imagination since it promised to reveal what kind and how much of knowledge was inborn and what kind and how much of knowledge had to be learned. In this sense, studies of early perception essentially constitute experimental tests of nativist and empiricist theories of knowledge.

Developmental studies of perception provide many important kinds of information on normative processes in early perception concerning, for example, the quality, limits, and capacities of the sensory systems as they function and first develop. Textbooks in pediatrics portrayed the infant as "perceptually incompetent"; more recent studies of perception at the beginning of life contradict the validity of this characterization. Determining how the senses function in infancy also helps to specify the perceptual world of babies. If a substance tastes sweet to adults they may suppose that it tastes that way for infants too, and even that infants like it; in fact, however, taste receptors for sweetness may not even be present in infants or, if present, may not function or signal the same perception to infants as to adults. Defining normative capacity in early life also permits developmental comparisons of mature versus immature perceptual function, and studies of perception in infancy provide baseline data against which the normal course of maturation and the effects of experience over time can be assessed.

For these reasons, much of the impetus to study perceptual development has derived from philosophy, and much perceptual study has focused on infancy. Further, in the study of perceptual development both theory and methodology have played critical roles. The discussion of perceptual development in this chapter begins with a consideration of philosophical foundations and motivations for studying perceptual development experimentally, and then turns, almost immediately, to the contribution that theory—in particular, the nature–nurture controversy—has made to the understanding of perceptual development. The

---

[1]Early empiricists and nativists were interested in epistemology for both philosophical and theological reasons. Empiricism as championed by Locke, Berkeley, and Hume arrived in the eighteenth century and was greeted into a milieu of strong religious dogma: If ideas—faith and morals—were inborn in men, then God would transcend. But the empiricists rejected this supposition on epistemological grounds, and thereby inadvertently questioned articles of faith. If the mind of the babe is a *tabula rasa*, they reasoned, knowledge (even of God) must be acquired through sense experience. But no one has witnessed God or can know God this way. (Moreover, in Berkeley and Hume's analyses even mind degenerated into frail perceptions, memories, and feelings.) Kant parried for science as well as for religion: Perhaps skepticism is not an ultimate but a limited authority, and there is room for instinct and emotion alongside the knowledge and morality inherent in the mind's nature and structure.

next section of the chapter overviews perceptual development cum a taxonomy of methodologies used in studying it. This scheme of psychophysiological and behavioral methods is organized both to reflect different contemporary strategies of addressing major questions in perceptual development, and to underscore the fact that different perceptual methodologies require different degrees of inference. Although the chapter focuses on perceptual development in early life, reflecting the evolution of theory and of contemporary research, some significant principles of perceptual development in later childhood and in old age are also reviewed. Following the history of developmental research, this chapter emphasizes the "higher" senses of sight and hearing, but also includes some data about the "lower" senses—taste, smell, and touch—and about how sensory abilities interrelate and coordinate. The chapter concludes with a brief evaluation of the developmental effects engendered by altered perceptual worlds.

PHILOSOPHICAL UNDERPINNINGS

Among all of the different subject disciplines of developmental psychology, perception has historically been the one most intimately tied in with nature–nurture questions. What do we know before we have any experience in the world? How do we acquire knowledge about the world? The two main positions are *empiricism* and *nativism*.

Empiricism

The empiricist argument is described in several steps: Empiricists assert, first, that there is no endowed knowledge at birth; second, that all knowledge comes through the senses; and third, that perceptual development proceeds through associative experience. In specific, empiricists argue that stimuli in the world naturally provoke bodily sensations which, occurring close together in space or in time, give rise to more global "ideas" and thereby begin to invest the perceptual world with meaning. It is through association, empiricism explains, that separate raw sensations aggregate into meaningful perceptions. The empiricist's view of the nature of the mind was fostered by two separate, if similar, schools of thought. One derived from John Locke (1632–1704) who is reputed to have expressed the opinion that the infant mind is a *tabula rasa:* Mental life begins with nothing, and understanding of the world depends wholly on the accretion of experiences. A slightly different empiricist view can be attributed to William James (1842–1910): The world of the infant is a "blooming, buzzing confusion" out of which, presumably, the infant's experience helps to organize and create order and knowledge. According to empiricist belief, the naive infant does not share the perceptual world of the experienced adult. Empiricism is inherently developmental because, by whatever mechanism is postulated, children develop from perceptually naive to perceptually sophisticated beings.

Nativism

The belief that human beings begin life empty-headed, so to speak, is to many both philosophically intolerable and logically indefensible. Nativists originally argued that God did not create human beings as mindless, and that the knowledge which humans possess could not be achieved by learning alone in so short a span of time as childhood. As a consequence, philosophers like René Descartes (1596–1650) and Immanuel Kant (1724–1804) conceived of humans as endowed from birth with ideas or categories of knowledge that assist perceptual functions. They postulated innate perceptual categories for size, form, position, and motion, as well as for the more abstract conceptions of space and time. The nativist argument, contrary to the empiricist, holds that the mind naturally and from the beginning of life imposes order on sensory input, thereby transforming sensations into meaningful perceptions. According to the nativist account, the infant and adult share many of the same perceptual capacities, and the two perceive the world in much the same way. For abilities that are congenital, nativism is not a developmental theory; for abilities that mature, nativism is developmental in outlook.

Reflecting on the extreme nativist and empiricist opinions that have been championed and the vigor with which they have been argued, many have observed that perceptual development stands as a kind of battleground between nativists and empiricists on how the mind works. We can examine one exemplary skirmish, the question of how depth in space is perceived. This example is suitable for several reasons. First, depth perception is crucial to determining the spatial layout of the environment, to recognizing objects, and to guiding motor action. Second, the study of depth perception addresses an interesting psychophysical question, namely how the three-dimensional layout of the environment is constructed when the retina first codes only two-dimensional information. Third, debate on this question exemplifies the typical historical course: It originates with hotly contested nativist–empiricist philosophical debates that spanned the seventeenth to nineteenth centuries and culminates with experimentation in infancy and with contributions of animal physiology in the twentieth century.

A Nativist–Empiricist Debate

How Do Human Beings Come to Perceive Depth in Visual Space?

The Phase of Philosophy. Writing in *La Dioptrique* in 1638, René Descartes offered a straightforward answer to this question that assumed the mind's intuitive grasp of basic mathematical relations. Descartes believed that human thought operated as a system driven by natural law; knowledge was inborn. Thus Descartes introspected: Our two eyes form the base of a triangle whose apex is the object under our gaze. When we look at a faraway object, our eyes are nearly parallel and the base angles of the triangle approach 90°; whereas when our eyes converge on a nearby object, the base angles are acute. The closer the object, the more acute the angles. Descartes (1638/1824) concluded that distance is given by "an act of thinking which, being simple imagination [pure thought], does not entail [explicit] reasoning" (pp. 59–66). All of us are born with two eyes, and our eyes converge more for near than for far points of interest. But are we born with trigonometric tables in our heads?

A counterexplanation for depth perception (that actually built on Descartes') was put forward by empiricist George Berkeley (1685–1753) in his *Essay Towards a New Theory of Vision* of 1709. Berkeley (1709/1901, sect. xix) argued that humans do not deduce distance by "natural geometry":

> Since I am not conscious, that I make any such use of the Perception I have by the Turn of my Eyes. And for me to make those Judgments, and draw those Conclusions from it, without knowing that I do so, seems altogether incomprehensible.

Rather, Berkeley argued (sect. iii) that we come to know depth and distance through experience. He reflected:

> . . . when an *Object* appears Faint and Small, which at a near Distance I have experienced to make a vigorous and large Appearance; I instantly conclude it to be far off. And this, 'tis evident, is the result of *Experience;* without which, from the Faintness and Littleness, I should not have infer'd any thing concerning the Distance of *Objects.*

In essence, Berkeley claimed, we associate the large apparent size of objects (their "vigorousness") with bringing our two eyes close together in conjunction with the small cost of small arm movements when we reach for nearby objects; and we associate the small apparent size of objects (their "faintness") with the parallel position of our two eyes in conjunction with the large cost of large arm movements when we reach for faraway objects. Berkeley hypothesized that infants' consistent reaching in association with convergence of the eyes and the appearance of objects eventuates in their visual understanding of depth and distance.

Nativists objected to this experiential argument on logic. In the *Critique of Pure Reason* of 1781, Kant asserted that the human mind does not rely on experience for meaning, but innately organizes sensations into meaningful perceptions. Kant (1781/1924) argued that "Space is a necessary a priori idea":

> Space is not an empiricial conception, which has been derived from external experiences. For I could not be conscious that certain of my sensations are relative to something outside of me, that is, to something in a different part of space from that in which I myself am. . . . No experience of the external relations of sensible

things could yield the idea of space, because without the consciousness of space there would be no external experience whatever. (pp. 22–29)

Kant buttressed his theoretical argument with two compelling observations: First, that depth perception arises early in life and could not wait for extensive experience and learning; and, second, that individuals with limited experience give evidence that they perceive depth. The philosopher Arthur Schopenhauer (1788–1860), in support, invoked the case of Eva Lauk: Born without limbs and consequently restricted in her experience, Eva reportedly possessed normal intelligence and perceptions of space. (Eva could, of course, still move about. Modern studies of profoundly handicapped infants, like thalidomide babies, demonstrate that the inability to act motorically does not inhibit the development of normal perception and cognition; see Décarie, 1969.) Fueled thus, nativists deduced that (at least) some capacity to perceive depth must be inborn or directly given. This deduction impelled some investigators to seek specific biological substrates which might underlie the ability to perceive depth. At first such mechanisms were only postulated, as for example by the notable nineteenth-century physiologist Ewald Hering (1834–1918). In more modern times, sensory physiologists recording from single cells in the cortex of the brain have found evidence for them.

Immediately after Kant, however, the debate continued with a defense of empiricism. In his classic 1866 *Handbook of Physiological Optics,* Hermann von Helmholtz (1821–1894) rebutted nativism with the logical and rational argument that "intuition theory is an unnecessary hypothesis." Helmholtz (1866/1925, Vol. III, sect. 26) asserted that it is uneconomical to assume mechanisms of innate perception, especially when:

It is not clear how the assumption of these original "*space sensations*" can help the explanation of our visual perceptions, when the adherents of this theory ultimately have to assume in by far the great majority of cases that these sensations must be overruled by the better understanding which we get by experience. In that case it would seem to me much easier and simpler to grasp, that all apperceptions of space were obtained simply by experience.

After that blow by Helmholtz, gestalt psychologists restored credibility to the nativist views of Kant primarily by appealing to experimentation. At that time in scientific history, experimental investigation began to supplant philosophical speculation. In fact, psychology, which began in that century, was specifically organized to address just such issues. Given the enormous significance attributed to these questions, and the power of an argument supported by the test of trial, it is hardly surprising that an experimental psychology of perceptual development captured the imagination, effort, and energy of subsequent generations of researchers.

Some Science. Three lines of investigation exemplify how developmental researchers have addressed the question of the origins of depth perception. The three together are valuable since no one alone provides definitive information, but as a group they converge to suggest how depth perception develops. The starting point for one is familiar:

> Human infants at the creeping and toddling stage are notoriously prone to falls from more or less high places. They must be kept from going over the brink by side panels on their cribs, gates on their stairways, and the vigilance of adults. . . . Common sense might suggest that the child learns to recognize falling-off places by experience—that is, by falling and hurting himself. But is experience really the teacher? Or is the ability to perceive and avoid a brink part of the child's original endowment?

Faced with this lingering conundrum, Gison and Walk (1960) began to investigate depth perception experimentally in human infants using a "visual cliff" (p. 64). Babies were placed on a centerboard to one side of which was an illusory precipitous drop, whereas the other side clearly continued the support of the centerboard. In fact, however, a glass sheet provided firm support for the babies on *both* sides of the centerboard. Gibson and Walk found that a majority of infants between 6 and 14 months crawled across the "shallow" side of the apparatus from the centerboard when the mothers called them, but only a few crawled across the "deep" side. On this basis, Gibson and Walk concluded that depth perception must be present in infants as young as 6 months of age. However, the method used in these studies to assess depth perception is obviously limited by the capacity of infants to locomote, which they begin to do only in the second half of the first year of life. By this time the child may have plenty of experience with depth. To meet the challange of this critique, Campos, Langer, and Krowitz (1970) monitored a different activity, heart rate, in precrawling babies suddenly exposed either to the deep or to the shallow drop. By 2 months of age, babies who were exposed to the apparently deep side showed a heart-rate change, whereas babies exposed to the shallow side showed no comparable heart-rate change. These differences suggest that babies may perceive depth long before they locomote. Of course, the two depths may stimulate babies differently and thereby affect their sensitivity differently without yielding a *perception* of depth.

The "visual cliff" experiments constitute one way investigators have sought to explore the infant's capacity to perceive depth. A related situation that taps perception of depth in space is "looming." Looming describes the motion of an object moving directly toward us on a "hit path," and our reaction normally is to avoid impending collision as the object moves closer in space. Bower, Broughton, and Moore (1970) and Ball and Tronick (1971) reported that babies only a few weeks old show an "integrated avoidance response" to impending collision:

They observed that infants threw back their heads, shielded their faces with their hands, and even cried when an object moved at them along a hit path, but that babies failed to show these defensive reactions when the same object moved along a "miss path" or receded in space. In the experimental situation these investigators created, infants were not actually threatened with a solid object, but viewed a translucent screen onto which a silhouette of the three-dimensional object was cast. This technique cleverly avoids cueing infants with air changes on the face as an actual approaching object would. However, Yonas (1981) insightfully reasoned that, insofar as magnification of an object's outline is the optical cue to impending collision, the object's upper contour naturally moves upward in the field of view as an object advances. In "throwing their heads back," infants may simply be tracking the rapidly changing upward contour of the advancing image, giving only an impression of "avoidance." Yonas therefore conducted a series of control experiments involving babies of different ages under conditions in which the object's image remained on a hit path but its upper contour either remained at a constant level or rose. He determined that babies probably do track upper contours and that the "looming response" could not be demonstrated reliably in babies less than approximately 4 months of age. However, Yonas also observed that babies as young as 1 month showed a reasonably consistent eye-blink response to approaching objects.

A third line of infant research that bears on the question of depth perception involves infants' sensitivities to isolated visual cues of depth. Psychophysicists traditionally categorize binocular convergence and accommodation as "primary" cues, and linear perspective, texture gradient, and shading as "secondary" cues (e.g., Hochberg, 1978). Convergence, for example, depends on an organism's capacities to fixate an object binocularly and to fuse the two separate retinal images into one. If infants rely on convergence of the eyes to respond to depth, as Descartes and Berkeley proposed, theorists need to show that the eyes indeed *can* converge. We have all noted, however, that in some babies one eye wanders, and many seem unable to fix an object with both eyes consistently. Empirical studies of infants' tracking stationary and dynamic targets have revealed only minimal convergence at 1 month, but more regular convergence by 2 to 3 months (e.g., Banks, 1980; Fox, Aslin, Shea, & Dumais, 1980). It is at this time that infants also first display sensitivity to the deep side of the visual cliff (Campos et al., 1970). Secondary cues do not seem to be available to infants before 6 months of age. One study showed that infants older than 6 months would direct their reaching to the apparently closer side of a photograph of a window rotated in depth, whereas infants only 1 month younger would not direct their reaching to the pictorially nearer side of the display although they would reach directionally when presented with a real window rotated in depth (Yonas & Granrud, 1985). When Granrud, Yonas, and Pettersen (1984) directly compared monocular and binocular cues for depth perception in a similar reaching experi-

ment, they found that infants' perceptions of object distances were more ver-
idical under binocular viewing than under monocular viewing.

Studies of the visual cliff, looming, and monocular and binocular sensitivity
in human babies together suggest that depth perception is relatively poor up until
about 2 months after birth, at which time this perceptual ability rapidly develops.
We still do not know, however, precisely when depth perception arises or what
course it follows in early development. Nor do these findings mean that the
development of depth perception is complete by 4 to 6 months of age. They only
show that infants have the capacity for *relative* distance perception by this time.
Although binocularity, for example, provides an organism with information
about *absolute* distance, it can do so only for known interocular distances; the
rapidly changing distance between the eyes in growing infants would require
frequent recalibration. Consequently, some investigators have argued that
achieving absolute distance calibration may depend on nonvisual sources of
information. Echoing Berkeley, they suggest that reaching is one valuable source
of calibrating absolute distance, and that self-produced locomotion is another.
More specifically, theorists such as Piaget (1954) have argued that infants can
tell the absolute distance of objects in near space only after they have had
experience with reaching, and the distance of objects in far space (i.e., beyond
reach) only after having crawled.

When perceptual psychologists studying infancy reach an impasse in their
efforts to resolve such questions, they frequently resort to other argumentation
and data such as behavioral and physiological information provided by infrahuman animals. Animals offer special circumstances for research since they
lend themselves to experimentation and manipulation that are sometimes not
possible with humans. So, for example, animals have provided valuable behavioral information about the ontogency of depth perception. A variety of species
has been tested in the visual cliff; some of these, like chicks, move about on their
own within a day after birth. All show avoidance of the cliff, suggesting that
depth perception may develop very early and independent of motor experience.
Of course, it is still possible that depth perception is innate and congenital in
some species but not in others, including human beings.

The general premise of the developmentalist's appeal to physiological data is
that perceptions ought to have identifiable neural substrates, and if those substrates are found they can contribute evidence to the nativist–empiricist argument. Continuing the example from depth perception: The fusion of two separate
images such as are produced by the two eyes to yield one image (stereopsis)
enhances depth perception. Hubel and Weisel (1970) and Barlow, Blakemore,
and Pettigrew (1967) identified single cells in the visual systems of cats and of
monkeys which are exquisitely sensitive to such fusion. Although these sorts of
results suggest some physiological basis for perception, developmentalists usually exercise caution about reductionism of this sort. Because such cells exist in

other mature species does not mean that they exist in infant forms of those species; because such cells exist in lower species does not mean that they exist in human beings; and because such cells exist at all, of course, does not mean that they signal "depth" in a psychologically or functionally meaningful way.

A Conclusion.   Although empirical studies such as these clearly advance the understanding of perceptual function beyond philosophical debate, scientific investigation does not necessarily guarantee resolution. Researchers on both sides of the issue are quick to point out that there can be no final triumph for nativism or for empiricism. *No matter how early in life depth perception can be demonstrated, the ability still rests on some experience; no matter how late its emergence, it can never be proved that only experience has mattered.*

Looking back over this example, it is clear that theoretical, philosophical, and even theological differences of opinion about epistemology have burned like embers in the minds of men for centuries, now and again igniting into flaming controversy over whether human ideas, abilities, and capacities are innately given or the products of experience. The sparks of speculation which flew in bygone days generated more heat than light. In modern times, science has added experimental behavioral evidence, in addition to observations from animals and from physiology, to fan the ancient fires.

Summary

By far the two most prominent themes in perceptual study have been nativism and empiricism—opinions about how much or how little organisms are capable of before they have had experience, and what sorts of roles experience plays in development. Indeed, in no other area of psychology has the nativism–empiricism controversy been perceived as so meaningful or legitimate as in the study of perceptual development. One connected line of thought and research, extending from Locke and Berkeley down to modern empiricists like D. O. Hebb, holds that perceptions arise out of experiencing the world. A parallel line, extending from Descartes and Kant down through modern nativists like Max Wertheimer, holds that perceptions are competences already a part of the armamentarium of even the very young child. Different theorists' arguments for depth perception exemplify these divergent points of view: Nativists see the child as immediately capable of perceiving depth because of how the nervous system functions, whereas empiricists see the child as capable of that only after repeated experience in associating movements of the eyes, arms, and body with small and large images of objects. Thus, constructionist theories such as Piaget's assume that the two-dimensional retinal image must be supplemented with movement to give a scale of depth; but direct perception theories, such as James and Eleanor Gibsons', maintain that space is automatically perceived in those relations among higher-order variables (such as texture) to which the sensory systems have evolved acute sensitivity. Not every theory or theorist fits neatly into a nativist or an empiricist perspective; there are elements of both in all developmental theories. More important, despite the fact that they are sometimes conceived as either-or contributors to development, nature and nurture interact.

NATURE AND NURTURE

The potential ways in which the forces of nature and nurture may interact in the course of development can be conceptualized in a simple and comprehensive manner. Figure 4.1 shows different possible courses of development before the onset of experience, and the several possible ways experience may influence eventual perceptual outcomes after. First, there is the possibility that perceptual abilities or functions develop fully before the onset of experience, after which they require experience only to be maintained—and that, without relevant experience, these abilities or functions may be lost. Second, perceptual abilities or functions may develop only partially before the onset of experience, after which experience operates in one of three ways: Relevant experience may facilitate further development of an ability or function or may attune that ability or function; experience may serve to maintain the ability or function at the partial level of development it attained before the onset of experience; or, without relevant

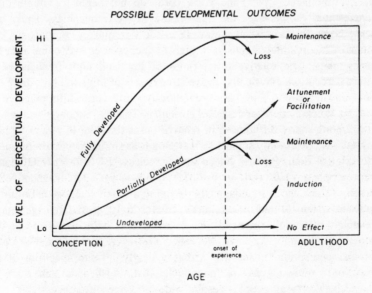

FIG. 4.1. Possible developmental outcomes given different levels of perceptual development before the onset of experience and different experiences afterward. (From Aslin, 1981. Copyright Academic Press. Reprinted with permission.)

experience, the ability or function may be lost. (Of course, experience per se may not be altogether necessary where the perceptual ability or function would continue to mature as a reflection of the genetic blueprint.) Finally, third, a perceptual ability or function undeveloped at the onset of experience may be induced by relevant experience; again, without such experience, the function or ability may not emerge.

To flesh out this skeletal introduction to how nature and nurture may interact in perceptual development, we can examine, however briefly, a perceptual domain in which these several possibilities occur. This domain is the narrow but perennially important one of *speech perception*. Just a bit of background is required before going into the scheme itself. Recall that sounds are essentially different sine-wave frequencies produced simultaneously, and that speech is the complex array of different frequencies produced at different intensities over time. Languages abstract particular subsets from the universe of all possible speech sounds (phonetics), which they invest with meaning (phonemics). One dimension along which certain phonemes in many languages are distinguished is their "voicing." Differences in voicing are heard when a speaker produces different frequencies of sound waves at slightly different times. In voicing, a sound like /b/ (pronounced "ba") is produced by vibrating the vocal cords and producing higher frequencies *before* or *at* the time the lips are opened and low-frequency energy is released—/b/ is a voiced phoneme. By contrast, for sounds like /p/ (pronounced "pa") the vocal cords do not begin to vibrate higher frequencies until some *after* the lips release lower frequencies. Thus, high-frequency components of a sound may precede low-frequency components, components may begin simultaneously, or high-frequency ones may come after low-frequency ones. The relative onset times of low and high frequencies cue phonemic perception. Physically, the relative onsets of low- and high-frequency components of a sound may vary *continuously;* however, adults perceive differences in voicing more or less *categorically.* That is, although we can distinguish among many differences in relative onset times of low- and high-frequency sounds, we classify some different sounds as similar while discriminating others. English distinguishes voiced and voiceless /b/ from /p/. Of course, different people say /b/ and /p/ in different ways, yet adult listeners seldom misidentify these speech sounds, as they employ implicit category definitions to allot a sound to the /b/ and /p/ categories. Interestingly, cross-language research has revealed that adults in nearly all cultures hear only one, two, or three categories of voicing: The three are called *prevoiced, voiced,* and *voiceless.* Categorical perception means that across a nearly infinite spectrum of possibilities, only three tokens are functionally distinguished; and they are distinguished by nearly all peoples despite wide language differences.

Many researchers speculate that phenomena so ubiquitous, consistent, circumscribed, and significant in human behavior as perceptual categories of speech might have a biological foundation. To test this assumption, Eimas,

Siqueland, Jusczyk, and Vigorito (1971) sought to discover whether preverbal human infants would perceive acoustic changes in voicing categorically; that is, in a manner parallel to adult phonemic perception. Using a technique called *habituation* that relies on babies first getting bored when the same sight or sound is presented over and over again, and then expressing interest in a novel sight or sound, these investigators arranged to "ask" infants some simple same–different questions about their auditory perceptions. They found that 1- and 4-month-olds behaved as though they perceived speech sounds in the adultlike categorical manner: Babies distinguished /b/ from /p/, but not examples of two different /b/s. That is, babies categorize different sounds as either voiced or voiceless long before they use language or even have extensive experience in hearing language. This might suggest that categorical perception is essentially innate. Returning to Fig. 4.1, it would seem that categorical perception of phonemes most closely fits the topmost developmental function.

However, this experiment did not in fact conclusively rule out the role of experience in development. The subjects were born into monolingual English-speaking families in which the voiced–voiceless distinction they discriminated is common, as in *ba*by versus *pa*pa. It could be that categorical perception is partially developed at the onset of experience, and facilitated or attuned over the 1 to 4 months of experience these babies had prior to the experiment. It could also be that categorical perception is undeveloped at the onset of experience, and that experience with the language, however little, quickly induces sophisticated auditory perceptions.

Recall that surveys of the world's languages show that only three categories of voicing are common—prevoiced, voiced, and voiceless—but that not all languages use all these categories. Eimas et al. (1971) had only tested an English category in their babies. Are all or only some of these categories universal among infants? That is, do infants from communities where different patterns of voicing prevail in the adult language make the same categorical distinctions? If infants everywhere had some or all of the same three categories, although the adults in their cultures did not, the data would go a long way toward classifying the possible developmental courses of categorical perception of speech. To address this question, Lasky, Syrdal-Lasky, and Klein (1975) tested infants from Spanish-speaking (Guatemalan) monolingual familes. Spanish was chosen because the voiced–voiceless distinction is not quite the same as in English. The 4- and 6-month-olds from Spanish-speaking families discriminated the English voiced–voiceless sound contrast rather than the Spanish one. Likewise, Streeter (1976) found that Kenyan 2-month-olds from families that speak Kikuyu categorized the English voicing contrast that is not present in Kikuyu as well as a Kikuyu prevoiced–voiced contrast that is not present in English. These two studies confirm that at least some perceptual capacities develop before the onset of experience; and the Kikuyu study also suggests that perceptions can be induced with just two months of experience (unless Kikuyu babies and American babies are biologically different in some way). Interestingly, Spanish-speaking and Kikuyu-speaking adults perceive (though they do not use) the universal English voicing contrast, but they perceive it only weakly. Between infancy and maturity, therefore, a perceptual discrimination that is present at birth atrophies because of lack of experience, although it is not wholly lost. Similarly, American infants only 2 to 3 months of age discriminate /r/ from /l/ (Eimas, 1975), and so presumably do Japanese babies; yet Japanese adults fail to discriminate these sounds (Goto, 1971; Miyawaki, Strange, Verbrugge, Liberman, Jenkins, & Fujimura, 1975). Without experience to maintain it, this discrimination, too, appears to be lost.

These phenomena have been investigated systematically and confirmed in other languages. One study found that English 6-month-olds could discriminate pairs of Hindi speech contrasts (not used in English) as well as Hindi adults do, although English speakers 4 years of age and older could not. A follow-up study tested the generalizability of these findings and attempted to pinpoint the developmental period when the loss of this discriminative ability occurred. English 6-month-olds distinguish pairs of Thompson (native Indian) speech contrasts not used in English as well as Salish (Thompson-speaking) adults, but this ability is lost in the first year of life: 6- to 8-month-olds were found to perform the discrimination, 8- to 10-month-olds were found to do so more poorly, and 10- to 12-month-olds were found to be as poor at discriminating as were older children and adults (Werker, Gilbert, Humphrey, & Tees, 1981; Werker & Tees, 1983).

The literature in categorical perception of phonemes has developed so as to illustrate almost fully the scheme depicted in Fig. 4.1. Certain perceptions seem to be universal and developed at birth; they are maintained by linguistic experiences of the child, but may be lost if absent from the language heard by the child. Other perceptions, present at birth, can be altered by experience. Still other perceptions can be induced in children through immersion in a particular linguistic environment.

PERCEPTUAL DEVELOPMENT
AND THE METHODOLOGIES USED TO STUDY IT

In practice, the study of perceptual development is virtually synonymous with studies of infancy. This is so for three reasons. First, as we learned, perceptual study as a whole was given strong impetus by the nature–nurture debate. To study perception was to address this controversy, and to do so effectively was to study perception near the beginning of life. Second, by the time human beings reach toddlerhood their perceptions are (thought to be) reasonably mature. Thus, much of the "action" in perceptual development seems to take place in infancy. The third reason that the study of perceptual development has been circumscribed to early life is that perceptual study in the balance of the life cycle, predominantly in adulthood, normally falls outside the province of developmental psychology; it belongs to a different area in psychology—the study of sensation and perception proper. Research on adults is included in studies of perceptual development only when certain ontogenetic comparisons are called for. However, the early developmental focus of perceptual study challenges research investigators formidably; the reason is clear.

Perception is private. There is no way for one person to know what other people's perceptions of *red, C-sharp, sweet, pungent,* or *soft* are like without drawing inferences from their reports or from their behaviors. From a developmental point of view, the study of perception from young adulthood through old age poses little difficulty in this respect since mature individuals can readily be instructed to report about or to behave in certain ways that communicate their perceptions. In childhood and especially in infancy, however, the communication barrier poses a fundamental impediment to perceptual study. Moreover, infants are motorically underdeveloped. As a consequence, therefore, our knowledge of early perception must be inferred from reports and behaviors of varying fidelity and credibility.

Different methodologies available for the study of perception vary in the power of *inference* they allow about another observer's perceptions. Some methods yield only weak inference, whereas others yield stronger inference. The term can best be defined with reference to an illustration. If we ascertain that a sound applied at the ear of an observer produces a regular pattern of electrical response in the brain, then we can feel certain that some internal connections between the peripheral sensory system (the ear) and the central nervous system (the brain) are present. However, regularity of brain response tells us nothing, unfortunately, about how or even whether the observer actually *perceives* the sound; hence, inference about perception based on electrophysiological data is weak. (Even if two different stimuli gave rise to two distinctly different patterns of electrical activity in the brain, we still would not know whether the two stimuli were perceived, or whether they were perceived as different.) If, however, we were able to instruct or train the observer to respond behaviorally to a sound, or in one way to one sound and in another way to another sound, our inference would be so strong that, barring artifact, we would possess incontrovertible evidence of perception. The two main response systems for the study of perception in nonverbal observers that have been explored are psychophysiological and behavioral; several different techniques within each have been developed. For purposes of comparison, the methodologies reviewed here are ordered along a hypothetical continuum roughly in terms of the strength of inference they permit. For purposes of illustration, examples are drawn mainly from the now extensive literature on infancy.

It is interesting to note that despite important differences among methodologies, virtually all techniques developed to study perception have been engineered to address a surprisingly small number of perceptual questions. Two important questions have to do with whether the observer detects the presence of a stimulus—in the psychophysicist's terms, whether the stimulus passes above an *absolute threshold*—and whether the stimulus is meaningful for perception. A third, related question has to do with whether the observer detects the difference between two stimuli—whether the stimuli surpass a *difference threshold*.

To forecast, this section of the chapter summarizes and illustrates main principles and findings in early perceptual development. To do so, it is necessary to view the data in different substantive domains of perception as inextricably linked with common methodologies used to obtain them.

The Foundations of Perceiving and Psychophysiological Techniques

Psychological investigations of perceptual development that have adopted physiological techniques have approached the study of development via assessment of both the central and autonomic nervous systems.

CNS Function.   Research efforts related to perceptual development focused in the central nervous system (CNS) have been pitched at three general levels—neurological anatomy, single-cell physiology, and gross cortical electrical activity. Questions asked at the level of anatomical investigation concern the structural ontogeny of the perceptual apparatus, with a view to its relation to function. A presumption of this research strategy is that structure (anatomy) is necessary for function (perception), and so understanding function is, in a sense, enriched by the knowledge of underlying structure. (Perceptual theorists have on occasion turned this argument on its head and postulated the existence of structures based on known function; an example is Teller & Bornstein, 1986.) Note, however, that structure is a necessary but not a sufficient condition for function: Babies have legs but do not walk. Thus, insofar as inference about perception is concerned, evidence based on anatomical structure alone is very weak.

The course of anatomical development of the sensory systems has received more than modest attention, leading to the conclusion that human beings are reasonably well prepared for perception once extrauterine life begins. By the midtrimester of prenatal life, the eye and the visual system (Bronson, 1974; Maurer, 1975), the ear and the auditory system (Hecox, 1975), the nose and the olfactory system (Tuchmann-Duplessis, Auroux, & Haegel, 1975), and the tongue and the gustatory system (Bradley & Stearn, 1967; Humphrey, 1978) are on their way to being structurally and functionally mature. In general, two principles of development operate within and among sensory systems. Within systems, maturation tends to proceed from the periphery to the center so that, for example, the eye differentiates structurally and reaches functional maturity before the visual cortex does (e.g., Abramov, Gordon, Hendrickson, Hainline, Dobson, & LaBossiere, 1982; Conel, 1939–1959). Among systems in all species of birds and mammals, different senses tend to come into functional maturity in sequence (Gottlieb, 1983): vestibular, cutaneous, olfactory, auditory, and visual. Turkewitz and Kenny (1982, 1985) have persuasively argued the biopsychological advantages of this staggered program of development in terms of reduced mutual competition as well as heightened organization and integration.

The second level of psychophysiological investigation has focused even more narrowly on the development and specificity of individual neurons in different sensory systems. Since the advent of microelectrode recording techniques in physiology, it has been possible to study the sensitivities of single neurons in the brain. Such neurophysiological recording reveals that individual cells code specific characteristics of the environment. So-called "trigger features" of environmental stimulation to which individual neurons in the visual system, for example, have been found to be sensitive include wavelength of light, orientation of form, direction of movement, and others. Though this area of research is exciting and very provocative for the study of perceptual development, several questions render it of limited current value and indicate that findings in the area can be adopted only with caution. For example, although single neurons are sensitive to properties of environmental stimulation, their actual rule (if any) in perception is largely undefined. Further, since virtually all studies of single units have been conducted in infrahuman species, usually in the cat or monkey, the direct relevance or applicability of single-unit studies to human perception is still open to question. Finally, a very intriguing but still largely open question for perceptual development in this field is whether single units are innately sensitive to their "trigger features"; it could be that sensitivity grows with or reflects experience.

The third level of research into central nervous system contributions to perception addresses perceptual development most directly in intact human beings, and derives from measures of overall electrical activity of the developing brain. The principal electrophysiological technique involved is the cortical evoked potential (CEP). The CEP derives from the complex sequence of electrical currents that are normally produced in the brain and can be derived from the electroencephalograph (EEG). When a stimulus is presented to the eye or to the ear, for example, it gives rise to a characteristic waveform of activity in particular parts of the brain. Through computer averaging techniques, this waveform can be isolated from the EEG as a whole.

Studies of the development of the CEP show that the waveform begins simply, is slower to start in response to a stimulus in infancy than in adulthood, but has a relatively stable amplitude across the life cycle. As is shown in the top panel of Fig. 4.2, the CEP for a visual stimulus can be detected in preterm babies when it assumes a simple form, and it is already relatively complex at birth. The waveform remains quite variable up to 3 years of age, however. As can be seen in the bottom panel, the time between stimulus onset and the appearance of the major positive crest (P_2) of the CEP shows a reasonably orderly decrease with age until it reaches adult values. The amplitude of the CEP (not shown) follows a more complex course of development: It diminishes with age up to birth, then increases to 3 years of age, then decreases again so that, in essence, adult and

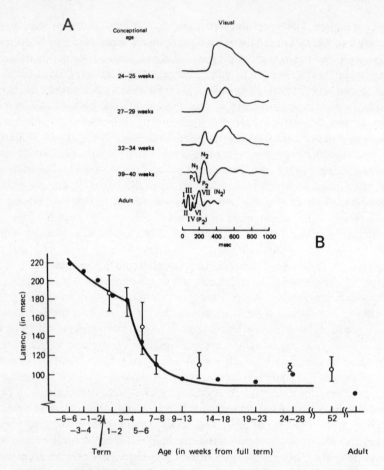

FIG. 4.2. Development of the form and latency of the cortical-evoked potential before and after term. A: Cortical responses evoked by visual stimuli in preterm infants, term newborns, and adults. (Derivations are bipolar: Oz-Pz for the visual response. Surface negatively in plotted upwards.) B: Latency (in msec) of the major positive component of the visual cortical-evoked response as a function of age (in weeks from term). (The solid and open dots represent data from two different experiments. The vertical lines passing through the open dots signify ± 1 SD for a group of 21 subjects.) (From Berg & Berg, 1979. Copyright John Wiley. Reprinted with permission.)

newborn show similar amplitudes. It is important to note that these principles, though broad (Berg & Berg, 1979), are descriptive of normal infants shown particular visual stimuli; variations among infants or stimuli compromise these generalizations.

Sound sensitivity in infants has also been measured via the CEP. Indeed, through unique placement of a miniature loudspeaker next to the ear and an electrode clipped to the scalp of the fetus *in utero*, Scibetta, Rosen, Hochberg, and Chik (1971) recorded auditory-evoked potentials in the last trimester of pregnancy. Since the middle ear reaches maturity in structure by the sixth month after conception (Hecox, 1975) and at this time fetuses respond to auditory stimuli behaviorally (Birnholz & Benacerraf, 1983), it may be that babies still in the womb can "overhear" parental conversations (Spence & De Casper, 1984). Of course, it is important to consider that human voice qualities may be altered for the fetus, given acoustic transduction characteristics of the uterus, amniotic fluid, and abdominal wall of the mother.

Studies of anatomy, single-cell physiology, and gross electrical activity of the brain all contribute to our understanding of perception, its bases, and its development. Perhaps evoked potential studies have provided the most useful data thus far.

ANS Function.   A second widely applied psychophysiological approach to gaining information about perception early in life has developed through monitoring infants' autonomic nervous system (ANS) responses in perceptual tasks. Orientation reflexes, respiration, and heart rate are commonly measured, even with the youngest observers. Figure 4.3 shows a newborn baby "wired" for perceptual study.

Among several measures, heart rate has proved to be particularly useful in the research on early perception (Berg & Berg, 1979; Porges, 1974). Heart rate has

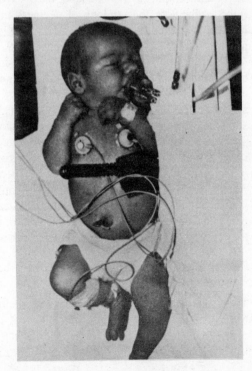

FIG. 4.3. Measurement of autonomic nervous system activity in the newborn. Two-day-old infant with heart rate electrodes attached (two on chest, and the indifferent electrode on right leg), pneumobelt between the abdomen and chest [to measure respiration], and an automatic nipple in place [to deliver fluid and measure amplitude and frequency of suckling] (From Lipsitt, 1977.)

been substituted for crawling in testing young infants' perceptions of depth on the visual cliff; heart rate has been widely used to assess other visual, auditory, gustatory, and olfactory perceptions in infants. Further studies have even connected heart rate to more complex social-cognitive perceptions. Campos (1976), for example, collected heart-rate data in the context of 5- and 9-month-old infants' global responses in unstressed and distressed situations. Infants in this age range are beginning to fear strangers. As a stranger enters, approaches, intrudes, and then departs from them, infants' facial expressions change, going from simple interest and becoming increasingly negative; they go from a frown to a wimper to a cry; and concomitantly their heart rates first decelerate from a resting level (a common index of interest) and then accelerate during distress (as much as 30 beats per minute in 9-month-olds). Thus, heart rate accompanies changes of affect and serves, as here, as a converging measure of perception.

Our understanding of the foundations of perception has been enhanced considerably by studies of nervous system structure and function. They inform us as to the existence and operation of structures, and of the connections among structures, that underpin perception. In immature organisms, psychophysiological indices often substitute valuably for behavioral ones as objective and sensitive measures of perception, though many factors other than those under experimental scrutiny can influence psychophysiological responses. The psychophysiological approach has also proved valuable for the light it sheds on atypical development. For example, the evoked potential has been used successfully to diagnose the etiology of deafness in infancy: If the infant does not respond to sound, the evoked potential can at least indicate whether or not brain pathways are intact (Hecox & Galambos, 1974; Schulman-Galambos, 1979).

Despite these several virtues, the contributions of psychophysiology to the understanding of perception have been limited, and they require the highest degree of inference. That a cortex exists, and a stimulus presented to the sensory system creates an identifiable pattern of cortical activity, is no guarantee that the stimulus registers in *perceptually meaningful and functional ways* for the observer, whether infant or adult. Some autonomic system measures fare somewhat better in this regard, but they still do not provide convincing evidence of *conscious perception* since the body may respond in the absence of awareness. Access to conscious perceptual function is only obtainable through behavioral report. Behavioral techniques constitute the second main class of approaches to perceptual development, and from the point of view of understanding perception they represent a profound improvement over psychophysiological techniques.

Perceptual Development in Different Modalities and Behavioral Techniques

To assess perceptual development early in life, developmental psychologists have invented a wide variety of behavioral techniques. Prominent measures depend on natural responses and reactions, preferences, and learning. Again, this list is at least implicitly ordered according to the strength of inference each paradigm yields about perception. Perception in infancy and early childhood can be illustrated with data from studies that use each of these techniques.

First Vision and Corneal Reflection.   In the 1960s, Kessen, Haith, and Salapatek argued in a series of experimental reports that it ought to be possible to assess visual function at birth simply by "looking at looking." These investigators photographed the reflection of a stimulus in the cornea of the baby's eye. They assumed that "perceiving" is in some degree implied by the infant's "fixating" the stimulus—voluntary visual orienting so as to bring a stimulus into the line of visual regard—and that where a baby looks thus indicates visual selectivity and, hence, visual perception. Until these studies, basic questions such as whether or not newborn babies see were unanswered. In more than 20 years since the technique was introduced, many experimenters have adopted the logic of this inquiry and its methodology (see Fig. 4.4), but the original findings are still among the most provocative and still demonstrate many basic principles: Even in the first hours after birth, infants tend to look at parts of stimuli where there is information (usually high-contrast features such as the angles and along the contours of figures) instead of scanning randomly about the background or over the central part of a figure. Scan patterns seem to indicate that infants from the first days of life consistently and actively orient to visual information in the environment, and studies of such patterns indicate not just what babies look at,

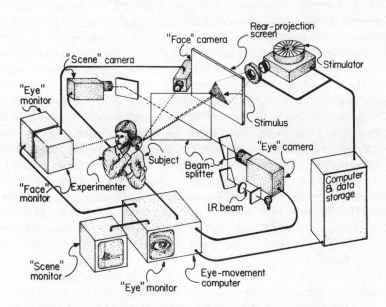

FIG. 4.4. A schematic representation of an eye movement recording system designed for use with infants. (From Hainline & Lemerise, 1982. Copyright Academic Press. Reprinted with permission.)

but how scan patterns develop and are distributed over different visual patterns. For example, scanning faces versus geometric forms speaks directly to perceptual processing (Hainline & Lemerise, 1982; Haith, 1980; Maurer, 1975, 1985).

Preferences and Natural Reactions in Different Modalities.   One day while playing with his daughter, James Mark Baldwin, one of the founders of modern developmental psychology, observed that the young girl would consistently reach for a yellow cube over a blue one. The girl preferred one to the other independent of where the toy cubes were located. From this Baldwin deduced that young Helen saw color because her preferential reaching gave evidence that she discriminated yellow from blue. Although at the time Baldwin's logic met with some resistance, in the late 1950s and early 1960s Fantz revived Baldwin's argument, grounding it this time in infant *looking* rather than reaching. Fantz argued that if a baby looked preferentially at one stimulus over another in a paired-choice design, irrespective of the spatial location of the two stimuli, that preference could be taken to indicate detection or discrimination. Today Fantz's argument is the bedrock of the most popular infant research techniques. Infants visually prefer and discriminate faces over nonfacial configurations of the same elements, some pattern organizations over others, and some colors over others; and they orient and attend preferentially and discriminatively to select sounds and smells.

Studies of organized scanning indicate at a minimum *that* newborns and young infants see something when they look at patterns, but do not reveal *how well* they see. In their study of acuity, Fantz, Ordy, and Udelf (1962) capitalized on the observation that infants prefer heterogeneous to homogeneous patterns. They posted pairs of patterns for babies to look at, in which one member of the pair was always gray and the other a set of stripes that varied systematically in width. (The two stimuli were always matched in overall brightness.) If pattern is consistently preferred, the stripe width which fails to evoke a preference for the baby is the one that marks the limit of the baby's ability to tell stripes from the solid gray. (At some point, stripe width can become so fine as to fade into homogeneity for all of us.) By this measure, 2-week-olds showed 20/800 vision (in Snellen notation), whereas 5½-month-olds showed 20/70 vision. Acuity improves steadily from infancy, until adult (20/20) levels are reached at about 5 years of age. In the 20 years since Fantz's original study, techniques for measuring infant visual acuity have grown in sophistication (e.g., Teller, 1979). Fortunately, measures of visual acuity by behavioral and electrophysiological methods agree well with Fantz's findings and also converge with one another (see Dobson & Teller, 1978).

Preferential looking and reaching have been used to investigate a wide variety of perceptual abilities in infancy, especially in pattern vision (Karmel & Maisel, 1975; Yonas & Granrud, 1985) and in color vision (Bornstein, 1981; Teller & Bornstein, 1986). Other sorts of preferences and reactions have been used to study perceptual development in other sensory systems as well. We know from experience that soothing pats can quiet a fussy infant, whereas the sharp stab of paper causes them distress; newborns can clearly feel, but research has not progressed far in helping us understand how acutely infants perceive stimuli by touch. Ruff (1984) filmed infants of 6, 9, and 12 months of age and later scored both general behaviors (e.g., touching) as well as specific ones (e.g., alternating between looking and mouthing). She found that mouthing decreased over the second half of the first year, whereas both fingering and more precise forms of manipulation increased (accompanying the further development of fine motor coordination). Ruff also found that infants vary their manipulatory activities to match the object being explored. When she changed stimuli for the infants once they had had the chance to explore them in some detail, Ruff found that infants changed in their patterns of tactual exploration so as to maximize the acquisition of information about the new stimulus. For example, they responded to a change in an object's shape by rotating it more, and to a change in its texture by fingering it more; and in both cases they threw, pushed, and dropped new stimuli less than familiar ones.

One of the clearest demonstrations of preference belongs to Steiner (1977, 1979), who investigated newborns' differential reactions to tastes and smells by their facial expressions. Psychophysical evidence is compelling that four basic qualities together exhaust taste experience: sweet, salt, sour, and bitter (Cowart, 1981). Tastes are, as we know, very powerful stimuli in learning: A single experience of nausea associated with a particular taste is enough for someone to avoid that taste virtually forever (Garcia & Koelling, 1966). Steiner gave newborn infants sweet, sour, or bitter substances to taste, and he photographed their "gustofacial" reactions—all prior to the very first time any of the babies ate. Figure 4.5 shows the results. A sweet stimulus evoked an expression of "satisfaction," often accompanied by a slight smile and by sucking movements. A sour stimulus evoked lip-pursing, often accompanied or followed by wrinkling of the nose and blinking the eyes. A bitter stimulus evoked an expression of dislike and disgust or rejection, often followed by spitting or even by movements preparatory to vomiting. These taste discriminations are organized at a primitive level of the brain, since they also appear, as Steiner reported, in babies who have no cortex.

Davis (1928) conducted a classic "cafeteria" study with babies. She reported on the food preferences of three infants allowed to choose what they wanted to eat beginning at 8 months when they were still exclusively breast-fed. At each meal, infants were served a tray with a variety of meats, vegetables, cereals, fruits, and liquids. Infants began by trying everything that was available; then they chose what they liked (though different babies developed different preferences). Although they went on food binges and strikes from time to time, on the whole the babies selected a variety and amount of food adequate for good nutrition. One baby who had rickets reportedly drank cod liver oil until he was well!

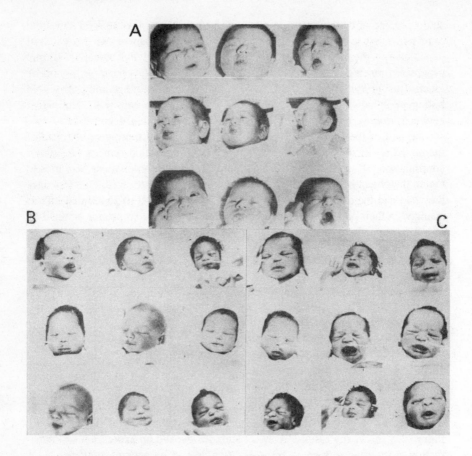

FIG 4.5. Gustatory and olfactory sensitivity in newborn babies. A: Infants' gustofacial response to the taste of sweet (left column), sour (middle column), and bitter (right column). B: Infants' nasofacial response to the smell of vanilla (B columns) and raw fish (C columns). (After Steiner, 1977.)

Steiner (1977, 1979) also observed neonates' "nasofacial" expressions and their attempts to withdraw from odors placed on cotton swabs held beneath the nose. Steiner found that newborns respond in qualitatively different ways to different food odors. Butter and banana odors elicit positive expressions; vanilla, either positive or indifferent expressions; a fishy odor, some rejection; and the odor of rotten eggs, unanimous rejection.

Cernoch and Porter (1985) systematically compared breast-fed with bottle-fed infants only 12 to 18 days old for their olfactory recognition of mother, father, and stranger. Babies were photographed while exposed to pairs of gauze pads worn in the underarm area by an adult on the previous night, and the infants' durations of orienting were recorded. Only breast-feeding infants oriented preferentially and exclusively to their own mothers' scents, thereby giving evidence of discriminating their mothers. Infants from neither group recognized their fathers preferentially, nor did bottle-fed infants recognize their mothers. This pattern of results suggests that, while they are breast-feeding, infants are exposed to and learn unique olfactory signatures. Similarly, the suckling young of nonhuman species are uniquely attracted to chemical signals (pheromones) produced by their lactating mothers (Porter & Doane, 1976); and, reciprocally, human mothers can recognize the scents of their babies after only 1 or 2 days (Porter, Cernoch, & McLaughlin, 1983; Russell, Mendelson, & Peeke, 1983).

Demonstrable preferences offer good evidence for the existence of absolute and discriminative thresholds; unfortunately, the preference paradigm suffers from a major shortcoming. It is that the observer's *failure to demonstrate* a preference is fundamentally ambiguous about the observer's ability *to detect* or *to discriminate* stimuli. A child in the laboratory, for example, may orient to mother and stranger equally, but still be able to smell them apart . . . and know which to prefer under particular circumstances. This is a nontrivial methodological drawback, and for this reason many investigators have turned to paradigms that draw even more actively on definitive behavioral acts to study absolute and difference thresholds in perception. Among the most widely used such paradigms today are conditioned head rotation and habituation.

Auditory Perception and Conditioned Head Rotation. Physical development tends to proceed cephalocaudally (from the head downward) and proximodistally (from the center of the body outward); as a consequence, the eye, head, and neck regions of the body are the most highly developed earliest in ontogenesis. Many of the response procedures discussed thus far call upon children's looking or orienting or sucking for use in the analysis of perceptual function.

One paradigm that taps infants' voluntary motor control to assess perceptual development is conditioned head turning. The baby sits on the mother's lap, otherwise unencumbered. There is a loudspeaker to one side. When a sound (tone or speech syllable) is played through the speaker and the baby responds by orienting to it, the baby is rewarded by activation of a colorful mechanical toy located just above the speaker. In recent years, developmental psychoacousticians have defined the growth of several abilities basic to sound perception—the detection of sounds of different frequencies, discrimination among frequencies, and localization of sounds in space—as well as responsiveness to complex sounds that specify speech. Head rotation has proved valuable in the study of each.

How loud must a sound be to be heard? For adults, the amount of energy defining the auditory threshold varies with the frequency of the sound across the hearing range (approximately 20 to 20,000 hertz [Hz] or cycles per second). Both low and high frequencies (above or below 1,000 Hz) require more energy than middle frequencies (around 1,000 Hz). Schneider, Trehub, and Bull (1980; Trehub, Schneider, & Endman, 1980) found that infant thresholds for complex noises (as opposed to pure tones) vary substantially with frequency; that they are higher than those of adults for very low frequencies (200 Hz), approach adult levels for middle frequencies (1000 Hz), are again higher than those of adults at high frequencies (10,000 Hz), and finally are nearly equivalent at very high frequencies (19,000 Hz). Further, they observed nearly continuous developmental improvements in hearing at low and high frequencies during the first two years. Maturation of the ear or the CNS could account for this increasing developmental sensitivity. Whatever the reason, infants appear to be more sensitive to high-frequency than to low-frequency sounds. In complementary studies, Olsho (1984; Olsho, Schoon, Sakai, Turpin, & Sperduto, 1982a, 1982b) explored frequency discrimination and found that for infants in the same age range difference thresholds were about twice those of adults at low (250–1,000 Hz) and middle (1,000–3,000 Hz) frequencies, whereas they were virtually the same as adults' at higher frequencies (3,000–8,000 Hz).

Vision and Audition through Habituation-Test.   The conditioned head rotation technique provides reasonably secure data about infant perception since babies actively, voluntarily, and definitely respond in that way and thereby directly "communicate" their perceptions to the experimenter. An equally demonstrative and reliable technique, and one that has been adopted widely in experimental studies of perception in the first years of life, is habituation–test. This procedure has the advantage that it can and has been used to investigate perception in every modality; for purposes of this exposition, vision will serve as the main example (Bornstein, 1985, provides a comprehensive review).

In habituation, a baby is shown a stimulus and the baby's visual attention to the stimulus is monitored. Typically, when placed in an otherwise homogeneous environment, the infant will orient and attend to the novel stimulus on its initial presentation. If the stimulus is available to the infant's view continuously, or if it is presented repeatedly, the infant's attention to the stimulus will wane. This decrement in attention, called *habituation*, presumably reflects two component processes: the infant's developing a mental representation of the stimulus, and the infant's continuing comparison of whatever stimulus is present with that representation. If external stimulus and mental representation match and the baby "knows" the stimulus, there is little reason to continue to look; mismatches, however, maintain the infant's attention. A novel (and discriminable) test stimulus, introduced after habituation to a familiar one, will typically re-excite infant attention. Habituation to familiarity and recovery to novelty have proved to be most versatile and fruitful infant testing methods, permitting investigators the wherewithal to assess myriad aspects of perception in infancy. In particular, developmental researchers have focused on ontogeny of perception of form, orientation, location, movement, and color.

Consider first *form* perception. The fact that an infant scans an angle of a triangle and even resolves contour well does not mean that the infant perceives the triangle (or even an angle of it) as a triangle. Until recently, the problem of form perception proved remarkably resistant to solution because almost any discrimination between two forms (e.g., a triangle from a circle) can be explained as a discrimination on some simpler, featural basis (as between an angle and an arc) without whole form perception being implicated (e.g., Pipp & Haith, 1984). Bornstein (1982) tested infants' sensitivity to symmetry, which is usually perceived in terms of a whole form. In one study, 4-month-olds were found to habituate to vertically symmetrical patterns efficiently (where both featural discriminations and contour explanations were controlled among comparison stimuli), thereby indicating their perception of symmetry as form (Bornstein, Ferdinandsen, & Gross, 1981); in subsequent studies, infants were found to use the global composition of symmetry in discriminating forms (Fisher, Ferdinandsen, & Bornstein, 1981), and vertical symmetry was found to be a general organizing principle of whole form perception (Bornstein & Krinsky, 1985).

Another strong source of evidence that infants perceive pattern wholes derives from demonstrations of form invariance (Bornstein, 1984). Form invariance arises through the perceived stability of an object despite variations in its sensory representations. For example, shape constancy describes the tendency for perceived object shape to remain stable even through the orientation of the object's image on the retina varies. Definitive studies of shape constancy have been conducted by Caron, Caron, and colleagues (1978; Caron, Caron, & Carlson, 1978 Caron, Caron, & Carlson 1979); they show that infants as young as 3 months of age treat as familiar a shape with which they have had diverse experience, even though they are seeing it in a new orientation or slant. Bornstein and his associates (Bornstein, Gross, & Wolf, 1978; Bornstein, Krinsky, & Benasich, 1986), Fagan (1979), and Gibson, Owsley, Walker, and Megaw-Nyce (1979) have provided converging evidence for the perceived constancy of simple and complex *shapes* in 2- to 7½-month-olds; McKenzie, Tootell, and Day (1980) have provided evidence for the perceived constancy of *size* in 4- to 8-month-olds. These several lines of research provide converging evidence that babies still only in the first year of life can perceive form *qua* form.

Objects are specified not only by their form, but also by their coordination in space; that is, by their orientation, location, and movement. Physical space extends outward from the central ego equally in all directions, yet perceived orientation is not uniform: For adults, vertical holds a higher psychological status than does horizontal, and horizontal is generally higher in status than oblique (Bornstein, 1982; Essock, 1980). We accept the statement that "5° is almost vertical" as somehow truer than the statement that "vertical is almost 5°." Vertical is the reference point for *orientation* (Rosch, 1975; Wertheimer, 1938).

Studies of detection, discrimination, and preference suggest that this hierarchy among orientations exists in early life for artificial geometric forms as well as for more meaningful patterns like the human face, and for static as well as for dynamic forms. Over the first year infants detect patterns aligned vertically or horizontally more readily than they do the same patterns aligned obliquely, and visual acuity for vertical and horizontal patterns increases more rapidly than does acuity for oblique patterns (Gwiazda, Brill, Mohindra, & Held, 1978; Leehey, Moskowitz-Cook, Brill, & Held, 1975). Babies know and like the vertical: 2- to 4-month-olds strongly prefer the normal vertical orientation of a face, compared to upside-down and left and right orientations along the horizontal axis, as measured by their smiling as well as by their looking (Hayes & Watson, 1981; Watson, 1966). Bornstein and his associates have shown both preference and perceptual advantages for vertical and horizontal early in life: 4-month-olds prefer to look at a simple grating pattern aligned on the vertical and horizontal (Bornstein, 1978a), and 12-month-olds prefer vertically symmetrical patterns to matched horizontal or oblique ones (Bornstein et al., 1981). A moving vertical or horizontal pattern also evokes significantly greater heart-rate deceleration (orienting) from a 4-month-old than does the same pattern oriented on the diagonal (Ivinskis & Finlay, 1980). Finally, babies still in the first half-year of life habituate more quickly when a given stimulus is oriented on the vertical than when it is oriented on the horizontal, regardless of whether the stimulus is static (Bornstein et al., 1981) or dynamic (Gibson, Owsley, & Johnston, 1978).

Young babies seem able to discriminate orientation well, not only in the discrimination of vertical from horizontal (Bornstein et al., 1978; Fisher et al., 1981; McKenzie & Day, 1971), but also when tested using variants of the habituation design: 5-month-olds discriminate horizontal from 35° off horizontal (Weiner & Kagan, 1976), 4-month-olds vertical from 45° off vertical (Bornstein et al., 1978), and 5- to 6-month-olds a vertical face from the same face at a 45° diagonal (Fagan, 1979). Four-month-olds discriminate even finer differences involving only obliques: a 50° disparity from 20° to 70° (Bornstein et al., 1978) and a 10° disparity from 5° to 15° (Bornstein et al., 1986).

We know, from studies of the kind reviewed in the introductory section of this chapter, that young babies perceive depth in space. They can also *locate* stimuli in space. Von Hofsten (1984) submitted babies' reaching for objects to longitudinal study, beginning at 4 months when babies first make reliable contacts. Recording their following motions, goal-directed behaviors, and types of reaches to objects located at different distances and moving at different velocities, he found that infants as young as $4\frac{1}{2}$ months will reach and contact an object even if it is moving (von Hofsten & Lindhagen, 1979), and that their reaching is accomplished in a way that indicates sophisticated predictive targeting of location (von Hofsten, 1980).

Infants also locate things in large-scale spaces. In anticipation of an event, infants in the second half of their first year incorrectly look in the same direction as was appropriate before they were moved to a different spot in the environment (Acredolo, 1978; Acredolo & Evans, 1980; Cornell & Heth, 1979); that is, they give priority to subjective (so-called *egocentric*) information in recalling spatial location. Toddlers in the second year of life rely on landmarks and possess an objective (so-called *allocentric*) knowledge of coordinated perspectives of space. These results give rise to speculation about a major developmental change over the first year with regard to the child's understanding of spatial location. It could also be, of course, that both egocentric and allocentric codes are available to babies at both ages, but that babies of the two ages elect to use or rely on different codes. In this connection, some researchers have speculated that the infants' own beginning locomotion in crawling and walking motivates their adopting a more mature, objective understanding of space (Benson & Užgiris, 1985; Bremner & Bryant, 1985). Pertinently, infants who crawl or have experience in a "walker," versus those who do not, extract form from a fluctuating display (Campos, Bertenthal, & Benson, 1980) and avoid the deep side of the visual cliff (Campos, Svejda, Bertenthal, Benson, & Schmidt, 1981); and infants who crawl to a search location find hidden objects more frequently than infants who are carried to the search location (Benson & Užgiris, 1985).

It has long been recognized that even newborns are attracted by *movement* (Haith, 1966): They fixate dynamic patterns and faces longer than static ones (Kaufmann & Kaufmann, 1980), and they visually lock onto moving heads and blinking eyes (Samuels, 1985). Research shows that the infant's perception of motion is quite acute. Ruff (1985) tested the abilities of young infants to recognize and to discriminate different motions of rigid objects. For example, she first habituated babies to a series of objects each one of which moved the same way (say, from side to side), and she then tested the same infants with a novel object moving in the familiar motion and with a novel object moving in a novel way (say, from side to side and rotating). Both $3\frac{1}{2}$- and 5-month-olds discriminated side-to-side from side-to-side plus rotation, and by 5 months infants discriminated side-to-side from rotation alone, rotation from oscillation around the vertical, and left versus right rotation. Finally, Slater, Morison, Town, and Rose (1985) showed that newborns perceive similarity between a stimulus when moving and stationary, can transfer what is learned between moving and stationary stimuli, and on these bases possess the potential for identity constancy.

One of the most basic aspects of the object environment revealed through motion is "figural coherence," the perceptual grouping of elements having an invariant set of spatial relations that may be extracted from coordinated relative motions among the elements. A compelling example of figural coherence is the so-called point-light walker display that specifies motion typical of humans. People perceive displays of lights attached to the joints of a human being shown in the dark not as an unrelated swarm of randomly moving dots, but as biochemical motion giving evidence of figural coherence. Johansson (1975) and Cutting, Profitt, and Kozlowski (1978) have demonstrated that adults observing such a dynamic light display can identify the motion and the object in less than 200 msec, whereas static displays of the same information are essentially uninterpretable. Infants, too, are sensitive to biomechanical motion (Fox & McDaniels, 1982). Bertenthal (Bertenthal, Profitt, & Cutting, 1984; Bertenthal, Profitt, Spetner, & Thomas, 1986) used habituation to evaluate infants' sensitivity to figural coherence in such dynamic point-light displays. He uncovered sensitivity to structural invariance in dynamic displays (but not in static ones) in infants as young as 3 months, and sensitivity to the three-dimensional structure of the human form at 9 months.

Objects in the environment not only have form and spatial coordination that help us to distinguish and identify them, they also have *color*. Additionally, color is an intellectually impressive and aesthetically attractive kind of physical information. Infants see colors and seem to do so pretty well. Charles Darwin (1877; see Bornstein, 1978b) speculated on children's seeing color in the 1870s, but real progress toward understanding the development of color vision only began in the 1970s. Studying color vision presents particularly formidable technical problems (Teller & Bornstein, 1986). For example, for both adults and infants, hue and brightness—the two major components of color—covary so that whenever the color of a stimulus changes, both its hue and brightness are changing. In order to compare two stimuli on the basis of hue alone, therefore, it is necessary to match the two in brightness. With adults, this is relatively easy since there exists a formula that relates the amount of change or difference in hue to the amount of change or difference in brightness; alternatively, adults can match colored stimuli for brightness directly. In babies, however, the precise relation between brightness and color was for a long time elusive, and babies certainly cannot be asked to match brightness. The anatomy of the immature eye is also different enough to suggest some perceptual differences between infants and adults (e.g., Abramov et al., 1982). As a consequence, an understanding of infant color vision needs to begin with studies of the infant's perception of brightness, and, on the basis of proper brightness controls, proceed to test discrimination, preference, and organization of hue.

Babies are nearly as acute as adults are when the task is to compare brightness differences between stimuli presented simultaneously (Peeples & Teller, 1978), although they are much less acute if comparison stimuli are separated in space or time (Kessen & Bornstein, 1978). Experiments comparing chromatic or spectral sensitivity using electrophysiological (Dobson, 1976; Moskowitz-Cook, 1979) and behavioral (Peeples & Teller, 1978) techniques agree that, across a broad range of conditions and across most of the visible spectrum, the infant's sensitivity is reasonably similar to the adult's. Thus, in studies where the task is hue discrimination per se, it is possible to adopt several different strategies to unconfound hue and brightness. It is possible to match colors in brightness by an adult standard in specific spectral regions where infant and adult are known to correspond, or in testing discriminations displaced in time (as did Chase, 1937, and Bornstein, 1975); to vary brightness against hue systematically or unsystematically so that brightness is not an influential factor in discrimination (as did

Peeples & Teller, 1975, and Schaller, 1975). Peeples and Teller (1975) capitalized on the preference babies have for heterogeneity by showing 2- and 3-month-olds two screens, one white and the second white with either a white or a red bar projected onto it. They then systematically varied the brightness of the bar around the adult match to the brightness of the background screen. When the white bar was darker or brighter than the screen, it created the bar pattern that babies favored relative to the homogeneous white comparison; at the bar–screen brightness match point, however, the babies did not show a preference. Thus, just a shade of difference between the white bar and white screen engaged the babies to look: Babies' brightness sensitivity is acute. However, babies preferred the red bar–white screen combination at all brightness levels, demonstrating that even when the red bar matched the white screen in brightness, they still distinguished its hue.

"Color-blind" people are called so because they make identifiable color discrimination errors; they also confuse certain hues with white. To assess the status of color vision in infancy, Bornstein (1976) studied both these characteristics using a habituation-test technique. Infants 3 months of age discriminated blue-green from white, and they discriminated between yellow and green; these are two sets of discriminations that individuals with the two major types of red–green blindness fail. Teller and her colleagues later confirmed these findings using the choice-preference procedure, extending them to infants as young as 1 month (Hamer, Alexander, & Teller, 1982; Packer, Hartmann, & Teller, 1985; Teller, Peeples, & Sekel, 1978). Thus, infants are not red-blind or green-blind. Adams, Maurer, and Davis (1986) showed essentially the same capacity in neonates only hours old. Teller also found that 1-month-olds give evidence they are not blue-blind, the rarer third kind of color-blindness (Varner, Cook, Schneck, McDonald, & Teller, 1984). The development of color vision right after birth has not been studied so well, and is doubtlessly immature. Yet infants 1 month and certainly 2 months of age and older are known to possess largely normal color vision, based on their discrimination of color stimuli in the absence of brightness cues.

Adults perceive the color spectrum as organized qualitatively into categories of hue: We commonly distinguish blue, green, yellow, and red as distinct hues, although we recognize blends in between. In specific, we normally see blue when the wavelength of light falls around 450 nm, green around 530 nm, yellow around 580 nm, and red around 630 nm; and we tend to regard lights of wavelengths around 450 nm all as blue, even though we see them as different blues; see Fig. 4.6. It could be that the way that the visual system functions lends vision this organization, or it could be that children learn to organize the color world, perhaps when they acquire language. Bornstein, Kessen, and Weiskopf (1976a, 1976b) studied infants' categorization of color using a habituation-test strategy. They found that 4-month-olds who were habituated to a light of one color readily noticed when a light of a different color was shown on a test trial following

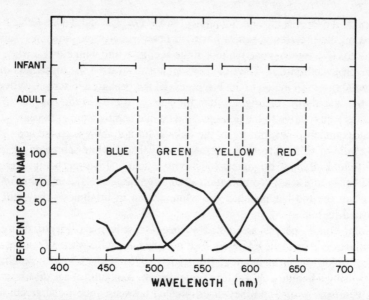

FIG. 4.6.   Wavelength groupings (I.e., hue categories) for 4-month-old infants and for adults. *Bottom:* Percentage color name as a function of wavelength for the color names blue, green, yellow, and red (after Boynton & Gordon, 1965). The rising function at very short wavelengths is for red. *Top:* Summary results for hue categories for infants and adults. The infant summary is derived from Bornstein, Kessen, and Weiskopf (1976a). The adult summary reflects a projection from the color-naming data at a psychophysical criterion of 70%. Infant and adult grouping patterns are highly similar, suggesting that by 4 months infants' hue categories are similar to those of adults.

habituation, even when the two lights were matched in brightness. These investigators then proceeded to determine whether babies regard two different blues, for example, as more similar qualitatively than a blue and a green. Babies were habituated to 480 nm, a blue near the boundary between blue and green, and on test trials following habituation the babies were shown lights of 450 nm, 480 nm, and 510 nm, all matched for brightness. Thus one test stimulus was the familiar hue, and two differed from the familiar hue by identical physical amounts; however, one new test light was blue (like the familiar stimulus) whereas the other was green. Babies shown the new blue stimulus treated it and the familiar blue as the same, whereas they treated the green stimulus as different. This result along with parallel results from other groups showed that preverbal infants categorize the visible spectrum into relatively discrete basic hues of blue, green, yellow, and red, which are similar to those of adults (Fig. 4.6); even though infants, like adults, can discriminate among colors within a given category (Bornstein, 1981).

Habituation has also been combined with learning in the study of infant perception. Siqueland and DeLucia (1969) observed that babies would suck with greater force more frequently than their baseline rate if their forceful sucks brightened a visual image or produced a sound. However, repeated presentation of the same image or sound would not maintain the babies' new high rate of sucking, but would eventually result in a decrement in the frequency of their high-amplitude sucking and in a return to their baseline. The introduction of a new discriminable stimulus, however, would re-excite infant sucking. An advantage of this paradigm is that it has proved to be applicable to the study of audition as well as of vision. This was the habituation procedure Eimas and colleagues (1971) adapted to study the speech perception of infants (discussed earlier in the chapter), and the technique has now been used to investigate a host of perceptions of speech and nonspeech sounds (see Jusczyk, 1985).

For example, very young infants are attracted to the global character of speech, and seem to find it reinforcing: Trehub and Chang (1977) found that the presentation of human speech contingent on infants' sucking would increase their sucking, whereas the withdrawal of speech, the noncontingent presentation of speech, and the presentation of nonspeech had equivalent and equally uneventful effects on infants' motivation to suck.

Intermodal Perception.   When we are by the ocean we see waves, hear the surf pound, smell salt air, and these sensations go together naturally to evoke an integrated experience. Seeing, hearing, and smelling are different percepts, but work in concert. There are many stimuli and events about which the different modalities provide integrated and consonant information, even though those stimuli and events may be specified in any of several modes. Some are relatively simple, like shape; some more complicated, like approach.

Cross-modal transfer reflects observer recognition of shape information across modalities. Meltzoff and Borton (1979) found that infants as young as 1 month of age would look more at a shape that matched a shape they had previously mouthed without seeing than at a shape they had not previously mouthed. Other studies of cross-modal transfer from touch to vision (see Rose & Ruff, 1987, for a summary) confirm that infants readily recognize object shape between modalities.

Approach is specified by an object getting both larger and louder, and recession by an object getting both smaller and softer. Young infants seem to be sensitive to coherence of intermodal information specifying such change, even when different senses are stimulated in distinctly different ways. Schiff, Benasich, and Bornstein (1986) tested infants' sensitivity to conjoint information of this type using the habituation technique. They found that 5-month-olds habituated more efficiently to coherent approach and coherent recession information (when both sound and image specified the same motion) than to incoherent information (when sound approached but image receded, or vice versa).

An engaging dispute has arisen among students of perceptual development concerning the origins of such multimodal sensitivity, a dispute that contests whether different sensations are initially integrated or initially differentiated. On the integrationist side, Bower (1977) proposed that newborns actually cannot distinguish among sensory inputs arriving at the brain via different sensory modalities. Bower (1977) wrote, "It seems that a very young baby may not know whether he is hearing something or seeing something. . . . Very rapidly, [however,] babies develop the ability to register not only the place, but also the modality of an input" (pp. 68–69). Some studies support this integrationist view, at least insofar as they show that newborns and very young infants respond in a similar fashion to, or treat as equivalent, visual and auditory or tactual stimuli. For example, Lewkowicz and Turkewitz (1980) habituated infants only 3 weeks old to a light of given luminance, and afterward divided infants into different groups and then tested them with different intensity levels of sound. Adults match certain sounds and lights at relatively fixed loudness and brightness levels. Lewkowicz and Turkewitz found that babies treated loudnesses that matched brightnesses as equivalent, at just the intensity levels that adults choose in cross-modality matching. Meltzoff and Borton (1979) were brought to an integrationist conclusion as well by their finding (described above) that infants in the first month of life visually identify a shape they have only experienced tactually. The fact that very young babies match cross-modally in these ways certainly supports the integrationist position, but does not supply evidence that infants do not or could not distinguish sensations—that they actually "think" that a sound and a light are the same.

A separate school of thought argues that the ability to coordinate information across the senses develops over the first year of life. The work of Rose, Gott-fried, and Bridger (e.g., 1978) on the development of class-modal transfer in infancy supports this view. They studied full-term and preterm infants on tasks that called for visual recognition of a shape that had been previously seen (*intra*modal recognition) or previously touched (*inter*modal recognition). They found that preterm 6-month-olds could perform neither the intramodal nor intermodal transfers successfully; that preterm 12-month-olds and full-term 6-month-olds could perform the intramodal transfer but still failed on the intermodal task, and that only full-term 12-month-olds could pass both the intramodal and intermodal transfer tasks.

Substance and Methodology of Early Perceptual Development

Investigators of early perception have overcome the major impediment their youngest subjects present to experimental research—silence—by establishing communication with infants in a variety of ingenious ways. Some investigators have relied on psychophysiological measurements of the central and autonomic nervous systems; others have employed behavioral measures of attention, response and reaction, and learning. Through the development of sophisticated methodologies developmentalists have glimpsed the perceptual world of the infant. In précis, what is that world like?

At birth, infants can see, hear, taste, feel, and touch; through these senses, they are well prepared for the new world that surrounds them. An important general aspect of sensation is that even from the very beginning of life babies actively seek out information in their environment. Moreover, they show distinct preferences for some kinds of information over other kinds: For example, soon after birth, newborns concentrate on contours and edges, where visual information is rich, and they prefer saturated colors, sweet tastes, and pleasant odors. Babies in the first month of life appear to discriminate among many physical stimuli that signify different sensory qualities. They can also recognize their mothers by voice and by scent. By 1 month of age, an infant's perceptual world is coming to be clearer and more organized in many ways. Babies' visual acuity and convergence are rapidly developing, and they are beginning to appreciate complex as well as simple visual patterns. At this age, babies see color and hear speech (although perhaps not yet as meaningful communication). By the end of their third month, their vision has much developed: They can focus on near or far objects, and they possess the rudiments of shape and size constancies. By 4 to 5 months of age, babies perceive gestalts and recognize objects in two or in three dimensions; they can discriminate sound differences at the beginning, in the middle, and at the end of syllables; they show sensitivity to all sorts of spatial coordination, including depth, orientation, location, and movement. By 6 months of age, their visual-auditory and visual-tactual information processing is already integrated so as to fuse perceptual wholes.

Most research in infant perception has focused on the related goals of, first, determining whether or not single particular perceptual capacities are present; and, second, tracing the emergence and the stability or change in those capacities over time. This was the logical and necessary point at which to begin basic developmental research, and the last twenty years have witnessed considerable progress in reaching these goals. Investigators of infant perception have progressed so far as to understand that the basic sensory systems are functioning and providing infants at a very early age with highly sophisticated information. In this way, modern investigators have systematically and forever eradicated the view of the perceptually incompetent infant, and are now moving on to new questions concerned with how information arriving at the different senses is processed into integrated precepts.

The exciting, sometimes startling results of these observations of infants does not mean that newborn perceptual capacities are fully developed. Even if rudimentary function is present, qualitative distinctions are often still lacking. In some systems, technical problems limit access to knowledge; in others, it is clear that development simply has not yet occurred. Some perceptual development remains to take place in the period after infancy, and much of this development, as is well known, is bound up with more comprehensive developments in cognition. An overview of these developments occupies the next section.

PERCEPTION IN CHILDHOOD, ADULTHOOD, AND OLD AGE

Historically, infancy has captured much of the attention of perceptual developmentalists for reasons already elaborated, and the most significant developments in perception seem to take place during this period. Nevertheless, two periods in the life span other than infancy hold considerable interest for perceptual developmentalists. Childhood and old age provide important basic information, and both provide further testing grounds for theories. Understanding perceptual capacity at these times is significant in a practical sense; in childhood because of the signal role of perception in learning to read (e.g., Gibson & Levin, 1975; Kavale, 1982), and in old age because of the significance of perceptual capacity to people's autonomy and self-reliance (Bromley, 1974). Comparing perception between childhood and old age is also theoretically important to determining whether deterioration of perceptual capacity follows a course parallel to its evolution (Comalli, 1970).

Childhood

Children are subjects of perceptual study for basic as well as for applied reasons. An example of the former is to trace cerebral specialization. In most right-handers, the left hemisphere of the brain is thought to be principally responsible for processing language, and the right hemisphere for processing visuospatial information. When do these specializations develop? Wittelson (1976) found them to be in place by 6 years of age; but more recently Rose (1984) found that 2- and 3-year-olds possess a left-hand (right hemisphere) superiority for shape recognition, though 1-year-olds do not.

Most applied investigators have been interested in perceptual development in childhood primarily because of its relation to schooling. How do children attend to and process perceptual information? The significance of these questions is truly brought home when children begin to learn how to read. For example, research shows that selective attention, visual integration of shape, and speed of visual information-processing vary enormously among individuals but nevertheless generally increase over childhood, reaching an adult asymptote around the onset of adolescence (e.g., Enns & Girgus, 1985, 1986; Nettlebeck & Wilson, 1985). Although visual perception per se may be mature by school age, visual functioning is not. Younger children are most distractible, less efficient, and slower than are older children.

Among the best-known experiments on the development of form perception in childhood are those conducted by the Gibsons to test a "differentiation" theory of perceptual learning. E. J. and J. J. Gibson (e.g., 1979, 1982) proposed that perceptual development involves increasingly efficient abstraction of invariants or constant stimulus features from an environmental array. Perceptual life begins as diffuse and through experience it differentiates, becoming more selective and acute. The Gibsons (1955) demonstrated perceptual differentiation of form in one cross-sectional experiment comparing children of 6 to 8 and of 8.5 to 11 years of age with adults. Each subject was shown a coil-like figure (ξ) and then asked to point it out again when shown a series of similar coils one at a time. The foils or distractors in the test looked very much like the original standard coil, except that they differed in number of turns, degree of compression, or orientation. Thus, successful identification depended on perceiving distinctive features of coils on these dimensions. There were 18 standards in all. Among the three age groups, adults initially scored the highest number correct and reached 100% recognition after only three exposures to each standard stimulus; older children scored fewer correct at first and took longer than adults to reach perfect recognition; and the youngest children scored the fewest correct initially and never met a learning criterion. Both measures give a good indication of children's increasing ability to differentiate perceptual features with age. In perception, we learn what to look for and what is distinctive versus what is irrelevant.

The Gibsons and their colleagues later applied this finding directly to the educational question of children's letter learning (Gibson, Gibson, Pick, & Osser, 1962). In this experiment, the investigators wanted to assess how children of 4 to 8 years learn to distinguish letterlike forms, a basic problem for shape constancy and a prerequisite for reading. This experiment also used a matching task, only this time letterlike forms were used (山), and foils varied systematically from the standard to assess what specific confusions children might make and whether their confusions might vary with age. Twelve types of foils were used; they included breaks (山), rotations (山), reversals (山), and perspectival transformations (山), Across ages, children detected figural breaks best, rotations and reversals less proficiently, and perspectival transformations least proficiently of all. Regardless of transformation, the children's performance improved with age. The fact that youngsters have particular difficulty with reversals reminds us of their common left–right reading and writing confusions (e.g., z for s, b for d, and so forth). Bornstein et al. (1978) offered a perceptual interpretation for this phenomenon: Because left–right reversals only occur in nature when they are twin aspects of the same thing (e.g., an object and its silhouette), they ought to be treated as the same (like a constancy) and need not be differentiated. In support of this hypothesis, Bornstein et al. showed that under many conditions very young infants treat left-right reversals as similar, although they distinguish other rotations of a stimulus. In the case of reversals in letters, children seemingly must unlearn a natural perceptual constancy.

Bornstein and his coworkers have looked at the continuity of one reading-related aspect of form perception across the life cycle. In a study of symmetry perception in children, Bornstein and Stiles-Davis (1984) found a clear developmental progression among 4- to 6-year-olds: Vertical symmetry possessed the highest perceptual advantage (as in discrimination and memory), then horizontal, then oblique. Fisher and Bornstein (1982) also found vertical and horizontal to be special vis-à-vis oblique in adults. Although the literature concerned with children's perception of form frequently has practical questions regarding reading in the background, few results have been directly applicable (Gibson & Levin, 1975). It is still not known how children gain perceptual access to this important symbol system. Some success rests on cognitive and social factors (Vellutino, 1977); clearly, however, achievement in reading depends as well on children's visual perception skills (e.g., Kavale, 1982): Fisher, Bornstein, and Gross (1985) found that, even with IQ controlled in the study, children who possess advanced visual skills read at higher levels. The practical importance of this area of research cannot be overemphasized, and there is clear need for continuing study.

The findings of children's perceptions of symmetry also address a question often posed to developmental investigators outside of infancy studies: Can studies of children converge with those of adults to advance our understanding of perceptual processes generally? It has frequently been suggested that development might parallel adult perceptual processing; unfortunately, few concrete examples exist. One may be the parallel between order of perceptual processing in symmetry by adults and development of children's learning or memory for symmetry. Many prominent models of symmetry perception postulate that adults process orientation in symmetry hierarchically, beginning with vertical, proceeding next to horizontal, and ending with oblique; empirical data support this hierarchy (e.g., Fisher & Bornstein, 1982; Palmer & Hemenway, 1978; Royer, 1981). The child studies show that detection and reproduction of symmetry follow the same orientation hierarchy ontogenetically (Bornstein & Stiles-Davis, 1984). In symmetry, perceptual biases that characterize stages of adult information processing seem equally apt to describe stages of perceptual development.

Old Age

One of the main principles of aging is that through a complex sequence of changes the body dies a little every day from its peak in early adulthood. Select intellectual functions and almost all bodily or vegetative functions decline in this way (Bromley, 1974). The consequences include changes and deterioration in perceptually related structures and functions: Brain weight reduces, cells in the CNS die and do not regenerate, nerve conduction velocity slows. Across the senses, perceptual deterioration is common and often regular.

A major question surrounding this decline of sensory–perceptual function in old age turns on the relative contributions of organ impairment, nervous system degeneration, and reduction of psychological judgment. Some poor performance in old age seems clearly to be based on physiological change. For example, conduction velocity of nerve fibers slows approximately 15 % between 20 and 90 years of age, and simple reaction time to lights and sounds concomitantly lengthens 50% over the same period (Bromley, 1974). Similarly, the lens of the eye grows like an onion over the entire course of the life span, adding layer upon layer. Each layer is pigmented, and as the lens grows light must traverse more and more absorptive material before it reaches the retina to be effective in vision. Since lens pigment selectively absorbs short-wavelength (blue) visible light, perception of blue systematically attenuates in old age; see Fig. 4.7. Other performance declines in old age may reflect a combination of central nervous system or anatomical deterioration with adverse changes in judgment.

The study of perception in aging is also of interest for the theoretical information it provides on the question of change across the life cycle. Some evidence supports progressive–regressive patterns in the life-span development of psychological abilities (Strauss, 1982). For example, many perceptual functions seem to improve during childhood, reach a peak or high plateau during adulthood, and subsequently decline in old age: Judgments of illusion magnitude, the apparent horizon, the rod-and-frame test, part–whole differentiation, visual span, and

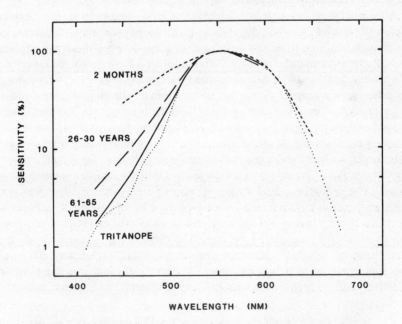

FIG. 4.7. In normal aging, the eye loses sensitivity to short wavelengths (blue light). Photopic spectral sensitivities measured near birth, at midlife, and near the end of life, in comparison with that of the average tritanope (blue-blind observer). (From Bornstein, 1977.)

tachistoscopic form discrimination are reported thus to wax and then wane during the life cycle (see Comalli, 1970). There is a need to determine how real these perceptual changes are versus how much they reflect criterion shifts in judgment.

Reprise: Nature and Nurture

The discussion of old age permits the opportunity to reconsider, if only briefly, the roles of nature and nurture in perception, this time in a somewhat different light. Consider the following.

Auditory sensitivity is measured by assessing absolute thresholds for sounds of different frequencies. One of the consequences of aging is deterioration in auditory sensitivity. In essence, the elderly require more energy to hear certain frequencies than do younger people. As the top panel of Fig. 4.8 shows, among Americans hearing loss in aging is more pronounced at higher frequencies. One prominent and straightforward explanation for this finding has been that aging entails the natural and regular deterioration of anatomical and physiological mechanisms that subserve hearing. An alternative hypothesis is that cumulative exposure to noise over the course of the life span deleteriously affects perception of high frequencies and is the first cause of the physiological change. How can we decide between the nature and nurture explanations?

Additional data—first, from individuals in other cultures with other experiences and, second, from individuals in our own society who have distinctive life histories of exposure to noise—help to distinguish between these two explanations. As the bottom panel in Fig. 4.8 shows, older American women experience less hearing loss than older American men; and Sudanese Africans, who show no sex differences in hearing with aging, sustain even less hearing deterioration than Americans of either sex. Contrary to the original biological hypothesis, gender and cultural data suggest that physiological aging alone is probably not the key factor in hearing loss. (It could still be, however unlikely, that sexes or races differ biologically in the integrity or susceptibility of their auditory mechanisms.) The data on elderly American men exposed to different amounts of noise over the course of their lifetimes lend further support to the experiential interpretation. Findings from this third research source—on noise history—strongly support the view that hearing loss in old age is related to amount of exposure to noise and less to natural physiological processes. The three research programs together supplement the original "descriptive evidence" with "explanatory evidence" and lend credence to a nurture view. Of course, the fact that noise history selectively affects high frequencies indicates that nature and nurture interact in development.

The influences of nature and nurture are often difficult to disentangle in developmental theory. Yet assessment of their differential contributions is critical to understanding the ontogeny of sensory and perceptual as well as other psychological processes. An especial virtue of developmental investigations de-

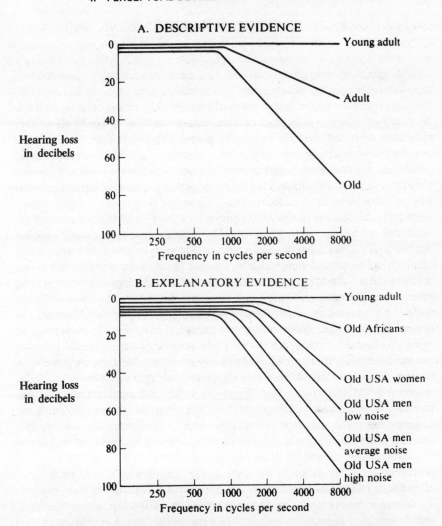

FIG. 4.8. Descriptive and explanatory evidence on auditory sensitivity in adulthood. (From Baltes, Reese, & Nesselroade, 1977. Copyright Wadsworth Publishing Company. Reprinted with permission.)

rives from information they afford regarding *prevention:* Whereas the descriptive evidence alone strongly implicates physiological deterioration, the alleviation of which might best be achieved through specialized hearing aids for the elderly, the explanatory evidence which derives from diverse biological and experiential comparisons of development suggests more productive intervention strategies that would effectively prevent sensory deterioration and hearing loss in the first place.

PERCEPTUAL MODIFICATION, ENRICHMENT, AND DEPRIVATION IN DEVELOPMENT

How do special rearing circumstances—modification, enrichment, and deprivation—affect perceptual development? As developmental research has evolved, this single question has reformulated itself into two. The first is quite literal: How do these factors affect perceptual development per se? Two opposite views have competed—without clear resolution—in answer to this question. Consider, for example, how deprivation in one perceptual system might affect development of other systems. One view is that by way of compensation the unaffected senses literally develop to a higher level of function, or that people develop a heightened level of awareness through them. Thus, according to this view, true auditory function in the blind is enhanced as some sort of physiological compensation for blindness; or, being visually deprived, blind people attend more closely to information arriving via other sensory channels, or analyze that information more efficiently. The second view is that an absence of information processing in one modality adversely affects the level of perceptual development or awareness other modalities achieve. On the first view, psychophysics has developed techniques (e.g., signal detection theory) which help to distinguish differences in sensory function from differences in psychological judgment. There is no good evidence, based on these procedures, that surviving systems reach a higher perceptual level, although there is good evidence that attention, awareness, or strategy can be enhanced in surviving perceptual systems (Hoemann, 1978; Warren, 1978). Of course, the degree to which enhanced attention in one modality compensates for loss of another varies. On the second view, research suggests that perceptual deprivation is specifically debilitating to a sensory system and to the information processing directly involved, but need not necessarily be detrimental to sensory systems generally.

The second formulation of the original question on how special rearing circumstances might affect perceptual development has been much more general. The question has been put this way: What effects do perceptual modification, enrichment, and deprivation early in life have on the later development of perceptual, cognitive, or social capabilities? Two separate approaches to this question have evolved as well. The first has involved the study of congenitally handicapped populations; and the second has involved normal populations who, by chance, have experienced special rearing circumstances, either in institutions, natural ecologies, or cultures that vary widely in the perceptual experiences they provide. In evaluating effects of perceptual modification of development on these diverse populations, it is imperative to bear in mind that other extraordinary conditions in these populations may surpass in significance their different perceptual experiences. Blindness, deafness, or other handicaps as well as institutionalization or cultural variation can have such profound social and emotional influences on development as to render studies of perception per se problematic.

192

For example, practical research problems revolve around defining the severity of a handicap, determining at what age the handicap began, disentangling physical, emotional, and intellectual disabilities the handicap has produced, and separating the handicapped child's limited general experience from his or her limited perceptual function. Unfortunately, there are no ready replies to these criticisms. As a consequence, what we have learned about perception from investigations of the handicapped is much more limited and uncertain than is commonly supposed.

For obvious reasons, studies of the effects of deprivation on perceptual development have usually involved animals; however, analogous effects may occur in humans in "natural experiments." Lewis, Maurer, and Brent (1985) capitalized on such a natural experiment in infants born with dense cataracts in one eye to study the effects of early light deprivation on visual development. Cataracts permit only diffuse light to be seen. They studied a number of visual functions in children who had such cataracts removed at different points in childhood, and found that, for example, visual acuity was better in those who had their cataracts removed after living with them the shortest amounts of time or who were visually deprived after 3 years of age, rather than from birth; indeed, acuity was worst in children deprived for the longest amounts of time and beginning at birth.

Other special populations present different solutions but new problems as well. Understandably, most studies involving institutionalized individuals have been concerned principally with elucidating the effects of deprivation on the development of cognitive and social skills. Although perception impresses us as a natural outgrowth of biological sensory processing, in the 1960s several theorists and researchers argued that early perceptual experience was critical for normal pscyhological growth and development (see Bornstein, 1987). For example, White and Held (1966) found that simply introducing a visually interesting stabile into institutionalized infants' otherwise bland environments at 1 month of age nearly doubled their visually directed reaching and visual attentiveness over that of comparable infants not enriched in this way. Similarly, Greenberg, Užgiris, and Hunt (1968) found that 1-month-olds who had a stabile strung over their cribs developed a visually defensive response to its sudden approach in half the time of matched-aged babies without comparable experience.

Though some have argued that such circumstances matter only inasmuch as they are accompanied by the absence of human beings in the child's life (Clarke-Stewart, 1973), several major investigations have yielded direct associations between perceptual experiences (or lack thereof) and cognitive development (e.g., Parke, 1978; Wohlwill, 1983). For example, Wachs and his associates (1979, Wachs, Užgiris, & Hunt, 1971) conducted studies attempting to overcome SES, institutional, and other confounds to delimit how exposure to inanimate physical stimulation—via perception—influences cognitive development in the first three years of life. Their findings support an "optimal match hypothesis" which posits that understimulation and overstimulation as well as disorganized stimulation are equally deleterious to development.

Bornstein initiated a series of studies designed to evaluate the positive effects on perceptual development of specific experiences in infants' natural ecologies. In one longitudinal study of 2- to 5-month-olds, Bornstein and Tamis-LeMonda (1987) examined the relation between mothers' prompting their infants' attention to themselves versus properties, objects, or events in the environment and their infants' visual and tactual exploration. Several specific experience-related associations were observed: Infants whose mothers encouraged attention to themselves had babies who attended more to them and less to the environment, whereas infants whose mothers encouraged attention to the environment had babies who explored objects more and their mothers less. Further, these effects were greater among infants whose mothers engaged in physical as opposed to verbal prompting. In a second experiment, Kuchuk, Vibbert, and Bornstein (1986) assessed how mothers' didactic interactions with their 3-month-olds influenced infants' perceptions: In the laboratory, infants displayed individual differences in sensitivity to a series of smiles that graduated in intensity; and concurrent observations of mother–infant interactions at home revealed that the mothers who more frequently encouraged their infants to attend to the mothers themselves when the mothers were smiling had infants who showed the greatest sensitivity to smiling.

The third human group to whom researchers have turned to address questions of how perceptual experiences may influence development includes children reared in contrasting perceptual environments. Indeed, one of the major ways in which extremes of perceptual experience have been investigated safely in humans has been to take advantage of such natural experiments (Bornstein, 1980). Since all human beings are believed to be endowed with roughly the same anatomy and physiology, it is reasonable to expect that most perceptual systems or abilities are essentially universal and that human beings all begin life on much the same footing. Do varying rearing circumstances influence perceptual development differently? Some perceptions seem to be affected, others not. For example, consider how the literature on the categorical perception of speech has evolved. As discussed earlier (see Fig. 4.1), prelinguistic infants distinguish certain categories of speech but not others, whereas adults sometimes distinguish the same categories but sometimes distinguish different ones. It must be the case, therefore, that a dearth of experience with certain distinctions fails to maintain some speech categories, just as experiences with other distinctions may facilitate or attune the development of other categories, or even induce new speech discriminations (Bornstein, 1979; Gottlieb, 1983).

In many ways our perceptual systems are unperturbed by large but normal variation in environmental stimulation. There can be little doubt, however, that experiences, or a lack thereof, play important roles in maintaining, facilitating and attuning, and inducing perceptions in infants' seeing and hearing, and in their tasting, smelling, and touching. Perception is somewhat malleable to experience, and future research will determine the limits of that plasticity as well as which experiences are most influential. Overall, our physical and perceptual experiences seem to be sufficiently common so as to render perceptions nearly the same for everyone everywhere.

SUMMARY AND CONCLUSIONS

Perception is among the oldest and most venerable fields in psychology and among the most closely tied to psychology's origins in philosophy. It is also among the most popular in developmental study. Studies of infancy constitute the bulk of research in perceptual development, and studies of perceptual development have, until recently perhaps, constituted the bulk of research in infancy for the many reasons outlined at the inception of this chapter.

In recent years, many perceptual secrets of infants and children—formidable and intractable as they once seemed—have been penetrated through a variety of ingenious techniques. Research shows that even the very young of our own species perceive beyond simply sensing. But several traditional and important questions about perceptual development are still open, left unanswered even by a wealth of research amassed in the last two decades. Moreover, many of the startling revelations that spring to mind even from our simplest introspections continue to spark curiosity about perceptual development. How do we develop from sensing patterns received and transduced at the surface of the body to effortlessly perceiving objects and events in the real world? How does a world that is constantly in flux come to be perceived as stable? As context is so influential in perception, how does selective attention to signal and figure develop in coordination with selective elimination of noise and ground? How do perceived objects come to be invested with meaning?

The study of perception in childhood is also very practical. For example, the relevance of perceptual research to social and emotional development as well as to medicine and education is readily apparent. Physical and social stimulation are perceptual stimulation, and many aspects of social development depend initially on perceptual capacity. Specific examples abound—from the neonate's perception and consequent ability to imitate facial expressions (Meltzoff & Moore, 1983), to the toddler's acceptance of photographs to mediate separation stress from his or her mother (Passman & Longeway, 1982), to perceptual prerequisites for reading in the child (Gibson & Levin, 1975).

In the past, many investigators expressed reluctance at adding a developmental perspective to the formal study of sensation and perception—developmental psychology often being treated as a different field—and the experimental study of sensation and perception was confined largely to adults and to infrahuman animals. Today, research progress with infant, child, and aged populations demonstrates the broadly informative contribution of the developmental point of view. Developmental study is now esteemed by all enlightened students of sensation and perception.

Perceptual development could serve as a model of developmental studies as good as that of any field described in this text. It encompasses philosophy and methodology, and it confronts all of the overarching theoretical and empirical issues in developmental study. Some perceptual capacities are given congenitally—even, apparently, in the basic functioning of the sensory systems—whereas other perceptual capacities develop between infancy and maturity. This ontogenetic change, in turn, has several possible sources: Development may be genetically motivated and transpire largely as a reflection of maturational forces, or it may be experiential and largely reflect the influences of the environment and of particular events. Perceptual development after birth (or whenever the onset of experience takes place) is doubtlessly some complex transaction of these two principal forces. At one time or another each of these possibilities has been proposed as determinative. Modern studies have informed a modern view, however. Through their systematic efforts in infancy and early childhood, perceptual developmentalists have determined that basic mechanisms in many cases can impose perceptual structure early in life, but that perceptual development is determined and guided by a transaction of these structural endowments in combination with experience. Thus, neither nativism nor empiricism holds sway over perceptual development; rather, innate mechanisms and experience together codetermine how children come to perceive the world veridically.

ACKNOWLEDGMENTS

Preparation of this chapter was partly supported by a research grant from the National Science Foundation (BNS 84-20017) and by research grants (HD20559 and HD20807) and a Research Career Development Award (HD00521) from the National Institute of Child Health and Human Development. I thank H. Bornstein, L. Hainline, and G. Turkewitz for valuable comments.

REFERENCES

Abramov, I., Gordon, J., Hendrickson, A., Hainline, L., Dobson, V., & LaBossiere, E. (1982). The retina of the newborn human infant. *Science, 217,* 265–267.

Acredolo, L. P. (1978). Development of spatial orientation in infancy. *Developmental Psychology, 14,* 224–234.

Acredolo, L. P., & Evans, D. (1980). Developmental changes in the effects of landmarks on infant spatial behavior. *Developmental Psychology, 16,* 312–318.

Adams, R. J., Maurer, D., & Davis, M. (1986). Newborns' discrimination of chromatic from achromatic stimuli. *Journal of Experimental Child Psychology, 41,* 267–281.

Aslin, R. N. (1981). Experiential influences and sensitive periods in perceptual development: A unified model. In R. N. Aslin, J. R. Alberts, & M. R. Peterson (Eds.), *Development of perception: Psychobiological perspectives. Vol. 2: The visual system.* New York: Academic Press.

Ball, W., & Tronick, E. (1971). Infant responses to impending collision: Optical and real. *Science, 171,* 818–820.

Baltes, P. B., Reese, H. W., & Nesselroade, J. R. (1977). *Life-span developmental psychology: Introduction to research methods.* Monterey, CA: Brooks/Cole.

Banks, M. S. (1980). The development of visual accommodation during early infancy. *Child Development, 51,* 646–666.

Barlow, H. B., Blakemore, C., & Pettigrew, J. D. (1967). The neural mechanism of binocular depth discrimination. *Journal of Physiology, 193,* 327–342.

Benson, J. B., & Užgiris, I. C. (1985). Effect of self-initiated locomotion on infant search activity. *Developmental Psychology, 21,* 923–931.

Berg, W. K., & Berg, K. M. (1979). Psychophysiological development in infancy: State, sensory function, and attention. In J. D. Osofsky (Ed.), *Handbook of infant development.* New York: Wiley.

Berkeley, G. (1901). *An essay towards a new theory of vision.* Oxford: Clarendon Press. (Originally published, 1709)

Bertenthal, B. I., Proffitt, D. R., & Cutting, J. E. (1984). Infant sensitivity to figural coherence in biomechanical motions. *Journal of Experimental Child Psychology, 37,* 1072–1080.

Bertenthal, B. I., Proffitt, D. R., Spetner, N. B., & Thomas, M. A. (1985). The development of infant sensitivity to biomechanical motions. *Child Development, 56,* 531–543.

Birnholz, J. C., & Benacerraf, B. R. (1983). The development of human fetal hearing. *Science, 222,* 516–518.

Bornstein, M. H. (1975). Qualities of color vision in infancy. *Journal of Experimental Child Psychology, 19,* 401–419.

Bornstein, M. H. (1976). Infants are trichromats. *Journal of Experimental Child Psychology, 21,* 425–445.

Bornstein, M. H. (1977). Developmental pseudocyananopsia: Ontogenetic change in human color vision. *American Journal of Optometry and Physiological Optics, 54,* 464–469.

Bornstein, M. H. (1978a). Visual behavior of the young human infant: Relationships between chromatic and spatial perception and the activity of underlying brain mechanisms. *Journal of Experimental Child Psychology, 26,* 174–192.

Bornstein, M. H. (1978b). Chromatic vision in infancy. In H. W. Reese & L. P. Lipsitt (Eds.), *Advances in child development and behavior* (Vol. 12). New York: Academic Press.

Bornstein, M. H. (1979). Perceptual development: Stability and change in feature perception. In M. H. Bornstein & W. Kessen (Eds.), *Psychological development from infancy: Image to intention.* Hillsdale, NJ: Lawrence Erlbaum Associates.

Bornstein, M. H. (1980). Cross-cultural developmental psychology. In M. H. Bornstein (Ed.), *Comparative methods in psychology.* Hillsdale, NJ: Lawrence Erlbaum Associates.

Bornstein, M. H. (1981). Psychological studies of color perception in human infants: Habituation, discrimination and categorization, recognition, and conceptualization. In L. P. Lipsitt (Ed.), *Advances in infancy research* (Vol. 1). Norwood, NJ: Ablex.

Bornstein, M. H. (1982). Perceptual anisotropies in infancy: Ontogenetic origins and implications of inequality in spatial vision. In H. W. Reese & L. P. Lipsitt (Eds.), *Advances in child development and behavior* (Vol. 16). New York: Academic Press.

Bornstein, M. H. (1984). A descriptive taxonomy of psychological categories used by infants. In C. Sophian (Ed.), *Origins of cognitive skills.* Hillsdale, NJ: Lawrence Erlbaum Associates.

Bornstein, M. H. (1985). Habituation of attention as a measure of visual information processing in human infants: Summary, systematization, and synthesis. In G. Gottlieb & N. A. Krasnegor (Eds.), *Measurement of audition and vision in the first year of postnatal life: A methodological overview.* Norwood, NJ: Ablex.

Bornstein, M. H. (1987). *The multivariate model of interaction effects in human development: Categories of caretaking.* Unpublished manuscript, New York University.

Bornstein, M. H., Ferdinandsen, K., & Gross, C. G. (1981). Perception of symmetry in infancy. *Developmental Psychology, 17,* 82–86.

Bornstein, M. H., Gross, J., & Wolf, J. (1978). Perceptual similarity of mirror images in infancy. *Cognition, 6,* 89–116.

Bornstein, M. H., Kessen, W., & Weiskopf, S. (1976a). The categories of hue in infancy. *Science, 191,* 201–202.

Bornstein, M. H., Kessen, W., & Weiskopf, S. (1976b). Color vision and hue categorization in young human infants. *Journal of Experimental Psychology: Human Perception and Performance, 2,* 115–129.

Bornstein, M. H., & Krinsky, S. (1985). Perception of symmetry in infancy: The salience of vertical symmetry and the perception of pattern wholes. *Journal of Experimental Child Psychology, 39,* 1–19.

Bornstein, M. H., Krinsky, S. J., & Benasich, A. A. (1986). Fine orientation discrimination and shape constancy in infants. *Journal of Experimental Child Psychology, 41,* 49–60.

Bornstein, M. H., & Stiles-Davis, J. (1984). Discrimination and memory for symmetry in young children. *Developmental Psychology, 20,* 639–649.

Bornstein, M. H., & Tamis-LeMonda, C. (1987). *Mother-infant interaction: The selectivity of encouraging attention.* Unpublished manuscript, New York University.

Bower, T. G. R. (1977). *A primer of infant development.* San Francisco: Freeman.

Bower, T. G. R., Broughton, J. M., & Moore, M. (1970). Infant response to approaching objects: An indication of response to distal variables. *Perception & Psychophysics, 9,* 193–196.

Boyton, R. M., & Gordon, J. (1965). Bezold-Brüke hue shift measured by color-naming technique. *Journal of the Optical Society of America, 55,* 78–86.

Bradley, R. M., & Stearn, I. B. (1967). The development of the human taste bud during the fetal period. *Journal of Anatomy, 101,* 743–752.

Bremner, J. G., & Bryant, P. E. (1985). Active movement and development of spatial abilities in infancy. In H. M. Wellman (Ed.), *Children's searching: The development of search skill and spatial representation.* Hillsdale, NJ: Lawrence Erlbaum Associates.

Bromley, D. B. (1974). *The psychology of human ageing.* Harmondsworth, England: Penguin Books.

Bronson, G. W. (1974). The postnatal growth of visual capacity. *Child Development, 45,* 873–890.

Campos, J. J. (1976). Heart rate: A sensitive tool for the study of emotional development in the infant. In L. P. Lipsitt (Ed.), *Developmental psychobiology: The significance of infancy.* Hillsdale, NJ: Lawrence Erlbaum Associates.

Campos, J. J., Bertenthal, B., & Benson, N. (1980). *Self-produced locomotion and the extraction of form invariance.* Paper presented at the meetings of International Conference on Infant Studies, New Haven, CT.

Campos, J. J., Langer, A., & Krowitz, A. (1970). Cardiac responses on the visual cliff in prelocomotor human infants. *Science, 170,* 196–197.

Campos, J. J., Svejda, M., Bertenthal, B., Benson, N., & Schmidt, D. (1981). *Self-produced locomotion and wariness of heights: New evidence from training studies.* Paper presented at the meetings of the Society for Research in Child Development, Boston, MA.

Caron, A. J., Caron, R. F., & Carlson, V. R. (1978). Do infants see objects or retinal images? Shape constancy revisited. *Infant Behavior and Development, 1,* 229–243.

Caron, A. J., Caron, R. F., & Carlson, V. R. (1979). Infant perception of the invariant shape of objects varying in slant. *Child Development, 50,* 716–721.

Caron, R. F., & Caron, A. J. (1978). Effects of ecologically relevant manipulations on infant discrimination learning. *Infant Behavior and Development, 1,* 291–307.

Caron, R. F., Caron, A. J., & Myers, R. S. (1982). Abstraction of invariant face expressions in infancy. *Child Development, 53,* 1008–1015.

Cernoch, J. M., & Porter, R. H. (1985). Recognition of maternal axillary odors by infants. *Child Development, 56,* 1593–1598.

Chase, W. (1937). Color vision in infants. *Journal of Experimental Psychology, 20,* 203–222.

Clarke-Stewart, K. A. (1973). Interactions between mothers and their young children: Characteristics and consequences. *Monographs of the Society for Research in Child Development, 38,* (6–7, Serial No. 153).

Comalli, P. E. (1970). Life-span changes in visual perception. In L. R. Goulet & P. B. Baltes (Eds.), *Life-span developmental psychology.* New York: Academic Press.

Conel, J. L. (1939–1959). *The postnatal development of the human cerebral cortex* (Vols. 1–6). Cambridge, MA: Harvard University Press.

Cornell, E. H., & Heth, C. D. (1979). Response versus place learning by human infants. *Journal of Experimental Psychology: Human Learning and Performance, 5,* 188–196.

Cowart, B. J. (1981). Development of taste perception in humans: Sensitivity and preference throughout the lifespan. *Psychological Bulletin, 90,* 43–73.

Cutting, J. E., Proffitt, D. R., & Kozlowski, L. T. (1978). A biomechanical invariant for gait perception. *Journal of Experimental Psychology: Human Perception and Performance, 4,* 357–372.

Darwin, C. (1877). A biographical sketch of an infant. *Mind, 2,* 286–294.

Davis, C. J. (1928). Self selection of diet by newly weaned infants. *American Journal of Diseases of Children, 36,* 651–679.

Décarie, T. G. (1969). A study of the mental and emotional development of the thalidomide child. In B. M. Foss (Ed.), *Determinants of infant behavior* (Vol. 4). London: Methuen.

Descartes, R. (Paris: np, 1824.) *La dioptrique.* In V. Coursin (Ed.), *Oeuvres de Descartes* (M. D. Boring, trans.). (Originally published, 1638)

Dobson, V. (1976). Spectral sensitivity of the 2-month-old infant as measured by the visually evoked cortical potential. *Vision Research, 16,* 367–374.

Dobson, V., & Teller, D. (1978). Visual acuity in human infants. A review and comparison of behavioral and electrophysiological studies. *Vision Research, 18,* 1469–1483.

Eimas, P. D. (1975). Speech perception in early infancy. In L. B. Cohen & P. Salapatek (Eds.), *Infant perception: From sensation to cognition* (Vol. 2). New York: Academic Press.

Eimas, P. D., Siqueland, E. R., Jusczyk, P., & Vigorito, J. (1971). Speech perception in infants. *Science, 171,* 303–306.

Enns, J. T., & Girgus, J. S. (1985). Developmental changes in selective and integrative visual attention. *Journal of Experimental Child Psychology, 40,* 319–337.

Enns, J. T., & Girgus, J. S. (1986). A developmental study of shape integration over space and time. *Developmental Psychology, 22,* 491–499.

Essock, E. A. (1980). The oblique effect of stimulus identification considered with respect to two classes of oblique effects. *Perception, 9,* 37–46.

Fagan, J. F. (1979). The origins of facial pattern recognition. In M. H. Bornstein & W. Kessen (Eds.), *Psychological development from infancy: Image to intention.* Hillsdale, NJ: Lawrence Erlbaum Associates.

Fantz, R. L., Ordy, J. M., & Udelf, M. S. (1962). Maturation of pattern vision in infants during the first six months. *Journal of Comparative and Physiological Psychology, 55,* 907–917.

Fisher, C. B., & Bornstein, M. H. (1982). Identification of symmetry: Effects of stimulus orientation and head position. *Perception & Psychophysics, 32,* 443–448.

Fisher, C. B., Bornstein, M. H., & Gross, G. G. (1985). Left–right coding skills related to beginning reading. *Journal of Developmental and Behavioral Pediatrics, 6,* 279–283.

Fisher, C. B., Ferdinandsen, K., & Bornstein, M. H. (1981). The role of symmetry in infant form perception. *Child Development, 52,* 457–462.

Fox, R., & McDaniels, C. (1982). The perception of biological motion by human infants. *Science, 218,* 486–487.

Garcia, J., & Koelling, R. (1966). Relation of cue to consequence in avoidance learning. *Psychonomic Science, 4,* 123–124.

Gibson, E. J. (1982). The concept of affordances in development: The renascence of functionalism.

In W. A. Collins (Ed.), *The Minnesota symposia on child psychology* (Vol. 15). Hillsdale, NJ: Lawrence Erlbaum Associates.

Gibson, E. J., Gibson, J. J., Pick, A. D., & Osser, H. (1962). A developmental study of the discrimination of letter-like forms. *Journal of Comparative and Physiological Psychology, 55,* 897–906.

Gibson, E. J., & Levin, H. (1975). *The psychology of reading.* Cambridge, MA: MIT Press.

Gibson, E. J., Owsley, C. J., & Johnston, J. (1978). Perception of invariants by five-month-old infants: Differentiation of two types of motion. *Developmental Psychology, 14,* 407–415.

Gibson, E. J., Owsley, C. J., Walker, A., & Megaw-Nyce, J. (1979). Development of the perception of invariants: Substance and shape. *Perception, 8,* 609–619.

Gibson, E. J., & Walk, R. D. (1960). The "visual cliff." *Scientific American, 202,* 64–71.

Gibson, J. J. (1979). *The ecological approach to visual perception.* Boston, MA: Houghton Mifflin.

Gibson, J. J., & Gibson, E. J. (1955). Perceptual learning: Differentiation or enrichment? *Psychological Review, 62,* 32–41.

Goto, H. (1971). Auditory perception by normal Japanese adults of the sounds "L" and "R". *Neuropsychologia, 9,* 317–323.

Gottlieb, G. (1983). The psychobiological approach to developmental issues. In P. H. Mussen (Ed.), *Handbook of child psychology (Vol. 2).* M. M. Haith & J. J. Campos (Vol. Eds.), *Infants and developmental psychobiology.* New York: Wiley.

Granrud, C. E., Yonas, A., & Pettersen, L. (1984). A comparison of monocular and binocular depth perception in 5- and 7-month-old infants. *Journal of Experimental Child Psychology, 38,* 19–32.

Greenberg, D., Užgiris, I. C., & Hunt, J. McV. (1968). Hastening the development of the blink response with looking. *Journal of Genetic Psychology, 113,*167–176.

Gwiazda, J., Brill, S., Mohindra, I., & Held, R. (1978). Infant visual acuity and its meridional variation. *Vision Research, 18,* 1557–1564.

Hainline, L., & Lemerise, E. (1982). Infants' scanning of geometric forms varying in size. *Journal of Experimental Child Psychology, 32,* 235–256.

Haith, M. M. (1966). The response of the human newborn to visual movement. *Journal of Experimental Child Psychology, 3,* 235–243.

Haith, M. M. (1980). *Rules that babies look by,* Hillsdale, NJ: Lawrence Erlbaum Associates.

Hamer, R. D., Alexander, K., & Teller, D. Y. (1982). Rayleigh discriminations in young human infants. *Vision Research, 20,* 575–584.

Hayes, L. A., & Watson, J. S. (1981). Facial orientation of parents and elicited smiling by infants. *Infant Behavior and Development, 4,* 333–340.

Hebb, D. O. (1953). Heredity and environment in mammalian behavior. *British Journal of Animal Behavior, 1,* 43–47.

Hecox, K. (1975). Electrophysiological correlates of human auditory development. In L. B. Cohen & P. Salapatek (Eds.), *Infant perception: From sensation to cognition* (Vol. 2). New York: Academic Press.

Hecox, K., & Galambos, R. (1974). Brain stem auditory evoked responses in human infants and adults. *Archives of Otolaryngology, 99,* 30–33.

Helmholtz, H. von. (1925). *Handbook of physiological optics* (J. P. C. Southall, Trans.). New York: Optical Society of America. (Originally published 1866)

Hochberg, J. E. (1978). *Perception.* Englewood Cliffs, NJ: Prentice-Hall.

Hoemann, H. W. (1978). Perception by the deaf. In E. C. Carterette & M. P. Friedman (Eds.), *Handbook of perception* (Vol. 10). New York: Academic Press.

Hofsten, C. von. (1980). Predictive reaching for moving objects by human infants. *Journal of Experimental Child Psychology, 30,* 369–382.

Hofsten, C. von. (1984). Developmental changes in the organization of prereaching movements. *Developmental Psychology, 20,* 378–388.

Hofsten, C. von., & Lindhagen, K. (1979). Observations on the development of reaching for moving objects. *Journal of Experimental Child Psychology, 28,* 158–173.

Hubel, D. H., & Weisel, T. N. (1970). Binocular interaction in striate cortex of kittens reared with artificial squint. *Journal of Physiology, 206,* 419–436.

Humphrey, T. (1978). Function of the nervous system during prenatal life. In U. Stave (Ed.), *Perinatal physiology.* New York: Plenum.

Ivinskis, A., & Finlay, D. C. (1980). *Cardiac responses in four-month-old infants to stimuli moving at three different velocities.* Paper presented at the International Conference on Infant Studies, New Haven, CT.

Johansson, G. (1975). Visual motion perception. *Scientific American, 232,* 76–88.

Jusczyk, P. W. (1985). The high amplitude sucking technique as a methodological tool in speech perception research. In G. Gottlieb & N. A. Krasnegor (Eds.), *Measurement of audition and vision in the first year of postnatal life: A methodological overview.* Norwood, NJ: Ablex.

Kant, I. (1924). *Critique of pure reason* (F. M. Müller, Trans.). New York: Macmillan. (Originally published 1781)

Karmel, B. Z., & Maisel, E. B. (1975). A neuronal activity model for infant visual attention. In L. B. Cohen & P. Salapatek (Eds.), *Infant perception: From sensation to cognition* (Vol. 1). New York: Academic Press.

Kaufmann, R., & Kaufmann, F. (1980). The face schema in 3- and 4-month-old infants: The role of dynamic properties of the face. *Infant Behavior and Development, 3,* 331–339.

Kavale, K. (1982). Meta-analysis of the relationship between visual perceptual skills and reading achievement. *Journal of Learning Disabilities, 15,* 42–51.

Kessen, W. (1967). Sucking and looking: Two organized congenital patterns of behavior in the human newborn. In H. W. Stevenson, E. H. Hess, & H. L. Rheingold (Eds.), *Early behavior: Comparative and developmental approaches.* New York: Wiley.

Kessen, W., & Bornstein, M. H. (1978). Discriminability of brightness change for infants. *Journal of Experimental Child Psychology, 25,* 526–530.

Kuchuk, A., Vibbert, M., & Bornstein, M. H. (1986). The perception of smiling and its experiential correlates in 3-month-old infants. *Child Development, 57,* 1054–1061.

Lasky, R. E., Syrdal-Lasky, A., & Klein, R. E. (1975). VOT discrimination by four- to six-and-a-half-month-old infants from Spanish environments. *Journal of Experimental Child Psychology, 20,* 215–225.

Leehey, S. C., Moskowitz-Cook, A., Brill, S., & Held, R. (1975). Orientational anisotropy in infant vision. *Science, 190,* 900–901.

Lewis, T. L., Maurer, D., & Brent, H. P. (1985). The effects of visual deprivation during infancy on perceptual development. *British Journal of Ophthalmology, 70,* 214–220.

Lewkowicz, D. J., & Turkewitz, G. (1980). Cross-modal equivalence in early infancy: Auditory-visual intensity matching. *Developmental Psychology, 16,* 597–607.

Lipsitt, L. P. (1977). Taste in human neonates: Its effects on sucking and heart rate. In J. M. Weiffenbach (Ed.), *Taste and development.* Bethesda, MD: DHEW.

Maurer, D. (1975). Infant visual perception: Methods of study. In L. B. Cohen & P. Salapatek (Eds.), *Infant perception: From sensation to cognition* (Vol. 1). New York: Academic Press.

Maurer, D. (1985). Infants' perception of facedness. In T. Field & N. Fox (Eds.), *Social perception in infancy.* Norwood, NJ: Ablex.

McKenzie, B. E., & Day, R. H. (1971). Orientation discrimination in infants: A comparison of visual fixation and operant training methods. *Journal of Experimental Child Psychology, 11,* 366–375.

McKenzie, B. E., Tootell, H. E., & Day, R. H. (1980). Development of visual size constancy during the first year of human infancy. *Developmental Psychology, 16,* 163–174.

Meltzoff, A. N., & Borton, R. W. (1979). Intermodal matching by human neonates, *Nature, 282,* 403–404.

Meltzoff, A. N., & Moore, M. K. (1983). The origins of imitation in infancy: Paradigm, phenomena, and theories. In L. P. Lipsitt (Ed.), *Advances in infancy research* (Vol. 2). Norwood, NJ: Ablex.

Miyawaki, K., Strange, W., Verbrugge, R. R., Liberman, A. M., Jenkins, J. J., & Fujimura, O. (1975). An effect of linguistic experience: The discrimination of [r] and [l] by native speakers of Japanese and English. *Perception & Psychophysics, 18,* 331–340.

Moskowitz-Cook, A. (1979). The development of photopic spectral sensitivity in human infants. *Vision Research, 19,* 1133–1142.

Nettlebeck, T., & Wilson, C. (1985). A cross-sequential analysis of developmental differences in speed of visual information processing. *Journal of Experimental Child Psychology, 40,* 1–22.

Olsho, L. W. (1984). Infant frequency discrimination. *Infant Behavior and Development, 7,* 27–35.

Olsho, L. W., Schoon, C., Sakai, R., Turpin, R., & Sperduto, V. (1982a). Preliminary data on frequency discrimination. *Journal of the Acoustical Society of America, 71,* 509–511.

Olsho, L. W., Schoon, C., Sakai, R., Turpin, R., & Sperduto, V. (1982b). Auditory frequency discrimination in infancy. *Developmental Psychology, 18,* 721–726.

Packer, O., Hartmann, E. E., & Teller, D. Y. (1985). Infant color vision: The effect of test field size on Rayleigh discriminations. *Vision Research, 24,* 1247–1260.

Palmer, S. E., & Hemenway, K. (1978). Orientation and symmetry: Effects of multiple, rotational, and near symmetries. *Journal of Experimental Psychology: Human Perception and Performance, 4,* 691–702.

Parke, R. D. (1978). Children's home environments: Social and cognitive effects. In I. Altman & J. F. Wohlwill (Eds.), *Children and the environment: Vol. 3. Human behavior and environment.* New York: Plenum.

Passman, R. H., & Longeway, K. P. (1982). The role of vision in maternal attachment: Giving 2-year-olds a photograph of their mother during separation. *Developmental Psychology, 18,* 530–533.

Peeples, D. R., & Teller, D. Y. (1975). Color vision and brightness discrimination in two-month-old human infants. *Science, 189,* 1102–1103.

Peeples, D. R., & Teller, D. Y. (1978). White-adapted photopic spectral sensitivity in human infants. *Vision Research, 18,* 49–53.

Piaget, J. (1954). *The construction of reality in the child.* New York: Basic Books.

Pipp, S., & Haith, M. M. (1984). Infant visual responses to pattern: Which metric predicts best? *Journal of Experimental Child Psychology, 38,* 373–399.

Porges, S. W. (1974). Heart rate indices of newborn attentional responsivity. *Merrill-Palmer Quarterly, 20,* 231–254.

Porter, R. H., & Doane, H. M. (1976). Maternal pheromone in the spiny mouse (*Acomys cahirinus*). *Physiology and Behavior, 16,* 75–78.

Porter, R. H., Cernoch, J. M., & McLaughlin, F. J. (1983). Maternal recognition of neonates through olfactory cues. *Physiology and Behavior, 30,* 151–154.

Rosch, E. (1975). Cognitive reference points. *Cognitive Psychology, 7,* 532–547.

Rose, S. A. (1984). Developmental changes in hemispheric specialization for tactual processing in very young children: Evidence from cross-modal transfer. *Developmental Psychology, 20,* 568–574.

Rose, S. A., Gottfried, A. W., & Bridger, W. H. (1978). Cross-modal transfer in infants: Relationship to prematurity and socioeconomic background. *Developmental Psychology, 14,* 643–652.

Rose, S. A., Gottfried, A. W., & Bridger, W. H. (1979). Effects of haptic cues on visual recognition memory in full-term and preterm infants. *Infant Behavior and Development, 2,* 55–67.

Rose, S. A., Gottfried, A. W., & Bridger, W. H. (1981). Cross-modal transfer and information processing by the sense of touch in infancy. *Developmental Psychology, 17,* 90–98.

Rose, S. A., & Ruff, H. A. (1987). Cross-modal transfer. In J. D. Osofsky (Ed), *Handbook of infant development* (2nd ed.). New York: Wiley.

Royer, F. L. (1981). Detection of symmetry. *Journal of Experimental Psychology: Human Perception and Performance, 7,* 1186–1210.

Ruff, H. A. (1984). Infants' manipulative exploration of objects: Effects of age and object characteristics. *Developmental Psychology, 20,* 9–20.

Ruff, H. A. (1985). Detection of information specifying the motion of objects by 3- and 5-month-old infants. *Developmental Psychology, 21,* 295–305.

Russell, M. J., Mendelson, T. & Peeke, H. V. S. (1983). Mothers' identification of their infants' odors. *Ethology and Sociobiology, 4,* 29–31.

Samuels, C. A. (1985). Attention to eye contact opportunity and facial motion by three-month-old infants. *Journal of Experimental Child Psychology, 40,* 105–114.

Schaller, J. (1975). Chromatic vision in human infants: Conditioned operant fixation to "hues" of varying intensity. *Bulletin of the Psychonomic Society, 6,* 39–42.

Schiff, W., Benasich, A., & Bornstein, M. H. (1986). *Infants' sensitivity to audio-visual coherence.* Unpublished manuscript, New York University.

Schneider, B. A., Trehub, S. E., & Bull, D. (1980). High-frequency sensitivity in infants. *Science, 207,* 1003–1004.

Scibetta, J. J., Rosen, M. G., Hochberg, C. J., & Chik, L. (1971). Human fetal brain response to sound during labor. *American Journal of Obstetrics and Gynecology, 109,* 82–85.

Schulman-Galambos, C., & Galambos, R. (1979). Brain stem evoked response audiometry in newborn hearing screening. *Archives of Otolaryngology, 105,* 86–90.

Siqueland, E. R., & DeLucia, C. A. (1969). Visual reinforcement of nonnutritive sucking in human infants. *Science, 165,* 1144–1146.

Slater, A., Morison, V., Town, C., & Rose, D. (1985). Movement perception and identity constancy in the new-born baby. *British Journal of Developmental Psychology, 3,* 211–220.

Spence, A. J., & De Casper, A. J. (1984). *Human fetuses perceive maternal speech.* Paper presented to the International Conference on Infant Studies, Austin, TX.

Steiner, J. E. (1977). Facial expressions of the neonate infant indicating the hedonics of food-related chemical stimuli. In J. M. Weiffenbach (Ed.), *Taste and development.* Bethesda, MD: DHEW.

Steiner, J. E. (1979). Human facial expressions in response to taste and smell stimulation. In H. Reese & L. Lipsitt (Eds.), *Advances in child development and behavior* (Vol. 13). New York: Academic Press.

Strauss, S. (Ed.) (1982). *U-shaped behavioral growth.* New York: Academic Press.

Streeter, L. A. (1976). Language perception of 2-month-old infants shows effects of both innate mechanisms and experience. *Nature, 259,* 39–41.

Tamis-LeMonda, C., & Bornstein, M. H. (1986). *Mother-infant interaction: The selectivity of encouraging attention.* Paper presented at the International Conference on Infancy Studies, Los Angeles, CA.

Teller, D. Y. (1979). The forced-choice preferential looking procedure: A psychophysical technique for use with human infants. *Infant Behavior and Development, 2,* 135–153.

Teller, D. Y., & Bornstein, M. H. (1986). Infant color vision and color perception. In P. Salapatek & L. B. Cohen (Eds.), *Handbook of infant perception.* New York: Academic Press.

Teller, D. Y., Peeples, D. R., & Sekel, M. (1978). Discrimination of chromatic from white light by two-month-old infants. *Vision Research, 18,* 41–48.

Trehub, S. E., & Chang, H. (1977). Speech as reinforcing stimulation for infants. *Developmental Psychology, 13,* 121–124.

Trehub, S. E., Schneider, B. A., & Endman, M. (1980). Developmental changes in infants' sensitivity to octave-band noises. *Journal of Experimental Child Psychology, 29,* 283–293.

Tuchmann-Duplessis, H., Auroux, M., & Haegel, P. (1975). *Illustrated human embryology* (Vol. 3). New York: Springer-Verlag.

Turkewitz, G., & Kenny, P. A. (1982). Limitations on input as a basis for neural organization and perceptual development: A preliminary theoretical statement. *Developmental Psychology, 15,* 357–368.

Turkewitz, G., & Kenny, P. A. (1985). The role of developmental limitations of sensory input on sensory/perceptual organization. *Journal of Developmental and Behavioral Pediatrics, 6,* 302–306.

Varner, D., Cook, J. E., Schneck, M. E., McDonald, M., & Teller, D. Y. (1984). Tritan discriminations by 1- and 2-month-old human infants. *Vision Research, 25,* 821–832.

Vellutino, F. R. (1977). Alternative conceptualizations of dyslexia: Evidence in support of a verbal-deficit hypothesis. *Harvard Educational Review, 47,* 334–354.

Wachs, T. D., Užgiris, I. C., & Hunt, J. McV. (1971). Cognitive development in infants of different age levels and from different environmental backgrounds: An exploratory investigation. *Merrill-Palmer Quarterly, 17,* 283–317.

Warren, D. H. (1978). Perception by the blind. In E. C. Carterette & M. P. Friedman (Eds.), *Handbook of perception* (Vol. 10). New York: Academic Press.

Watson, J. S. (1966). Perception of object orientation in infants. *Merrill-Palmer Quarterly, 12,* 73–94.

Weiner, K., & Kagan, J. (1976). Infants' reaction to changes in orientation of figure and frame. *Perception, 5,* 25–28.

Werker, J. F., Gilbert, J. H. V., Humphrey, K., & Tees, R. C. (1981). Developmental aspects of cross-language speech perception. *Child Development, 52,* 344–355.

Werker, J. F., & Tees, R. C. (1983). Developmental changes across childhood in the perception of nonnative speech sounds. *Canadian Journal of Psychology, 37,* 278–286.

Wertheimer, M. (1938). Numbers and numerical concepts in primitive peoples. In W. D. Ellis (Ed.), *A source book of gestalt psychology.* New York: Harcourt.

White, B. L., & Held, R. (1966). Plasticity of sensorimotor development. In J. F. Rosenblith & W. Allinsmith (Eds.), *The causes of behavior.* Boston, MA: Allyn & Bacon.

Wittelson, S. F. (1976). Sex and the single hemisphere: Specialization of the right hemisphere for spatial processing. *Science, 193,* 425–427.

Wohlwill, J. (1983). Physical and social environment as factors in development. In D. Magnusen & V. Allen, (Eds.), *Human development: An interactional perspective.* New York: Academic.

Yonas, A. (1981). Infants' responses to optical information for collision. In R. N. Aslin, J. R. Alberts, & M. R. Peterson (Eds.), *Development of perception: Psychobiological perspectives* (Vol. 2). New York: Academic Press.

Yonas, A., & Granrud, C. E. (1985). Reaching as a measure of infants' spatial perception. In G. Gottlieb & N. A. Krasnegor (Eds.), *Measurement of audition and vision in the first year of postnatal life: A methodological overview.* Norwood, NJ: Ablex.

5 Cognitive Development

Deanna Kuhn
Columbia University

INTRODUCTION

The primary aim of this chapter is to examine the succession of ways in which the study of cognitive development has been approached during the relatively brief historical period of its existence. Such an approach is based on the premise that an examination of this sort affords the greatest insight into the topic itself. The study of cognitive development, it can be claimed, has consisted of an overlapping historical succession of conceptualizations: (a) what it is that develops; (b) the process by means of which development occurs; and (c) how the study of this development is best conducted. These conceptualizations have dictated both the questions that are selected for investigation and how the products of those investigations are understood. They have thus provided a series of "windows" through which the topic might be viewed, and it is only by examining these windows themselves—these conceptual and methodological frameworks—that one can gain a sense of how our knowledge of cognitive development has progressed.

One thing a reader new to the field is likely to gain from this chapter is an appreciation of why the study of cognitive development has not yielded simple, straightforward answers to seemingly simple, straightforward, empirically researchable questions, such as, "Does basic memory capacity increase or remain constant as the individual develops?" The reader should come to appreciate why such questions themselves, as well as their answers, turn out to be considerably more complex than they appear on the surface. While the reader new to the field may be disillusioned to learn that the field is not comprised of simple, easily answered research questions or an accumulated body of perspective-free facts, there is actually considerable reason to be optimistic regarding the field's past and prospective progress. In fact, the field is in many ways at a turning point in its own development, with considerable promise for future progress. A number of longstanding polarities, controversies, and preoccupations that have detracted attention from the central questions crucial to an understanding of cognitive development have in recent years either been resolved, set aside, or recast; the result is that attention is now focused more directly on these key questions. Some might take the negative view that through the succession of those windows in terms of which the field has proceeded, it has done no more than repeat itself and thus in effect stand still. In this chapter I suggest instead ways in which these windows are becoming larger and clearer as the perspectives they entail increase in explanatory power.

THE COORDINATION OF MIND AND REALITY: BASIC PERSPECTIVES

An adequate account of cognitive development must, at a minimum, contain answers to two basic questions: First, what is it that develops? Second, how does this development occur? The answer to the first question, at least, might appear obvious: The profound differences in the intellectual functions exhibited by the newborn infant and the mature adult are evident to the most casual observer. It is this development that is the obvious object of concern. In fact, however, different theoretical and methodological approaches to the study of cognitive development represent a wide variety of views as to what is developing, ranging from individual stimulus–response connections to discrete, context-linked skills, to a smaller set of more general cognitive functions, to a single broad system of cognitive operations that underlies all more specific intellectual abilities and behaviors.

The second question also harbors greater complexity than is suggested on the surface. There is more to be explained than how it is that intellectual functioning, or mind, is transformed during the course of development, although formulating such an explanation is in itself a formidable challenge. The full question that must be addressed, rather, is how it is that mind comes to develop *in the particular direction,* or toward the particular end, that it does (rather than in the host of other possible directions in which it might develop) so as to become well adapted to the external world of which the developing individual is a part. The two questions are of course not independent. The answer to the second question to a large degree determines the answer to the first, although the reverse is less true. The following discussion, then, focuses on answers to the second question, while noting their implications with respect to the first.

Three broad answers to the second question have appeared and reappeared throughout the history of developmental psychology. All three have roots in classical philosophical traditions that predate psychology as a field of scientific study. Each of the perspectives can be classified in terms of which of these three answers it reflects.

The first answer, rooted in the philosophical tradition known as *rationalism,* is that mind and reality exist in preestablished coordination with one another. In other words, the development of the mind in a particular direction is predetermined, presumably through some form of genetic coding unique to the species. The second answer, whose roots lie in the philosophical tradition known as *empiricism,* is that the nature of reality is imposed on the mind from without during the course of development, and it is for this reason that mind and reality come to coordinate with one another. The third answer, rooted in the philosophical tradition known as *interactionism,* is that the mind is neither in preestablished coordination with reality nor molded by it from without; that rather, through a lengthy series of interchanges between individual and environment, the coordination is gradually achieved.

Maturationism

The first of the three answers is reflected in the first theoretical perspective to have a major guiding influence on the study of child development by North American psychologists, the doctrine of *maturationism.*[1] Until the appearance of the work of Arnold Gesell, the major advocate of maturationism, studies of children's development had been conducted largely within the atheoretical "child study movement," which had flourished in America during the early part of the twentieth century. It can be argued that the myriad of descriptive studies of children's knowledge and interests produced by the child study movement did not make a lasting contribution to our understanding precisely because these investigations were not guided by an overarching conceptual framework. Gesell's studies, in strong contrast, adhere clearly to a mold dictated by his theoretical view.

Gesell was struck by the regularity he observed in the emergence of various motor abilities during the first years of life, despite huge variability in environmental circumstances. These observations led him to the thesis that new skills emerge according to a regular sequence and timetable that are the product of a predetermined genetic code, similar, for example, to the code that governs the appearance of secondary sexual characteristics at puberty. Maturation, Gesell proposed, is the internal regulatory mechanism that governs the emergence of all new skills and abilities, cognitive as well as behavioral, that appear with advancing age. According to such a view, then, a sequence of discrete skills develops by means of predetermined unfolding.

---

[1]The theories of James Baldwin, as we note later, had an influence largely confined to Europe, despite the fact that Baldwin was an American.

Gesell and his coworkers engaged in meticulous cross-sectional and longitudinal observations of infants, which enabled them to describe in precise detail the sequence and timetable in terms of which early motor abilities appeared. Subsequent research of this sort in developmental psychology has been criticized as "merely descriptive," but one cannot lodge this criticism against Gesell's work, for there is a logical link between his research strategy and his theory: If the appearance of new behaviors is the product of an innate genetic code, the researcher's task is merely to provide a precise description of this unfolding; no further explanation is necessary.

An experimental methodology would seem to have no place in Gesell's work. One experiment Gesell performed, however, has become a classic. Gesell (1929) conducted the experiment for the purpose of demonstrating the secondary role of the environment, relative to the central role he believed to be played by the process of maturation. Quite unlike most modern experiments, Gesell's experiment had only two subjects, 11-month-old twin girls. At the onset of the experiment, neither twin exhibited any proficiency in the skill that was to be the focus of the experiment, stair-climbing. Gesell proceeded to subject one of the twins to daily training sessions on a specially constructed staircase, for a period of six weeks. At the end of this period, the trained twin was a proficient stair-climber, while the control (untrained) twin still showed no ability.

At this point, the experiment would appear to show exactly the opposite of what Gesell held; that is, it appears to show that the acquisition of motor skills is highly susceptible to environmental influence. The experiment did not end at this point, however. Several weeks later, the control twin spontaneously began to exhibit some stair-climbing proficiency. At this point, Gesell instituted a 2-week period of training of the same type that had been administered to the experimental twin. At the end of this period, the control twin equalled her experimental twin in stair-climbing proficiency, and the two remained equivalent in proficiency from then on.

What Gesell wished to demonstrate by this experiment, of course, is that the environment, or "experience," plays at most a superficial, secondary role in temporarily accelerating the emergence of a skill that is destined by the maturational code to appear at a later time. Although these results were initially accepted by some as evidence of the correctness of Gesell's maturational doctrine, a major criticism of the experiment was raised. Did the experimental design adequately control for the effects of experience? The untrained twin continued to have a variety of kinds of experience, even if not specifically stair-climbing, during the period the experimental twin was being trained. Could this experience legitimately be ruled out as having contributed to the eventual appearance of the untrained twin's skill?

At first, the issue appeared to be a problem in research design. Were it feasible on ethical and technical grounds to restrict totally the experience of the control twin during the training period, then experience could be ruled out as a contributing factor. Ultimately, however, the problem was recognized as a logical, not a methodological, one. As long as an organism has life, it is undergoing some experience, by the very definition of what it is to be alive. Thus, a process of maturation can be observed only in the case of a living organism that is undergoing experience of some sort during the period of observation. One cannot, in turn, rule out the possibility of this experience having played a role in the emergence of new behaviors exhibited by the organism.

Following this recognition of the impossibility of eliminating experience as a factor contributing to development, interest in the maturational doctrine declined, and attention turned instead toward investigating *how* experience influences development. Few if any current developmental psychologists would categorize themselves as maturationists. The modern-day theorist to whom the maturationist (or the more common modern term, *nativist*) view is often attributed is the linguist Noam Chomsky. It is important to note, however, that Chomsky does not subscribe to a nativist doctrine in anything like the strong sense that Gesell did. Chomsky regards the *capacity* to acquire language as an innate capacity unique to the human organism (in contrast to Jean Piaget, who regards the capacity for language as evolving out of sensorimotor activity during infancy). Chomsky (as well as Piaget), however, regards experience as an essential aspect of the *process* of the language acquisition.

The pure doctrine of maturationism, then, is significant because of its historical influence, rather than as a guiding perspective in the present-day study of cognitive development. However, it should be emphasized that rejection of a doctrine of maturationism does not imply rejection of underlying biological changes as critical to the emergence of new cognitive or behavioral skills. On the contrary, developments in the brain and nervous system that appear to be critical for behavioral development have become a topic of intense interest and research effort. Such physical developments, however, do not by themselves initiate related behavioral developments. At most, they are enabling conditions that make it possible for the behavioral developments to take place; the process of behavioral development itself remains to be explained.

Empiricism

Although Gesell's studies were theoretically motivated, his descriptions of developmental patterns were attended to more for their practical than their theoretical significance, most likely because the field at this point—under the influence of the child study movement—was still very practically oriented. In fact, the series of books by Gesell and his coworkers describing developmental norms are still referred to today. It is probably accurate to say, then, that when the empiricist movement that had come to occupy the mainstream of academic psychology by the middle of the century embraced the field of child development, it was the first time that the field's research efforts became dominated by an overarching theoretical framework.

The empiricist view represented a striking counterinfluence following Gesell's maturationism. If developmental change does not arise from within the organism, then perhaps it is imposed from without by the environment. This solution represents the second of the three answers presented earlier: Mind and reality come to be coordinated with one another because reality imposes itself on and hence shapes the mind over the course of development. Mind, then, is in the beginning John Locke's classic *tabula rasa,* or blank slate.

The name of B. F. Skinner is the one most closely identified with the empiricist doctrine of behaviorism. Skinner explored the full implications of the Law of Effect originally proposed by E. L. Thorndike at the turn of the century: Organisms tend to repeat those behaviors that have satisfying consequences and to eliminate those that do not. Thus, the behaviors an organism comes to exhibit are a function of the behaviors' environmental consequences. The organism is thereby shaped by its environment.

Bijou and Baer are the two theorists most widely known for applying Skinner's doctrine to child development. The child, they have proposed, is best conceptualized as "a cluster of interrelated responses" (Bijou & Baer, 1961); and development, in turn, consists of the progressive shaping of these responses by the environment. Like Skinner, Bijou and Baer claimed as one of their most important tenets that the temptation of relying on unobservable internal constructs to explain behavior must be avoided. Only external, observable behaviors are the proper object of scientific study in their view, and in turn these observable behaviors are a function of observable external events. They believed that speculation about processes internal to the individual only obscures the direct connection between external behavior and the external stimuli that control it.

One might wonder what relevance such a doctrine could have for the study of cognition and its development, as cognition almost by definition is a process internal to the individual. Bijou and Baer take the position, however, that cognition is nothing more than a particular class of behavior and as such is under the same environmental control as any other behavior. For example, consider what (mistakenly) might be regarded as an internal concept that a young child has of, say, *animals.* What this so-called "concept" actually consists of, Bijou and Baer held, is a common behavioral response the child has learned to exhibit (as a function of external reinforcement) in the presence of objects or events that have a certain set of properties (e.g., movement, four legs, eyes, nose, mouth, perhaps fur or a tail). It is thus not fruitful to regard the concept as either inside the child's head or existing in nature. Rather, such "conceptual" behavior is under the control of the environmental agents who administer the appropriate reinforcement contingencies (i.e., signify approval if the child emits the proper response when the defining properties are present). It could well be a different set of properties (and hence a different "conceptual" behavior) that the agents choose to reinforce. (See Bijou, 1976, Chapters 3 and 4, for an elaboration of this view of concept development.)

A few fundamental principles have governed research in cognitive development carried out within the empiricist framework; the most important are the principle of reductionism, the related principle of parsimony, and the principle of experimental control. *Reductionism* has been influential both as a theoretical principle and as a research strategy. As a theoretical principle, reductionism is the assertion that any complex behavior is in fact a constellation of very simple behaviors. As a research strategy, reductionism dictates that the smallest possible behavioral units that make up a complex behavior be isolated and investigated individually. Once the process governing each of these individual units is understood, explanations of more complex forms of behavior should follow.

The related principle of *parsimony* holds that an explanatory mechanism that accounts for the broadest range of phenomena is to be preferred over one that accounts for a narrower range of phenomena. In the case of behaviorist theory, this had meant that more complex explanations must be rejected if a behavior can be accounted for in terms of the simple mechanism of operant conditioning, or control by means of external reinforcement. Applied in the field of developmental psychology, the major implication is that developmental phenomena can (and should) be regarded as the accumulated effects of the operation of the simple conditioning (or learning) mechanism. In other words, development can be reduced to the simpler process of learning. Hence, there is no need to retain the more complex term.

The parsimony principle is also reflected in the assumption that the basic learning mechanism functions in an identical way throughout the individual's development. An implication of this assumption with respect to research strategy is that there is no need to compare individuals at different points in development. If a particular learning process is observed to operate at one age level, it is assumed that it will operate in the same way at any other age level. Thus, researchers studying cognitive development within an empiricist framework have tended to utilize a single age group in their studies. Rarely have they engaged in the cross-sectional and longitudinal age comparisons characteristic of much developmental research.

The principle of *experimental control* has led to the almost exclusive choice of an experimental laboratory method. Because the laboratory provides a controlled environment, the researcher can introduce the environmental variable believed to control a particular behavior, with reasonable assurances that some other (uncontrolled) variable has not actually produced the behavior, as might be the case in a natural setting.

A research program conducted within the empiricist framework that illustrates all of these principles is the laboratory study of paired-associate learning that was prevalent in the 1950s and 1960s. In a paired-associate learning experiment, a subject is exposed to pairs of nonsense syllables (e.g., PIF and LER) until the subject establishes a connection between the two members of the pair, such that presentation of one syllable enables the subject to recite the other. The choice of arbitrary (nonsensical) material to be learned is not itself arbitrary but rather is an important part of the research strategy, dictated by the objective of experimental control. Arbitrary associations between meaningless syllables will be completely, and therefore equally, new to all learners. Individual differences in past learning and reinforcement are thus controlled for.

Paired-associate learning experiments were conducted both with children and adults as subjects. The purpose of these experiments, however, was not to compare the performance of different age groups. Rather, the large number of studies conducted were all devoted to identifying the variables (for example, exposure time or distinctiveness of syllables) that affect the learning process; it was assumed that these variables would function in an identical way for all subjects at all ages.

The tremendous effort devoted to the study of paired-associate learning was justified on the assumption that it represents one of the simplest, most basic forms of learning, and that an understanding of how it operates would provide a key to understanding more complex and significant forms of learning that occur in schools and other natural settings. To critics who argue that it would be preferable to devote research effort to studying these more complex forms of learning directly, proponents of the reductionist strategy counter that the learning that occurs in natural contexts is simply too complex to be amenable to investigation. The reductionist strategy, they would claim, provides the only avenue to eventual understanding. The controversy between pro- and antireductionist positions has continued in various forms within the field of psychology to the present day. Later, we shall examine further how the reductionist strategy has fared in the study of cognitive development.

The maturationist and empiricist perspectives that have been described in this section reflect two of the three answers to the basic question posed at the outset: How does the mind develop so as to become coordinated with the external world it inhabits? The answers that underlie these two perspectives are diametrically opposed. The maturationist answer is that this coordination is preestablished within the individual, whereas the empiricist answer is that this coordination is imposed on the individual from without by the external world. Let us turn now to the perspective that reflects the third of these answers.

PIAGET AND CONSTRUCTIVISM

Rediscovering the Child's Mind

American developmental psychology was in many ways ripe for its "discovery" of Piaget in the 1950s. The Piagetian influence brought something that was new—and that many would argue had been conspicuously absent in the study of the child's cognitive (as well as social) development: the "rediscovery of the child's mind," as one observer (Martin, 1959/60) put it at the time. Some would go so far as to claim that the study of cognitive development began with Piaget;

before Piaget, there existed a psychology of learning, not a psychology of development. Many of Piaget's ideas are evident in the work of the philosopher and psychologist James Mark Baldwin (Wozniak, 1982), as well as Piaget's contemporary, Heinz Werner (1948). Yet it was Piaget who was to have the major influence on the study of cognitive development in American psychology, even though his scholarly career had been underway in Europe for several decades before American psychologists became interested in his work.

Piaget's descriptions of "childish" thought intrigued a wide audience of psychologists and educators. His revelations of the beliefs of young children— that liquid changes when poured into a differently shaped container, that names are a part of the objects they represent, that the sun follows one around and thinks and feels as humans do, that one's own thoughts and dreams are material objects apparent to observers, to cite a few of the most well-known examples—were startling to many who regarded themselves as knowledgeable about children. Such features of children's thought had evidently been "there to be seen" for centuries, but in most cases had never been noted before.

Yet Piaget himself found these observations of childish thought significant not so much for their own sake as for their implications regarding the mechanisms by means of which the mind develops. Consider, for example, the container of liquid portrayed in Fig. 5.1. If asked to draw the liquid as it would appear while the container is tilted at a 45-degree angle, young children tend not to represent the liquid by a line parallel to the true horizontal (left side of Fig. 5.1). Instead, they draw the line representing the liquid as parallel to the top and bottom of the container (right side of Fig. 5.1). No child has ever seen liquid in a container in this way. The child's drawing, therefore, cannot be a direct reflection of his or her experiences with objects and events in the physical world. Instead, Piaget argued, it must be an intellectual construction—the child's understanding of what he or she sees.

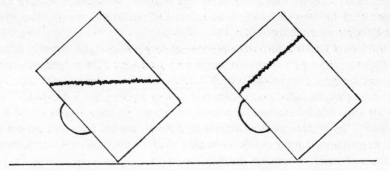

FIG. 5.1.   When asked to draw a line indicating the level of liquid in a tilted container, young children typically draw the line parallel to the top and bottom of the container (right) rather than on the true horizontal (left).

Each observation of this sort was significant in Piaget's view as testimony to the fact that the child is engaged in an extended intellectual "meaning-making" endeavor. In other words, the child is attempting to construct an understanding of self, other, and the world of objects. "Childish" beliefs, such as nonconservation (e.g., of the true horizontal, following a perceptual alteration such as tilting of the container, or of quantity, following transfer to a differently shaped container), are significant for the reason that they cannot have been directly internalized from the external world. Nor is it plausible that such beliefs are innate and simply appear, uninfluenced by the child's experience in the world.

In discounting these opposing alternatives, Piaget proposed at least the general form of a third solution to the question posed earlier of how mind and reality come to be coordinated with one another. Through a process of organism–environment, or subject–object, interchanges, the child gradually constructs an understanding of both its own actions and the external world. The most important feature of these interchanges is that they are bidirectional: The organism and the external world gradually come to "fit" one another; neither makes any radical or unilateral accommodations to the other. Each new "childish belief" that is discovered—that is, each new belief that directly reflects neither the external world nor the child's innate disposition—provides further evidence of the occurrence of some such bidirectional interchange and hence constructive process.

The Doctrine of Stages

It has been suggested that the single most central idea in Piaget's wide-ranging theorizing is that the intellectual effort to understand one's own actions and their relation to the world of objects—that is, the individual's extended "meaning-making" enterprise—motivates or energizes a constructive process directed toward progressively greater equilibrium between individual and environment. Thus, when Piaget's influence became prominent in American psychology, one might have expected that it would be this constructive meaning-making enterprise, or at the very least the "rediscovery of the child's mind," that Piaget would come to stand for.

Instead, it was the derivative doctrine of *stages* that Piaget's theory became identified with in American developmental psychology. The individual's meaning-making effort, Piaget believed, was marked by a striving for coherence, with the result that the individual's ideas had a unity to them, even if the ideas were largely incorrect by external, or mature, standards. In other words, stated more formally, these ideas were reflections of a broad, unified cognitive system that had its own unique form and that mediated all of the more specific manifestations of the individual's cognitive functioning.

Furthermore, it was this system as a whole that allegedly underwent developmental change. As a result of the interactive process directed toward adaptation, or greater equilibrium between organism and environment, the cognitive system underwent a series of major reorganizations each reflecting an improved equilibrium; that is, mind and reality were better coordinated with one another than they had been previously. These newly and better organized mental structures, or "stages," were held to appear in an invariant sequence universal to the human species, each new structure reflecting the most probable organization to emerge from the organism–environment interactions that characterized the preceding level. Each new structure represented a new set of principles or rules that governed the interaction between organism and environment. One reason the doctrine of stages may have become the focus of attention for American developmental psychologists, then, is that it respresented a challenge (and what looked like an empirically testable one) to prevailing empiricist theories, as it implied both the inevitability of the sequence of stages and their resistence to environmental influence.

Following from this structuralist theoretical perspective is an inductive research strategy, aimed at inferring the nature of the underlying cognitive system by observing a varied sampling of intellectual behaviors and postulating a model of mental structure that might underlie them. Implied in this strategy is the view that any one of these individual behaviors cannot be fully understood and appreciated in isolation. It is only by understanding their relation to each other, and to the underlying mental structure they reflect, that their true nature can be appreciated.

Following from the theoretical claim that the cognitive system undergoes a series of major transformations, is a developmental research strategy. The functional rules that describe interaction between organism and environment do not remain constant, as assumed from the empiricist perspective. Rather, these rules themselves undergo transformation, as part of the transformation of the cognitive system as a whole. Each new structure is unique, and consequently the individual at each new stage of development must be studied as a unique organism, different from what it was earlier and from what it will be at a later stage of development.

In Piaget's work these postulated structures are represented in the symbolic medium of formal logic, and each of the major structures—sensorimotor, preoperational, concrete operational, and formal operational—is regarded as a broad system of logical operations that mediates and hence unites a whole range of more specific intellectual behaviors and characteristics (Piaget, 1970). The most appropriate structure for us to examine as an example of Piagetian stage structures is the structure labelled *concrete operations*, alleged to emerge in the age range of 6 to 8 years, since it is the one that has received the most attention both in Piaget's own work and in subsequent research by others.

The central feature that defines the concrete operational thought structure and differentiates it from the earlier preoperational thought structure, Piaget claimed, is the reversibility of mental operations. Mental acts emanating from the preoperational thought structure are irreversible; they cannot be reversed and performed in the opposite direction. Thus, judging that A is smaller than B does not entail the identical judgment made from the reference point of B rather than A, that is, that B is larger than A. For this reason, the child conceptualizes phenomena in absolute rather than relative terms. For example, a young child who regards a ball as *large* is likely to find it difficult to subsequently regard this same ball as *small*, relative to another, larger ball.

The underlying irreversibility of preoperational thought, Piaget claimed, is what is responsible for many of the unique features of young children's thinking described in his investigations. Most central are the absence of operations reflecting the logic of *relations*, as just illustrated; and the logic of *classes*—that is, the ability to conceptualize elements as having multiple membership in a set of hierarchical classes (e.g., living things, human beings, man, father). It is this absence of class logic to which Piaget attributed one of his most widely cited examples of preoperational reasoning: A young child, asked if there are more roses or more flowers in a set of four roses and three tulips, is likely to reply "more roses." Such a reply, Piaget claimed, reflects the child's inability to simultaneously (and hence reversibly) regard the roses as both a subclass and a part of the larger class (flowers). Hence, the child compares the subclass *roses* to its complement *tulips*, rather than to the class *flowers*.

The complete system of operations proposed by Piaget as the concrete operational thought structure is an integrated system of the reversible operations of (a) *classification*—the combining of elements into groups based on their equivalence; and (b) *relation*—the linking of one element to another in an equivalence relation of symmetry (A is to B as B is to A, as in the case of two brothers), or in a difference relation of asymmetry (A is less than B and B is greater than A). The evolution of this structure was also postulated by Piaget to underlie the attainment of conservation: With concrete operations the child can mentally reverse the transformation (for example, the pouring of the liquid from the original to a differently shaped container), and hence deduce that the quantity must remain invariant despite its altered appearance. In addition, the irreversibility of thought prior to the evolution of the concrete operational structure was alleged by Piaget to underlie all of the characteristics of young children's thinking that he labeled "egocentric": inability to assume another perspective (role-taking), attribution of one's one psychological characteristics to material objects (*animism*), and elevation of the products of one's own psyche (thoughts, dreams) to the status of real, material events visible to others (*realism*).

Summary: Constructivism and Empiricism

In summary, the constructivist perspective that has just been described and the empiricist perspective described previously have been the two major guiding theoretical influences leading up to the present-day study of cognitive development. The two perspectives differ from one another on a number of major dimensions. The constructivist views what it is that develops as the *internal cognitive system as a whole*, the central feature of which is the individual's "meaning-making" effort to understand his or her own actions and the external world. The empiricist views what it is that develops as independent *units of external, observable behavior,* each under the individual control of environmental variables.

With respect to how development occurs, the empiricist posits a *cumulative* process in which each new behavior unit is acquired independently through operation of the same basic mechanism of shaping by the environment. The constructivist posits a *bidirectional interaction* between individual and environment, leading to a series of major qualitative reorganizations in the cognitive system as a whole and reflecting progress in the individual's "meaning-making" enterprise.

The research strategy employed by the empiricist is a nondevelopmental experimental laboratory strategy devoted to examining the process by means of which an individual behavior is shaped by environmental contingencies. Empirical investigations are therefore devoted to detailed analysis of a single simple behavior. The research strategy employed by the constructivist is inductive, as well as developmental. The researcher samples a wide range of behaviors as a basis for hypothesizing the nature of the underlying cognitive system as a whole that is presumed to generate these behaviors. Cross-age comparisons are conducted as a basis for inferring changes that occur in the cognitive system.

It is probably because the two perspectives are so diametrically opposed that the study of cognitive development during the 1960s to a large extent became polarized into two camps, with a good deal of the research and theoretical writing during this period directed toward demonstrating the merits of one of the approaches and deficiencies of the other. Since then, serious weaknesses have become apparent in each of the approaches. As a result, at most only a few theorists or researchers studying cognitive development today would classify themselves as adhering to either the empiricist or constructivist perspectives in the pure forms in which they have described here. In turn, several new perspectives have evolved and gained adherents; while each of these new perspectives retains certain aspects of empiricism or constructivism, none is in such polar opposition to another as were the original constructivist and empiricist perspectives that preceded them. Let us turn now to the weaknesses that became apparent in the empiricist and constructivist perspectives.

THE LIMITS OF EMPIRICISM

It has been suggested by some observers that researchers who conducted studies of children's learning and memory in the 1950s within the empiricist tradition that dominated at the time had no interest in childhood per se, but rather used children as subjects of convenience to investigate the processes of learning that were the real focus of their interest. Whether this claim is justified or not, a sizeable accumulation of such research supported a conclusion that gained wide acceptance: The basic mechanisms of learning function in an identical way across species and across humans of different ages. A psychology of learning is therefore applicable to children and adequate to explain development.

The Study of Learning

Subsequent research has forced a modification of this basic conclusion. The most influential series of studies, by Kendler and Kendler, originated directly in the discrimination-learning paradigm prevalent at the time. (See Kendler & Kendler, 1975, for an interesting historical review of this work.)

An example of the stimuli and reinforcement contingencies used in the basic experimental paradigm is shown in the left column of Fig. 5.2. Reinforcement is always administered if the response is made in the presence of either of the two top stimuli (designated +) and is never administered if it is made in the presence of either of the bottom stimuli (designated −). This initial "training" phase of the experiment continues until the subject reaches a preestablished criterion of some number of errorless trials—that is, repeated presentations of the four stimuli during which the subject always makes the response in the presence of a reinforced (+) stimulus and never in the presence of a nonreinforced (−) stimulus. This basic experimental paradigm was employed with quite diverse types of subjects, and so the response and reinforcement themselves might be anything from a lever press and a food pellet in the case of an animal to verbal responses and reinforcers in the case of a college student.

At this point the training phase of the procedure ends and the test phase

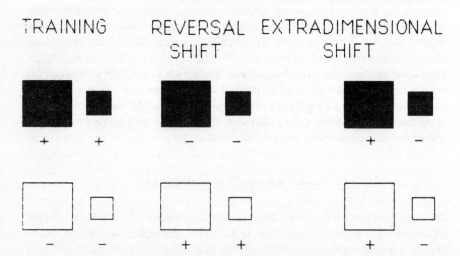

FIG. 5.2.   An example of the stimuli and reinforcement contingencies used in the basic experimental paradigm.

begins. The stimuli remain unchanged during the test phase; only the reinforcement contingencies associated with them change. The contingencies are changed in one of two ways. One of the ways (labeled *reversal shift*) is portrayed in the center column of Fig. 5.2. The other (labeled an *extradimensional shift*) is portrayed in the right column of Fig. 5.2. The question of interest is how long it takes the subject to learn the new response so as to reattain the criterion of errorless responding; that is, to respond consistently in the presence of the + stimuli and never in the presence of the − stimuli. In particular, which of the two altered contingency patterns portrayed in Fig. 5.2 should result in more rapid learning, in other words more rapid reattainment of the criterion? Readers unacquainted with this research may wish to study Fig. 5.2 and make their own prediction before reading on.

Classical empiricist theories of learning yield a clear prediction. The response (or nonresponse) to each stimulus is regarded as an associative bond that is built up as a function of the reinforcement contingencies. When the shift to the test phase occurs, at least some of these bonds must be relearned. The number of such bonds that need to be relearned, however, depends on the type of shift. The reader can verify from Fig. 5.2 that in one case (extradimensional shift), only two bonds must be relearned; the other two remain unchanged. In the other case (reversal shift), in contrast, all four must be relearned. It can be predicted, therefore, that the former will be easier to master.

Kendler and Kendler compiled substantial evidence confirming this prediction in the case of animals and young human subjects (less than 6 years of age). Uncharacteristic of researchers studying learning, however, they also studied subjects at a range of different age levels, including adulthood. They discovered that older subjects performed contrary to the learning theory prediction: For them, the reversal shift was easier to relearn than the extradimensional shift.

The inability of traditional learning theory to account for the performance of older subjects in these experiments led the Kendlers to develop a new, modified theory that they termed *mediation theory*. What the older subject is learning in the training phase of the experiment, the Kendlers proposed, is not a set of discrete associations between stimuli and responses, but rather a covert (internal) "mediational" response. In the instance portrayed in Fig. 5.2, for example, a subject may in effect say to herself, "Oh, it's the color that matters; the size has nothing to do with it." This covert response mediates, or controls, the overt responses (that is, responding in the presence of the black stimuli and inhibiting response in the presence of the white stimuli). The Kendlers initially emphasized the verbal nature of these mediating responses; that is, it was verbal labels that could be applied to the stimuli (size, color; black, white) that older subjects had learned and verbalized to themselves during the experiment. Subsequently, however, the Kendlers broadened their theory somewhat to regard mediating responses as any covert symbolic responses the subject makes to common features of the stimuli.

If older subjects do indeed make mediational responses during the training phase, then the predicted relative difficulty of the two kinds of shift changes. In the extradimensional shift, not only the overt responses but the covert mediating response must be relearned (e.g., size instead of color). In the reversal shift, only the overt responses must be relearned (e.g., respond to white, not black). Therefore, the reversal shift should be easier, exactly what the Kendlers found for subjects above the age of 5 or 6.

The Kendlers therefore proposed what was in effect a developmental theory of learning. The traditional model of formation of discrete stimulus–response bonds characterizes the learning of children until the age of 5 or 6. At about this age children develop mediational learning capacity, and at this point the mediational model becomes a more accurate description of the learning process. The historical significance of the Kendlers' formulation of mediation theory is twofold. First, their theory represented a refutation of the behaviorist maxim that the basic learning process functions in an identical way across the life cycle. How an individual learns, the Kendlers' work indicates, depends on the individual's developmental level; as a result learning cannot be studied independent of development.

Second, mediation theory represented a departure from the behaviorist maxim that observable behavior is the only proper object of scientific study, and that it is not fruitful to postulate unobservable internal constructs that mediate this observed behavior. The Kendlers' work indicated that speculating about internal processes was in this case the only route to an adequate conceptualization of the external behavior that was observed. By not doing so, one ran the risk of serious misinterpretation. In the shift experiments, the achievement of laboratory rats, 5-year-olds, and college students appears equivalent at the end of the training phase (though one group may require more trials to reach the criterion than another). Performance of the respective subject groups during the test phase, however, indicates that the learning that takes place during the training phase, though it appears equivalent in its external manifestations, is actually quite different across subject groups. A theory that makes reference to the processes underlying these seemingly equivalent observable performances seemed the only way to explain the differences in performance that the subsequent test phase revealed to be present. In other words, the Kendlers' work pointed to the importance of a distinction that would become critical in future work in cognitive psychology: the distinction between product (performance) and the process that generated it.

The Study of Memory

Some notable parallels exist between historical developments in the study of learning and historical developments in the study of memory, to which we now turn our attention.

Memory as Storage.   From the empiricist perspective that dominated psychology in the 1940s and 1950s, learning and memory were two sides of a single coin. As an example, recall the paired-associate paradigm discussed earlier. *Learning* refers to the process by which the associative bond (between the two nonsense syllables) is formed; *memory* refers to the retention or storage of that bond, once it has been formed. Because the stimuli are meaningless to the subject—that is, because the subject has no prior history of associations to them—they were considered as the ideal medium through which to study the basic processes of learning and retention in their pure form. By employing these elementary, "neutral" stimuli, basic properties of the human learning and memory apparatus might be identified. For example, how many exposures are required for an association to be formed, and what is the organism's storage capacity for associations, once formed? From such a perspective, the only role that development might play in the operation of memory processes is to increase the individual's storage capacity. Memory, then, could be regarded as a set of storage compartments that become larger with age.

Memory as Construction.   Memory became a popular research topic in the 1960s, and many laboratory studies of it were conducted with both children and adults as subjects. The findings from much of this research, however, were difficult to reconcile with the concept of memory as a storage of associations, or of development as the expansion of storage space. Consider, for example, memory for an arrangement of chess pieces on a chessboard after a subject studies the board and it is then removed. One might anticipate that studies of this nature would provide indices of the capacity of the human visual memory system. Such estimates, however, have been found to be dependent on the subject's familiarity with the stimulus material, and on the constraints imposed on the stimulus material to be remembered; that is, whether the pieces are arranged on the board randomly or in a pattern conforming to the rules of chess. If the arrangement is random, chess experts and nonchess players show equal memory capacity; if the arrangement is legitimate, however, chess experts display greater memory capacity than nonchess players, even when the chess experts are children and the nonplayers adults (Chi, 1978). Other studies have shown exceptional memory capacity in very young children within domains in which they have a great deal of knowledge and experience (Chi, 1985, in press; Chi & Koeske, 1983). Thus, one cannot speak of any absolute memory capacity, even one that increases in an age-linked manner. It all depends on what it is that is being remembered, relative to the remember's existing cognitive system.

A great many other studies have suggested that, when processing a piece of information to be remembered, an individual does not store it in its intact form as an isolated unit. Instead, the individual assimilates the new information into a framework provided by the individual's existing knowledge, often altering or elaborating the new information in a way consistent with this existing knowledge base. In a series of studies, Paris and his coworkers asked children simple questions to assess their memory of short narratives. Even young children were willing to reply "yes" to a question such as "Did she use a broom?", the story having stated only, "She swept the kitchen floor" (Paris & Carter, 1973). Moreover, by the age of 9, children were able to recall a sentence such as the preceding one from the cue "broom" as effectively as from the cue "swept" (Paris & Lindauer, 1976), even though one had been explicitly and the other only implicitly present.

It appears, then, that individuals integrate new material into a framework provided by their existing knowledge and draw on this existing knowledge to make inferences that go beyond what is explicitly presented. As a result, newly acquired material cannot be clearly separated from what is already known. Memory, then, is more aptly conceptualized as a process of construction, or reconstruction, than as a process of storage. As such, it cannot be strictly separated from broader processes of reasoning and comprehension; that is, from the individual's more general "meaning-making" activity.

Memory and Development.   If memory is part of the broader cognitive system, then developmental changes in this system ought to have implications for memory functions. That this is the case has been demonstrated in both a narrow and a broad sense. In the narrow sense, the level of a subject's comprehension of material to be remembered should affect how and how well it is remembered. A simple demonstration of this influence has been provided by studies of children's ability to draw an ordered set of sticks of graduated length after they have viewed it and it is then removed (Inhelder, 1969; Liben, 1977). Children who do not comprehend the logic of asymmetrical relations (as indicated by their inability to construct a seriated array from a set of randomly ordered sticks of different lengths) have been found less able to draw a seriated array from memory after viewing one; instead they report very different-looking configurations as what they "remember" having seen (Fig. 5.3).

In the broad sense, transformations of the cognitive system ought to affect the memory function itself. A wide range of studies has been conducted indicating such developmental changes. The bulk of these have centered around the utilization of strategies to enhance memory. Organization of material to be remembered into conceptual categories, and rehearsal, for example, are both strategies that aid memory. Children below the age of Piaget's concrete operational stage show negligible use of these or other strategies to aid memory (Brown, Bransford, Ferrara, & Campione, 1983). For example, given a list of items to memorize containing foods, animals, toys, and items of clothing in a random order, older children and adults tend to recall the individual items within these superordinate categories; young children show no such organizational tendency in their recall. The absence of strategic devices in young children's performance on memory

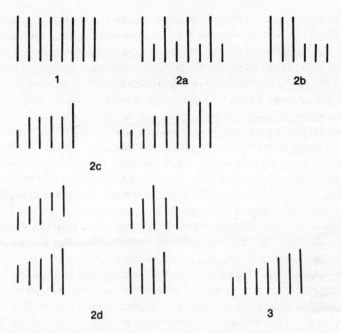

FIG. 5.3.   Various arrays produced by subjects in Inhelder's studies of memory development in children (Inhelder, 1969).

tasks is further substantiated by the finding that young children perform equivalently in a memory task whether they are instructed to try to remember the presented items or simply to look at them (Flavell, Beach, & Chinsky, 1966). Later we consider further what governs the development and utilization of memory strategies and other kinds of cognitive strategies. The most important implication to note here is that, as the Kendlers' work demonstrated with respect to learning, memory functions cannot be studied without regard to the developmental status of the subject.

Summary: The Limits of Reductionism

In summary, we have traced the ways in which both the study of learning and the study of memory came to take on both a more cognitive and a more developmental cast. Neither learning nor memory can be studied profitably as a basic process that functions uniformly, independent of what it is that is being learned or remembered and of its relation to what the learner already knows. Given this to be the case, there are the two following implications for the study of the development of learning and memory, each of which has received considerable empirical support (Brown, Bransford, Ferrara, & Campione, 1983; Paris & Lindauer, 1982; Paris, Newman, & Jacobs, 1985; Siegler, 1983; Siegler & Klahr, 1982). First, developmental change in the cognitive system influences learning and memory performance in the narrow sense that the level of comprehension of new material affects how and how well it is both learned initially and remembered. Second, developmental change in the cognitive system affects learning and memory in the broad sense of influencing the learning or memory function itself, that is, the strategies the individual utilizes in executing the task.

Perhaps the most telling indicator of the evolution that has been described is that in contrast to the 1950s and 1960s, few current psychologists classify their work as devoted exclusively to the study of learning or memory. Instead, they tend to classify themselves as cognitive psychologists, interested in the study of the cognitive system as a whole. In some ways the evolution described here might be interpreted as a failure on the part of the principle of reductionism. As described earlier, the principle of reductionism and the related principle of parsimony led to the invocation of a single basic mechanism to account for acquisition of new behavior, irrespective of the behavior, the organism, or the relation between the two. The research reviewed here indicates that this assumption is incorrect. As a research strategy, reductionism dictated that very simple behaviors be isolated and studied independently. Once the acquisition mechanism governing these very simple isolated behaviors was understood, understanding of more complex and significant forms of behavior would follow. It is fair to say that this promise has not been realized. It is now largely accepted that the search for a single content- and context-free acquisition mechanism will not be fruitful, and that mastery of new cognitive material cannot be investigated independent of the broader context of the meaning the subject attributes to the material and to the task.

The implications for methodological practice are substantial. In the case of the paired-associate research paradigm described earlier, strong critics (e.g., Riegel, 1978) have characterized the studies themselves, not just the task material, as nonsensical and bound to have failed on the grounds that the learning that is observed is of no meaning or relevance to the learner; because such learning occurs completely out of any context, it cannot possibly provide insight into natural context-bound processes of learning. At a minimum, it has been established that context and meaning have a profound effect on performance (Paris, Newman, & Jacobs, 1985), an issue we shall further explore later on. Thus, studying the acquisition of arbitrary (meaningless) material in artificial settings offers at best limited insight into the acquisition of meaningful material as it occurs in complex, meaning-rich contexts. This limitation has been particularly severe in the study of memory development, in which work has been confined largely to the laboratory study of memory for arbitrary stimuli (Brown & De-Loache, 1978; Brown et al., 1983). The last decade, however, has seen an increasing concern with the investigation of cognitive functions and their development in contexts that are meaningful to the individuals being studied; this is a trend we shall have more to say about later on.

Even a rejection of reductionism, and the resulting theoretical and methodological concepts of a context-free acquisition mechanism, however, does not force a total repudiation of the empiricist view. A few theorists, such as Bijou and Baer, have retained an orthodox behaviorist perspective. More common, however, are the "neobehaviorist" formations proposed by the Kendlers and several others (Gagné, 1968; Gholson, 1980; Rosenthal & Zimmerman, 1978). Largely abandoned by the neobehaviorists are the refusal to speculate about internal processes, reductionism in its radical form, and the nondevelopmental research strategy. Common to all of the neobehaviorist formulations, however, is endorsement of the empiricist solution to the question of mechanism: Mind is shaped from without by the unidirectional effects of the environment.

THE LIMITS OF CONSTRUCTIVISM

Empirical evidence incompatible with the theory brought into focus the limitations of orthodox behaviorism as an explanatory framework for cognitive development. During the 1960s and 1970s, American developmental psychologists conducted extensive research related to Piaget's work, much of it disconfirming predictions derived from Piagetian theory. One might have expected, then, that this work would, in a similar way, have brought into focus the limitations of constructivism as an explanatory framework for cognitive development. In this case, however, matters are more complex, for it was not constructivism to which researchers principally addressed their studies, but rather Piaget's doctrine of stages.

Stages

The most straightforward prediction derived from stage theory is that the various behaviors that are the alleged manifestations of the underlying stage structure ought to emerge in synchrony, as indicators of the emergence of the underlying structure. In the case of the various behaviors alleged to be manifestations of the concrete operational structure, a large number of studies were performed that replicated Piaget's findings that these behaviors emerge in the age range of 6 to 8 years. Researchers then went on to investigate whether, within individual children, the behaviors appear synchronously at some point during this age period— an issue with respect to which Piaget himself had not reported empirical data. A substantial amount of data has now been collected; none of it has yielded strong evidence that concrete operational concepts, such as hierarchical classification, seriation, transitivity, conservation, and various forms of perspective-taking, emerge synchronously, even though they all appear during the same general age range.

In the face of such findings, some developmentalists came to Piaget's defense, objecting that Piagetian theory did not proclaim a precise synchrony but rather only emergence during a broader period of several years, by the end of which the various abilities had consolidated into the structured whole specified by the theory. Others objected on methodological grounds to the studies showing lack of synchrony: The set of tasks administered to a subject to assess the various concepts, they claimed, had not been equated with respect to their more superficial performance demands, having little to do with the concept itself. One assessment task, for example, may have been presented in such a manner that it made greater demands on the subject's verbal skills than did the other tasks, and for this reason display of the concept being assessed by this task was delayed relative to the concepts assessed by the other tasks.

This second objection, however, points to what is an even more fundamental problem for stage theory: Even slight and what one would expect to be insignificant modifications in task format can drastically alter the likelihood that subjects will exhibit the concept being assessed. For example, whether children will recognize the subclass as part of the class (class inclusion) in the example of roses and flowers given earlier is affected by the numerical ratio between the two. Thus, even *within* a single task or concept domain, whether the concept is judged to be present or absent depends to a considerable extent on particulars of the assessment procedure. The sizeable literature that accumulated on children's attainment of Piagetian concepts showed this to be the case for every one of the concepts investigated. Using one assessment procedure, for example, 30% of 6-year-olds might be assessed as having attained a particular concrete operational concept. Using a slightly different procedure, perhaps 70% of the same group of 6-year-olds would be assessed as having attained the concept. On what basis does one decide which procedure yields the "true" incidence of attainment?

These demonstrations of so-called task variance were particularly significant because they suggested that Piagetian assessment tasks were not "pure" measures of an underlying reasoning competency, in the way that Piaget's descriptions of them implied. Rather, a number of distinguishable skills appeared to be involved in successful performance on a task, many of which were not an integral part of the reasoning competency that was the focus of the assessment. Consider, for example, the concept of *transitivity*, alleged to be part of the concrete operational structure. Piaget theorized that once the child's mental actions involving relational comparisons of the form $A > B$ are organized into a reversible mental structure, such that $A > B$ is recognized as entailing $B < A$, this reversibility should enable the child mentally to construct a seriated array— that is, $A > B > C > D$—as well as to derive additional order relations from those given. For example, given $A > B$ and $B > C$, the child should be able to make the inference $A > C$. Because B is understood as participating in dual relations, in one as less than A and in another as greater than C, it can serve as the mediator linking A and C. Piaget referred to this inference as the inference of transitivity.

A number of subsequent studies of the transitivity inference, however, by

Trabasso, Bryant, and others (Bryant & Trabasso, 1971; Trabasso, 1975) aimed to demonstrate that there is more involved in making an inference of transitivity than the inference itself. Each of the individual relations—that is, A > B and B > C—must first of all be attended to and encoded by the subject. Each relation must then in some manner be represented and retained in the subject's cognitive system. Failure with respect to any of these steps would be sufficient to prevent the inference from being made, for example if the subject forgot one of the initial relations. The studies by Trabasso and Bryant endeavored to show that, if successful execution of these initial components were insured (for example, by exposing subjects to extended training with respect to the initial relations), children several years younger than the ages reported by Piaget would show successful performance on a transitivity task. Similar analyses of other concrete operational concepts have been proposed, such as, for example, an analysis of the class inclusion concept by Trabasso et al. (1978).

In addition to suggesting that multiple skills enter into performance on a Piagetian reasoning task, the Trabasso and Bryant studies were examples of the numerous so-called "training" studies conducted in the 1960s and 1970s; these are examined in more detail later, in a discussion of methods for studying developmental change. In these studies, attempts were made to induce a particular concept alleged to be part of the Piagetian stage structure by exposing children who had not yet attained the concept to some form of training in an experimental laboratory session. Whether the changes from pretest to posttest assessment that occurred in many of these studies were superficial or genuine became the topic of extended debate. At the very least, however, the studies demonstrated that with relatively minimal instruction children could be taught to display some of the behaviors characteristic of the stage structure they had not yet attained naturally, bringing into question the claim that such behaviors are integral parts of a structured whole.

All the forms of evidence described so far—evidence of asynchrony in emergence, of heterogeneous skills contributing to performance on assessment tasks, and of susceptibility of this performance to environmental influences—contributed to an increasing disenchantment with the Piagetian doctrine of stages during the 1970s. Positing a single, unified structure, the evolution of which is totally responsible for all of the more specific changes in intellectual functioning that occur over the course of development, appeared an oversimplification that did not fit with a growing body of research data. In a certain sense, stage doctrine in its strong form appeared to be a kind of reductionism of an opposite sort to that adopted by those working within the empiricist framework: Instead of the accumulation of large numbers of individually governed small behavioral units, development could be reduced to the evolution of a single, unitary, all-encompassing structure. For further discussion of the debate surrounding stage theory, the reader is referred to articles by Brainerd (1978) and Flavell (1982), and a volume by Levin (1986).

Further disenchantment with stage theory arose from the fact that Piaget's descriptions of the major stage structures such as concrete operations were not closely linked to the actual mental processes in which a subject might engage when responding to one of the typical assessment tasks. Rather, as was illustrated earlier, these structures were described in terms of formal logical models sufficiently abstract and removed from surface behavior that readers of Piaget's descriptions were left uncertain as to how such models might ever be validated as true portrayals of the individual's mental structure.

In the absence of satisfying answers to such questions, large numbers of developmental psychologists turned away from stage theory, in search of what they hoped would be more promising models of cognitive development. The problem came, however, in articulating what might replace stage theory. To conclude that the positing of a single unified structure as what develops is an oversimplification does not dictate the opposite extreme: that discrete competencies develop entirely independent of and unrelated to one another. The truth is almost certain to lie between these two extremes (Flavell, 1982). The central theoretical and research challenge, then, becomes one of characterizing the interdependencies that exist between developments that occur within distinct domains. But note that the question being posed is a question about developmental process: To what extent and in what manner do developmental changes that occur within domains interact with one another as they take place?

In many ways, theorists and researchers in cognitive development were not in a particularly strong position at that point to formulate theoretical models or research hypotheses regarding developmental process. As we have observed, Piaget's views with respect to developmental process had received relatively little attention from American developmental psychologists in favor of the derivative theory of stages. The tendency in many circles, then, was to discount Piaget's theory in its entirety in rejecting the stage doctrine. On the other hand there was little enthusiasm, following American developmental psychology's absorption with Piaget, to return to an empiricist conception of mechanism, which had become widely perceived as inadequate to deal with the complexity of human cognition and cognitive development.

I describe later in this chapter the directions in which the study of cognitive development did turn, following the disillusionment with Piaget's stage doctrine. First, however, it is important to consider the evolution that has occurred with respect to the understanding of developmental process, for during the field's preoccupation with stage theory, a few developmentalists continued to focus their attention on questions of process, or mechanism, and therefore on an examination of the merits of Piaget's constructivist hypothesis.

Constructivism

Questions about structures, it has been suggested, are really questions about the process of construction of such structures. It can be argued that the study of stages within American developmental psychology came to the dead end it did because one cannot study structures apart from the constructive processes that give rise to them.

Piaget, however, portrayed the constructive process in somewhat the same manner as he did structures, that is, in a very general, abstract form, and to some extent this mode of characterization has given rise to a similar set of problems. The process Piaget described was one in which the individual's own actions on the external world generate feedback that leads to the modification of those actions and their reorganization into new interrelations with one another. In other words, individuals themselves produce their own development (Lerner, 1982; see also Dixon & Lerner this volume). To many, this conception of developmental change seemed a welcome and desirable corrective to the empiricist view of the individual as the passive recipient of effects produced by the environment.

The effort of those who undertook to explore Piaget's constructivist model, either theoretically or empirically, however, led to articulation of two related weaknesses in the model. First, the actions generated by the individual's cognitive system that give rise to change are described by the model in such general abstract terms that it is not easy to draw on the model in conceptualizing the varieties of more specific, cognitively salient acts the individual engages in, and their likely influence on cognitive development. For example, cross-cultural findings indicating that conservation of quantity develops more rapidly in cultures that emphasize certain kinds of experiences (Newman, Riel, & Martin, 1983) are not incongruent with Piaget's model, but the model offers no way of predicting the effects of such specific variations in experience.

The second limitation, related closely to the first, is that in emphasizing the role of the individual's own self-generated actions, the constructivist model neglects the social context in which these actions, and therefore cognitive development, necessarily occur. The constructive process, whatever its precise nature, does not take place in a vacuum. In the course of their everyday experience, children encounter all sorts of implicit or explicit examples of the higher level concepts which they themselves will acquire. That does not imply that they internalize the examples to which they are exposed in any direct or automatic way. But it is equally unlikely that they systematically ignore them. Indeed, specific evidence is now accumulating to show that children attend to external models of higher level concepts in a sustained and deliberate manner (Morrison & Kuhn, 1983). The objective, then, must be to understand the specific ways in which the individual's constructive activity utilizes these external data.

Summary: Neoconstructivist Directions

The preceding discussion briefly traces the impact that Piaget's work has had on American developmental psychology from its introduction in the 1950s to the present day. During this period, American researchers collected data suggesting asynchrony in emergence of stage-related competencies, the contribution of heterogeneous skills to performance on assessment tasks, and susceptibility of this performance to environmental influence. All of these kinds of evidence contributed to a disillusionment with stage doctrine in its strong form—the doctrine that all of cognitive development can be accounted for by the evolution of a single, unitary structure. The lesser attention devoted to Piaget's more central constructivist hypothesis also revealed a set of serious problems and limitations, however, centering around the effects of specific forms of experience on the individual's cognitive development.

Faced with the limitations they perceived in Piaget's constructivist formulation, a number of developmentalists concerned with questions of process sought ways to modify or to expand on the Piagetian model to take into greater account the specific influence of the environmental context in which development takes place. Fischer (1980; Fischer & Pipp, 1984), for example, while maintaining many of the central features of Piaget's structuralism, has proposed a model in which new cognitive skills are at least initially wedded to the concrete contexts in which they are acquired; they are not the totally general, content-free acquisitions implied by Piaget's theory. Also, to a large extent in reaction to the neglect of social context in Piaget's constructivism, a renewed interest occurred in developmental theories originating within Soviet pscyhology, notably those of Luria (1976) and Vygotsky (1978). The Soviet perspective has had a substantial impact in recent years with respect to methodology as well as theory, as we discuss later. The attention of a large number of researchers in cognitive development, however, turned in another direction.

THE INFORMATION-PROCESSING APPROACH

The information-processing approach to the study of cognitive development is not as readily classifiable as have been the theoretical perspectives examined up to this point. The major reason is that by the admission of its own adherents, it is not a comprehensive theory of development or even of cognition but rather an approach to the study of cognition and, to a lesser extent, of its development. Thus, it does not take an explicit position on some of the questions a theory of cognitive development must address.

The Computer Metaphor

The origins of the information-processing approach are in cognitive rather than in developmental psychology. A major impetus for its development was the technological innovation of the modern electronic computer. At the heart of the approach is the concept that the human intellect may function as an information-processing system, of which a mechanical information-processing system—that is, the computer—is a fruitful model. How did it happen that this approach so rapidly attracted the attention and enthusiasm of a large number of developmental psychologists? It is not difficult to trace the major reasons.

Recall our earlier example of the transitivity inference. Piaget attributed the child's ability at the level of concrete operations to infer A < C, given the information A < B and B < C, to the underlying thought structure acquiring the characteristic of reversibility: The operation A < B entailed the reverse operation B > A, and B could thus be regarded as simultaneously greater than A and less than C, thereby serving as the mediator linking A and C. This explanation in terms of underlying logical structure, however, does not identify the specific mental processes by which the child produces a judgment of transitivity in a particular instance. And thus critics of Piaget's structural approach complained that there was no way to ever prove or disprove the correctness of such models as explanations of the child's behavior.

Moreover, researchers studying the transitivity inference identified a number of specific processes that must go into its correct performance such as encoding and retention of the initial relations. From such work it is only a short step to the suggestion that performance of a cognitive task is made up entirely of the serial execution of a number of individual processes such as these. The computer-inspired information-processing model from cognitive psychology offered a formal model of just such a possibility, for it is by means of such serial execution of operations that the computer functions. The guiding assumption underlying the model is that human cognitive functioning is composed of a set of individual processes that operate sequentially and that are not necessarily governed by the same principles of operation. The information-processing approach can be characterized, then, as one that focuses on these individual processes and the manner in which they operate individually and combine serially to produce the subject's performance.

What are these individual processes? The major source of influence in defining them has been the information-processing operations executed by a computer. Thus, it is assumed that information from the environment must be encoded and stored in symbolic representational form. Various processes then operate on the contents of this representation, manipulating and transforming it in ways that create new representations. These processes may be constrained by the fixed processing capacity of the system, and representations may be constrained by a fixed storage capacity. When processing is completed, output is generated in the form of a final performance, or solution to the problem.

A few information-processing psychologists have taken the computer metaphor quite literally, and have attempted to describe the cognitive operations generating a performance by means of a very exact and detailed model that could actually serve as a program enabling a computer to produce the performance. This approach has the attractive feature of containing a ready test of the model's sufficiency: Does the program successfully simulate performance on a computer? Klahr and Wallace (1976), for example, modeled performance of a number of the Piagetian concrete operational tasks, using as the basic elements of their models a collection of "condition–action" links termed "productions." In sharp contrast, however, to the study of "condition–action" (or stimulus–response) links by behaviorists of the 1950s, the work of information-processing psychologists like Klahr and Wallace is focused squarely on modeling those processes inside the "black box" that behaviorists sought to bypass. An example of the production system proposed by Klahr and Wallace to produce a transitivity judgment is shown in Fig. 5.4, which illustrates the extremely precise, detailed nature of such a model. Every minute aspect of the process must be represented explicitly or the model will fail to meet the sufficiency criterion. The computer cannot make any decisions itself that the program has left unspecified.

Klahr and Wallace's models were criticized by some as substituting one formalism (i.e., Piaget's models employing symbolic logic) with another; and indeed, following Klahr and Wallace's pioneering effort, only a few attempts to construct similar models appeared. A good deal of work followed, however, by researchers who endorsed the general spirit of Klahr and Wallace's approach without casting their models in the form of explicit computer simulations. Interestingly, these researchers continued to employ Piagetian tasks in their work,

```
03000    QUANTIFIER:(CLASS SUBIT COUNT ESTIMATE)
03100
03600    APPQUANT:(OPR CALL) simulate quant opr selection
03700                  results in (GOAL * QQQQ(X)) where QQQQ
03800                  is SUBIT, COUNT or EST
03900
04200    REL.WORD:(CLASS MORE LESS LONGER SHORTER BIGGER SMALLER EQUAL SAME)
07900
08000                  transitivity rules
08100    PTRAN:((* GOAL TRAN)(X QREL Y QREL Z) --> SAT (X ===> OLD X) SEREAD)
08200    PTR789:((* GOAL TRAN)(X QREL Z)(X QREL Y)(Y QREL Z) --> MARKREL (X QREL Y QREL Z))
08300    PTR1:((* GOAL TRAN) (X QGT Y)(Y QGT Z) --> (X QGT Z))
08400    PTR2:((* GOAL TRAN) (X QLT Y)(Y QLT Z) --> (X QLT Z))
08500    PTR3:((* GOAL TRAN) (X QEQ Y)(Y QEQ Z) --> (X QEQ Z))
08600    PTR.RE:((* GOAL TRAN)(X QREL Y)(Z QREL X) --> (NTC (Z QREL X)))
08700    PTR4:((* GOAL TRAN)(X QGT Y) --> (X ===> OLD X)(Y Q< X))
08800    PTR5:((* GOAL TRAN)(X QLT Y) --> (X ===> OLD X)(Y Q> X))
08900    PTR6:((* GOAL TRAN)(X QEQ Y) --> (X ===> OLD X)(Y Q= X))
09000    PTRAN.FAIL:((* GOAL TRAN) --> (* ==> -))
09100
09200    MARKREL:(ACTION (NTC (X Y)(OLD **)(NTC (Y Z)(OLD **)
09300             (NTC (X Z)(OLD **))
09400    SEREAD:(OPR CALL) read series for desired relation
11400
11600                  main productions
11700    P1A:((* GOAL GET.REL X Y)(X QREL Y) --> SAT (NTC (X QREL)(OLD **) SAY.IT)
11900    P1B:((* GOAL GET.REL Y X)(X QREL Y) --> SAT (NTC (X QREL)(OLD **) SAY.IT)
12100    P2:((* GOAL GET.REL)(TS)(X- GOAL CON) ABS --> (* GOAL CON))
12200    P3:((* GOAL GET.REL)(X- GOAL TRAN) ABS --> (* GOAL TRAN))
12300    P4:((* GOAL GET.REL X Y) --> (* GOAL COMPARE X Y))
12600    P6A:((* GOAL COMPARE X Y) (X QREL Y) --> SAT)
12700    P6B:((* GOAL COMPARE X Y) (X QREL Y) --> SAT)
12800    P7:((* GOAL COMPARE X Y) (QS (X)) (QS (Y))   --> RELATE)
13100    P9A:((* GOAL COMPARE X Y)(X VALUE Y) -->(VALUE ===> OLD VALUE) (* GOAL QUANTIFY (X)))
13300    P9B:((* GOAL COMPARE X Y)(X VALUE Y) --> (VALUE ===> OLD VALUE)(* GOAL QUANTIFY (Y)))
13500    P10:((* GOAL QUANTIFY (X)) (GOAL + QUANTIFIER (X)) --> SAT)
13600    P11:((* GOAL QUANTIFY (X)) --> APPQUANT )
14500
14700    PS.TRAN:(PTRAN PTR789 PTR1 PTR2 PTR3 PTR.RE PTR4 PTR5 PTR6 PTRAN.FAIL)
14800    PSM2:(P1A P1B P2 P3 P4 P6A P6B P7 P9A P9B P10 P11)
14900    PSEXEC:(PA PZ PSVERB PSVS PS.TRAN PS.CON PSM2 PQ)
```

FIG. 5.4.   PS.QC6, a model for quantitative comparison, including conservation and transitivity rules (from Klahr & Wallace, 1976).

and they began to include tasks from Piaget's formal operational stage as well as the concrete operational stage.

In an approach advocated by Siegler (1983), for example, the child's performance on a task is described by the "rule" to which that performance conforms. The rule specifies a sequence of acts that are performed in order to execute the task. A test of the adequacy of the rule in characterizing the child's behavior is the extent to which it predicts performance over a variety of specific task items. The most widely cited example is Siegler's (1976) rule-based model of performance on Piaget's balance scale task. The subject is shown a balance scale on which weights are placed at various distances from the center, and the subject must predict whether one or the other (or neither) side of the scale will go down following the removal of a supporting block. Siegler showed that the performance of 5- and 6-year-old children on such problems conformed to what he termed Rule I, in which only the number of weights is considered: Predict that the side with more weights will go down; if the weights are equal, predict balance. Older children's performance conformed better to Rule II—identical to Rule I except that in the case of equal weights, predict the side with weights at a greater distance from the fulcrum will go down—or to Rule III, which includes processing of both weight and distance information but lacks a consistent rule for integrating them. Not until mid- to late adolescence did a fully correct rule (Rule IV) begin to characterize some subjects' performance (consistent with Piaget's findings on this task). The major virtue of this kind of rule-based model of performance on a cognitive task is its explicit characterization of the sequence of mental operations the individual allegedly utilizes to execute the task.

A somewhat different approach originated with Pascual-Leone (1970) and later Case (1978a, 1978b, 1985). At the heart of their work is what they term "task analysis" of the operations a subject would have to perform in order to execute a cognitive task. An example is their task analysis of Piaget's isolation-of-variables task. In one form of the task, Piaget asked children and adolescents to experiment with a set of rods that differed on several dimensions (e.g., length, thickness, material) to discover what determined their flexibility. Not until early adolescence, Piaget found, do subjects employ an isolation-of-variables strategy: to hold the level on all other variables constant while systematically varying the level of one variable to assess its effect. Piaget linked this development to emergence of the cognitive structure of formal operations.

Based on his task analysis, Case (1978b) argued that what the subject needs in order to perform this task is very simple:

All the subject must do is to identify an object with an extreme position value on the dimension to be tested (e.g., a long stick), then identify an object with an extreme negative value (e.g., a short stick), and then check to see if there is any *other* difference between these two objects that might affect the result of interest (e.g., bending). (p. 199)

Portrayed more formally, the subject must execute the set of procedures shown in Table 5.1 (from Case, 1978b).

The virtues of the information-processing approach to analyzing performance on cognitive tasks are readily apparent, and it is easy to see why the approach was particularly attractive to those developmentalists who had become disillusioned with Piagetian stage theory. In contrast to Piagetian models of cognitive competence—which seemed vague, abstract, removed from specific behavior, and unverifiable—information-processing analyses offered explicit, precisely articulated models of the series of cognitive operations a subject actually executes in performing a cognitive task. Less readily apparent, however, were several of the strengths of the constructivist approach that one sacrificed in adopting the information-processing approach. The reason this loss was less apparent has to do with what we have already noted with respect to the way American psychologists interpreted Piaget; that is, their focus on the theory of stages at the expense of the theory of constructivism.

A Return to Reductionism

The constructivist and information-processing perspectives differ radically in two respects. One is the information-processing perspective's explicit commitment to reductionism, in contrast to the constructivist perspective's explicit commitment to antireductionism, or holism. The other is the focus within the constructivist perspective on reflective aspects of cognition, in contrast to their de-emphasis within the information-processing perspective. Consider the issue of reductionism first.

The dual respects in which the modern-day information-processing approach is committed to reductionism closely parallel the respects in which the behaviorist approach of the 1950s and 1960s was described as committed to reductionism. First, in a theoretical vein, molar behavior is regarded as composed of a number of smaller, individually controlled elements. Second, in a methodological vein, the most fruitful research strategy is considered to be focused on a particular, well-specified task domain (such as our earlier example of paired-associate learning), which, once well understood, will permit generalization to broader (and more significant) domains of behavior. Piagetian theory and research strategy, of course, are notable, in contrast, as nonreductionistic—individual elements can be properly interpreted only in relation to the whole.

Methodologically, the result has been a series of exceptionally meticulous, detailed models of the procedures subjects employ in performing a particular task, ones that serve as pioneering examples in some sense of the precision to which psychological models might aspire. One of the major criticisms, however, that has been leveled against these task analyses of specific cognitive tasks pertains to their verifiability. Although closer to observable performance than Piaget's logical models, task analyses by no means constitute a magical key that

TABLE 5.1
Detailed Model for Control of Variables[a] (from Case, 1978)

Step or Operation	Specific Schemes	Symbol[b]
1. Identify the object with extreme positive value on the dimension to be tested (e.g., long).	(1) Operative scheme corresponding to the working definition of the positive pole of the dimension to be tested (e.g., for length, if the object sticks out the most, call it the longest).	ψ Dimension to be tested (+)
	(2)[c] Figurative scheme representing the array of the objects in the visual field.	ϕ Array
2. Identify the object with value at the other extreme of dimension to be tested.	(1) Operative scheme corresponding to the working definition of the other pole of dimension to be tested (e.g., for length, if the object is recessed the most, call it the shortest).	ψ Dimension to be tested (−)
	(2)[c] Figurative scheme representing the array of the objects in the visual field.	ϕ Array
3. Check to see if there is any difference between the two objects, other than the one to be tested.	(1) Figurative scheme representing the dimension to be tested.	ϕ Dimension to be tested.
	(2) Operative scheme representing the routine for scanning back and forth between the two objects and isolating any salient difference between them.	ψ Find difference
	(3) Figurative scheme representing object A.	ϕ Object A
	(4)[c] Figurative scheme representing object B.	ϕ Object B
4. If a difference is found recycle to Step 2.		
5. If no difference is found, conduct the test for property (i.e., see if object A > B on property of interest, e.g., bending).		

Note: Adapted from "Structures and Structures: Some Functional Limitations on the Course of Cognitive Growth" by R. Case, *Cognitive Psychology*, 1974, *6*, 544–573. Copyright 1974 by Academic Press. Reprinted by permission.

[a]Problem Question: Given a set of multidimensional objects with property X (e.g., bending), does dimension Y effect magnitude of X?

[b]ψ = operative scheme; ϕ = figurative scheme.

[c]Scheme activated by perceptual field. No M-power necessary.

235

unlocks the secret of how a correct (or incorrect) performance is produced. How do we know that a particular task analysis is correct? Researchers might collect converging behavioral evidence, such as eye movement patterns or reaction times, that are in accordance with what would be predicted by a given task analysis, but alternative hypotheses always remain possible. Indeed, researchers engaged in task analysis of cognitive tasks have tended to produce as many different analyses of a given task as there are analyzers of it. Empirical data have not as yet served in the role of *disconfirming* a task analysis that has been proposed.

Another criticism of task analysis and the information-processing approach more generally has been that it limits itself to proposing models of performance on specific tasks, and has not undertaken to integrate those models into a broader theory of human cognitive performance. Adherents of the information-processing approach, on the other hand, have defended this omission as a matter of appropriate sequence: Precise models of performance in very specific, restricted domains are alleged to be prerequisites for the formulation of broader, more comprehensive theories. Stated differently, the information-processing psychologist justifies, in the short term at least, sacrificing explanatory breadth for explanatory precision. Here again, the parallel to the historically earlier reductionist research strategy adhered to by behaviorists is clear. And so the debate over reductionism continues, with the information-processing approach assuming the proreductionist role.

Theoretically, the concept promoted by the information-processing approach—that multiple, largely independent processes are likely to be involved in performance of a cognitive task—has contributed valuably to thinking about cognitive development; it has served in particular, as an antidote to Piagetian stage doctrine, which treated performance as the manifestation of a single underlying stage structure. But the problem, and the reductionism debate, arises in deciding whether it is justified to go on to maintain that the performance is *nothing but* the serial execution of a specified set of individual processes, or whether some higher order organizing entity must be invoked. This brings us to the second major way in which the constructivist and information-processing perspectives differ.

The most serious criticism that has been lodged against the information-processing approach is that it has concerned itself predominantly with "strategy execution," and scarcely at all with "strategy selection." Consider for example Case's analysis of the isolation-of-variables strategy portrayed in Table 5.1. One can agree with Case that the sequence of strategies he specifies is not difficult to execute, and it is not surprising to learn that he was successful in teaching 8-year-olds to execute it (Case, 1974). But if not specifically directed to do so, how would an individual know that this set of strategies *ought* to be applied to such a problem? Without such knowledge, knowledge of how to execute the strategies is of limited value.

In comparison to knowledge of the first type—that is, knowledge of how to execute strategies, which is to a considerable extent ascertainable from the surface features of performance—knowledge of this second type is subtle and complex (Kuhn, 1983). In order to select a strategy as the appropriate one to apply in solving a problem, the individual must understand the strategy, understand the problem, and understand how the strategy and problem intersect or map onto one another, which entails understanding the range and limits of the strategy's appropriate application. In the case of the isolation-of-variables strategy represented in Table 5.1, such knowledge includes an understanding of (a) why the isolation or "all other things equal" method is the only means of achieving the task objective; (b) how and why each component of the strategy (such as ". . . check to see if there is any *other* difference between these two objects that might affect the result") constitutes an essential step in correct application; and (c) why any other strategy would not yield a correct solution.

To be convinced of the importance of this second kind of knowledge, one need only note that it is this knowledge that will determine whether or not an individual utilizes the strategy when an appropriate occasion arises in other situations, in the absence of direct instruction. It is the absence of such knowledge that is responsible for the common failures of generalization following training interventions: The subject learns the strategy in the particular context in which it is taught, but fails to apply it subsequently in other contexts in which it is equally appropriate. This problem of transfer of training, or more precisely failure of transfer, is one that has occupied psychologists from early (James, 1890) to modern times (Ferrara, Brown, & Campione, 1986).

Knowledge of one's own cognitive strategy as it applies to a task implies a *reflection on* the strategy that clearly differentiates it from *execution of* the strategy. The reader may recognize such a developing reflection on one's actions as at the heart of the constructivist account of cognitive development, originating with Baldwin and Piaget. It is just such reflection that is involved in strategy selection, to use the language of information-processing, but is difficult to incorporate into the information-processing model. Another way to characterize the distinction between execution of and reflection on a strategy is as a distinction between implicit and explicit knowledge of the strategy (Gelman, 1985; Kuhn, Amsel, & O'Loughlin, in press). A subject may be regarded as having implicit knowledge of a strategy if his or her performance reflects the use of that strategy or rule (e.g., the subject always predicts that the side with more weights will go down, in the balance scale example considered earlier). Implicit knowledge may exist only from the third-party perspective of an observer. Subjects whose performance reflects implicit knowledge of a strategy may or may not have explicit knowledge of it, as indicated both by their awareness that this is the strategy they are applying and by their ability to articulate this fact.

A slightly different aspect of this reflection on a strategy is implicated in another concept central to Piagetian theory, that of logical necessity. Consider once again the example of the transitivity inference. In the research by Trabasso and his colleagues described earlier, young children who did not show the transitivity concept were trained with respect to each of a set of individual relations, that is A < B, B < C, C < D, D < E, using a set of sticks of graduated lengths. It was hypothesized that subjects encoded and represented the set of relations as a visual image, that is, A < B < C < D < E. If so, this would explain how a child was able to answer questions about the relation between nonadjacent elements, for example, A and C, correctly: The child could simply refer to the internal pictorial array that had been formed, and produce the information A < C. These findings have prompted an extended debate as to whether such children had indeed been shown to have mastered the concept of transitivity (Breslow, 1981); and Piagetians were quick to make the distinction between an "empirical" judgment of transitivity and a judgment of transitivity that had the characteristic of logical necessity. In other words, the child just indicated might "read off" from her mental representation the fact that A < C; but it does not follow that she sees the relation A < C as an inevitable logical necessity following from the relations A < B and B < C, rather than as an empirical fact that happened to be true but could have been otherwise. The distinction is a difficult one to assess empirically, yet it is this logical necessity of the transitivity judgment that was the heart of the matter for Piaget. And such concepts of logical necessity can only come about as a product of reflection on one's own mental actions—in this case the mental actions of relating A to B and B to C.

Why is it that those utilizing an information-processing approach have tended not to focus on the processes of reflection on one's own cognition, processes that are the core of the constructivist perspective and that are implicated in the concept of logical necessity or the exercise of strategy selection? This neglect is most likely ascribable not to accident but to the fact that the information-processing perspective does not lend itself readily to the incorporation of this aspect of cognition, precisely because its underlying metaphor, the information-processing computer, does not—indeed cannot—reflect on what it is doing at a level differentiated from the "doing" itself. Unlike humans, computers do not "know" what they are doing. The computer can contemplate or evaluate its own actions only in the limited sense represented by the programmer specifying the operations that will constitute such an "evaluation;" for example, a condition—action link directing that processing be terminated once a certain set of conditions is met. But, again, such "evaluating" operations are not at a level distinct from the processing operations themselves.

Summary: Toward a Developmental Information-Processing Model

There are both strengths and limitations of the currently popular information-processing approach to the study of cognitive development. The major strength is the explicitness and precision with which it attempts to model specific kinds of cognitive performances. In addition, the information-processing approach is responsible for the concept that such performance is composed of a set of sequentially operating individual processes. This specificity and precision, however, are tied closely to a significant limitation—the scant attention that has been paid to integrating specific models into a broader theory of cognition and, particularly, cognitive development.

The major limitation that has been focused on is the lack of attention to what we have referred to as *reflective cognition.* If the information-processing approach is not to restrict itself unduly in explaining cognitive development, it can be argued that it will eventually have to go beyond a literal model of the computer to incorporate the reflective, or evaluative components of cognition and cognitive development. One indication of its need to do so is the frequent finding that subjects are able to execute all of the component strategies that a task analysis requires for performance, and yet the subjects do not assemble those components to produce the performance. Something else appears necessary for success.

This "something else" is often referred to as *metacognition,* that is, cognition about cognition. The term *metacognition* has been employed in such broad and diverse ways, however, that its usefulness as a scientific construct has been jeopardized (Forrest-Pressley, MacKinnon, & Waller, 1985). In its most general sense, the term metacognition has been used to refer to an "executive" function that selects, controls, and monitors the use of cognitive strategies, but it is often left unclear as to whether this function entails conscious awareness. Theorists who have an information-processing perspective and have concerned themselves with metacognition (e.g., Sternberg, 1984, this volume; Sternberg & Powell, 1983) have tended to regard metacognitive processes as functioning in an unconscious, automatic manner. This approach to metacognition thus does not incorporate the reflective aspects of metacognition—that is, individuals' reflective awareness of the cognitive operations they perform. The much earlier view expressed in Vygotsky's (1962) writing, in contrast, regards reflective awareness and deliberate control as the dual aspects of metacognition. The two can be regarded as describing the subjective (or *phenomenological*) and the objective (or *behavioral*) aspects of the same phenomenon: Someone aware of his or her own mental acts is able to reflect on those acts as objects of cognition, and is also likely to be able to access and apply them in a manner under voluntary control.

The rapidly increasing attention that is being addressed to metacognition and specifically to strategy selection (Paris & Oka, 1986; Pressley, Borkowski, & O'Sullivan, 1984; Siegler, in press; Siegler & Shrager, 1984; Sternberg, 1984) suggests a growing belief in the significant role it is likely to play in understanding cognitive development. What is necessary, however, is a fruitful conceptual and methodological framework in terms of which metacognitive processes can be studied, one that can accommodate the reflective as well as the control aspects of metacognition. Despite its centrality to his theory, Piaget's treatment of the topic has proven too abstract and divorced from specific contexts to be useful in generating much empirical research. At the same time, the computer model that underlies the information-processing approach, as we have noted, is not well-suited to capture the reflective aspects of metacognition.

One further limitation of the information-processing approach, that has only been alluded to until now, is one that has been widely noted and acknowledged by both adherents and critics of the approach—information-processing models offer no explanation of change. This limitation is obviously crucial if the approach is to provide an account of development. Why and how is the information-processing system modified over the course of development? However, information-processing is in good company here, for it is the mechanism of change that has proved the most difficult and formidable problem for all theories of cognitive development. Let us turn, then, to the more general question of mechanisms of developmental change.

MECHANISMS OF DEVELOPMENTAL CHANGE

Only a decade or two ago, it appeared that the question of mechanism in cognitive development was a clear-cut one. There were only two possibilities, and it seemed, moreover, that the data from a set of critical experiments would make it easy to choose between the two. Either the learning theorists were right, and the same basic processes of learning could account for development as well; or Piaget was right, and a small number of reorganizations of the cognitive system as a whole that occurred only a few times during the course of the individual's development were sufficient to account for all developmental change.

To decide between these two alternatives, it was thought, one needed only to conduct some so-called "training" studies. In the training study the investigator attempts to induce, via simple learning mechanisms, competencies held by Piaget to be manifestations of a global stage structure. If such studies were successful, the developmental process could be explained by simple learning mechanisms. If they were unsuccessful, Piaget's concept of global stage transformation would be implicated.

Remarkably, several hundred such training studies were carried out in the decade from the early 1960s to the early 1970s. Even more striking, the vast majority of these studies was devoted to inducing a single Piagetian competency, the conservation of quantity. The one thing that can be concluded about these studies is that they did not clearly decide the issue, and "the issue" indeed is now recognized to be much more complex than just portrayed. Many of the studies showed significant changes in children's performance on conservation tasks following training of a variety of different kinds, ranging from telling the children the correct answer ("The amount doesn't change") and rewarding them for making it, to more cognitively oriented attempts to get children to appreciate the logic that dictates the invariance. However, exactly what these results implied about how and why children shift during the natural course of development from believing that quantity varies with perceptual rearrangement to believing that it is invariant, is far from clear.

In what is perhaps the most widely cited conservation training study, one often praised as a model of elegant experimental design, Gelman (1969) claimed that young children fail to conserve because they do not attend to the relevant attribute—for example, to the number of elements rather than the length of the row in the case of number conservation. She demonstrated that by reinforcing children over many trials for choosing as "same" (as a standard) the row with the same number of items but different length (rather than the row of the same length by a different number of items), she could induce many of them to subsequently respond correctly in the standard conservation task; that is, to respond that the number of items in two rows remained the same after one of them was spread out so as to be of greater length than the other. In the terms used by Gelman, she taught such children to discriminate which of two possibilities (spatial magnitide or number) the term "same" refers to. Gelman, however, quite pointedly did not go on to draw from her findings the conclusion that natural attainment of the conservation concept involves "nothing but" (i.e., is reducible to) simple processes of discrimination learning and reinforcement. Nor have the many others who have cited her study seemed prepared to draw such a conclusion.

Exactly what conclusions are to be drawn from such studies, then, is far from clear. Much of the uncertainty can be traced to two major sources of ambiguity surrounding experiments that have utilized the training study methodology. First, many observers questioned the authenticity of the experimentally induced attainments: Had the child merely acquired the surface behaviors indicative of an understanding of conservation, or had some genuine change in understanding—that is, cognitive reorganization—taken place? Although much debate ensued, the matter was largely unresolvable inasmuch as opinion differed widely as to what conservation attainment in fact consists of: Is some underlying cognitive reorganization involved or merely the acquisition of a simple empirical fact or rule (e.g., quantity doesn't change through perceptual rearrangement)? In others words, what is it that is developing?

Even if these fundamental issues were agreed upon, however, and the experimentally-induced changes were accepted as genuine, a second and even more fundamental and troubling issue remains with respect to the method itself: the issue of *can* versus *does*. If a particular treatment is sufficient to produce a behavior in an experimental laboratory situation, it does not follow that the salient features of such a treatment are always, or ever, involved in the emergence of that behavior during the natural course of development. It is this second issue that is probably most responsible for the disillusionment with the training study as a tool for investigating mechanisms of developmental change. Perhaps the most striking testimony to its limitations is the fact that despite the 200 or more training studies of conservation conducted in the last three decades, there continues to exist a remarkably wide variety of theories regarding the process by which conservation is attained (Acredolo, 1981; Anderson & Cuneo, 1978; Brainerd, 1979; Pinard, 1981; Shultz, Dover, & Amsel, 1979; Siegler, 1981). Thus, the vast conservation training study literature has not significantly constrained our theories of the developmental process that underlies the attainment of conservation.

Multiple Dimensions and Mechanisms of Change

Along with abandoning the idea of training studies as providing a critical test of empiricist versus constructivist explanations of change, there came a gradual abandonment of the idea that either explanation could provide a comprehensive theoretical account of developmental change in cognitive functioning. One reason is that, following in part from work done within the information-processing approach, a considerably more complex picture of what it is that is developing has emerged—a "what" that encompasses a diverse set of competencies, rather than only a single entity. As a result, it is likely to require a more complex process, or set of processes, to explain that development. A range of possibilities exists with respect to what it is that may develop, including basic processing capacity, processing efficiency, processes of encoding and representation, knowledge, strategies, and metacognitive processes of strategy selection and regulation. Developmental changes in each of these conceivably could be governed by different mechanisms; moreover, changes in some (for example, processing capacity) might be invoked to account for changes in others (for example, strategy usage).

Processing Capacity.   A possibility that is very attractive because of its simplicity is that the change responsible for most if not all advances in cognitive functioning with age is an increase in basic processing capacity, presumably as the result of neurological development. Thus, this alternative attributes cognitive development most directly to an underlying biological process of maturation. Pascual-Leone (1970) and Case (1985) have advanced separate versions of an elaborate "neo-Piagetian" theory of cognitive development founded on the assumption of age-linked increase in absolute processing capacity. The fact that performance increases with age on tests of basic processing such as digit span appears to support such a view. A 3-year-old can repeat an average of only three digits, where a 10-year-old can repeat an average of six digits.

That such improvements in performance are attributable to increases in processing capacity, however, is extremely difficult, if not impossible, to prove since a number of hard-to-discount alternative explanations exist. In the instance of digit span, for example, the older child may be employing some strategic device, such as rehearsal or chunking, that the younger child is not. In other words, it is difficult to prove that children of the two ages are executing the task in exactly the same way, the only difference being that the older children have a quantitatively greater capacity. Furthermore, as discussed earlier, capacity is highly influenced by familiarity with the material: If the domain is one in which a particular child is highly experienced (e.g., chess boards), that child's recall performance may exceed that of much older children less familiar with the domain. Similarly, Case and his colleagues demonstrated that the capacity of adults drops to that of 6-year-olds if the adults are required to execute a digit memory task using a newly learned set of digit symbols (Case, Kurland, & Goldberg, 1982).

Processing Efficiency. Case (1985) has argued, in opposition to Pascual-Leone, that improvements with age in performance on tests such as digit span only appear to be the result of an absolute capacity increase. Actually, he claims, improved performance is ascribable to an increase in the efficiency with which basic operations, such as encoding, are executed; accordingly, less capacity is required for their execution. This leaves the individual with a greater remaining "functional" capacity for holding the products of those operations in memory, even though total capacity remains unchanged. In support of his view, Case cites recent evidence that performance on measures of basic operations—for example, counting an array of objects—becomes faster and more efficient with age, making plausible his view that such increases in efficiency are at least in part responsible for increases in functional capacity and hence in performance on processing tests such as digit span. Whether the fundamental change is one of processing efficiency, as Case claims, or of total processing capacity, as Pascual-Leone claims, both argue that such change itself is a function of underlying neurological development; Case raises the possibility, however, that experience of a very broad general sort may also contribute to increased efficiency.

An issue even more crucial to debate, however, is the extent to which age-related increases in processing capacity (whether absolute or only "functional") underlie all forms of developmental change in cognitive functioning, as both Case and Pascual-Leone claim. The fact that performance on measures of basic processing improves with age has been established, as previously indicated. But we also know that cognitive functioning changes developmentally in many other ways. Children acquire new, qualitatively different strategies they did not have previously: they integrate existing strategies in new ways, they encode new and different kinds of information and represent it in new and different ways, and they develop new forms of executive, or metacognitive, control over their cognitive functioning. Most developmentalists today would agree with the view that increases in basic processing efficiency and/or capacity are implicated at most as necessary conditions for many of these other kinds of changes. But they fall far short of being by themselves sufficient to explain how these changes come about.

Let us turn then to these other kinds of changes and the mechanisms that may underlie them.

Encoding and Representation.   Another factor that undergoes developmental change, and might account for improvements in performance on many kinds of cognitive tasks, is improved encoding and representation of information essential to successful execution of the task. No matter how efficiently they are developed, operations cannot be performed on material that has not been attended to, encoded, and in some manner represented within the cognitive system. Siegler (1976; Siegler & Klahr, 1982) demonstrates this point nicely in the case of the balance beam task described earlier: At a certain level children encode information about weight but do not encode information about distance of the weight from the fulcrum, as evidenced by their ability to reproduce weight but not distance information in tests of recall. The encoding of distance information is an obvious prerequisite to the execution of the more advanced strategies in which distance is taken into account, although Siegler's work does not prove that it is a change in encoding behavior that causes the change in strategy. Conceivably, the causal relation is the reverse: The child's intent to use a new strategy leads the child to encode new kinds of information.

Knowledge.   Still another factor that clearly undergoes developmental change is the particular knowledge the child possesses within specific content domains. The growth of domain-specific knowledge was long ignored by developmental researchers, or considered incidental to, or a by-product of, what were presumed to be more fundamental changes in modes of cognitive processing and strategy use. Yet older children have acquired a much larger knowledge base than have younger children, with respect to virtually any content domain in which we might examine their cognitive functioning. Is it not likely that these variations in knowledge play a role in the difference in performance observed across age groups? Keil (1981, 1984) has argued that the acquisition of domain-specific knowledge in fact plays the major role in developmental change, and that more general changes in process or strategy play a lesser role. In research on the ability to understand metaphors (Keil, 1986), for example, he notes that very young children are able to understand metaphorical relations between certain domains (e.g., animal terms and automobiles, as in "The car is thirsty"), but that relations between other domains are comprehended only at a much later age (e.g., human food consumption and reading, as in "She gobbled up the book"). Based on such evidence, Keil argues that what is most significant developmentally is not the ability to understand metaphor—that is, the juxtaposition of semantic fields—itself, but the gradual extension of this ability to new semantic fields, in a sequence that Keil argues is predictable from an analysis of the structure of those fields. Consistent with his emphasis on domain-specific knowledge, Keil (1984) advocates a research approach in which the investigator focuses attention on the structure of the knowledge that is acquired, and from this analysis makes inferences about how transitions in cognitive development occur, rather than searching for general mechanisms of change. The approach taken by Chi (1978) in her research on memory for chess boards, described earlier, is similar in its emphasis to Keil's, as is the view expressed by Glaser (1984). Carey (1985) makes an argument for the even stronger position that all of cognitive development is reducible to changes in domain-specific knowledge. Critics of the domain-specific view, such as Sternberg (1984, 1985), claim that proponents of this view—in their zeal to correct what they see as the neglect of domain-specific knowledge and overemphasis on general strategies in prior work—are guilty of the reverse overemphasis. What produces variations in the knowledge base individuals have acquired? Or, to put the question in its most fundamental form, what are the *processes* by means of which knowledge is acquired? This question leads inevitably to a consideration of strategy.

Strategy Execution.   How does an individual come to use new or modified strategies in performing a cognitive task? Constructivist accounts traditionally have emphasized the role of self-regulatory mechanisms within the individual: The individual gradually constructs a more adequate, comprehensive, and better equilibrated set of cognitive operations to be applied to the external world. But, as noted, such accounts have tended to minimize the role of the external environment. Within some versions of the constructivist account, exposure to material reflecting the higher level structure toward which the individual is developing is a necessary condition for change; other theories within the constructivist framework hold to the more radical position (reflected in Piaget's writings) that the individual literally constructs anew each more advanced mode of cognitive functioning based on the discrepant feedback produced by actions executed at the existing level. According to this formulation, then, simply the functioning of the cognitive system leads to its modification, a view endorsed by theorists operating from such disparate frameworks as Piaget (1971) and Klahr and Wallace (1976).

This stronger version of constructivism ignores the fact that models of the more advanced concepts or strategies the individual will acquire are often prevalent in the individual's environment, as emphasized by the Soviet theories of Luria and Vygotsky mentioned earlier. Case's (1978b) work on the isolation-of-variables strategy suggests that an individual can be taught to execute this strategy through social facilitation, at least in a laboratory context. The role of social influence in its acquisition in natural contexts is another question. But the role of both these processes (individual construction and social facilitation) must be considered in positing an explanation of how an individual masters execution of a new strategy. Even though external models are not directly or automatically internalized, it is most unlikely that they are systematically ignored.

Strategy Selection and Regulation.   With respect to one final factor, the individual's metacognitive decision to utilize particular strategies, the power of social facilitation is less clear. An individual might be instructed successfully in exactly how to execute a particular strategy and even be instructed regarding the conditions under which it is appropriate to apply the strategy, provided these conditions can be well specified. But whether the individual will choose to use the strategy in contexts that are not identical to the instructed one is more problematic. For example, children might be taught to use rehearsal to facilitate memory and yet not employ the strategy in their own activities, a finding that has, in fact, been reported by Paris and Lindauer (1982). As was suggested earlier, whether or not a strategy is selected in noninstructed, natural contexts is likely to depend on individuals' metacognitive understanding of the strategy itself; that is, their understanding of their own actions. In other words, the individual must understand the value and significance of the strategy as well as how to execute it, and the acquisition of this appreciation, or metacognitive understanding, is likely to be the more difficult, complex attainment of the two.

Piaget proposed that the mechanism underlying the development and application of new strategies was *equilibration,* the functioning of which he described only in rather general and formal terms. Strategies become consolidated and coordinated with one another through exercise. The feedback from this exercise, however, causes the individual to perceive the limitations of these strategies; and it provides the impetus, or *disequilibrium,* necessary for the construction of new strategies that will be more adequate for dealing with the tasks encountered and so leave the organism in a state of improved equilibrium with its environment. Several information-processing theorists have undertaken to introduce a developmental mechanism into their models by describing such a process in the language of information-processing (Klahr, Langley, & Neches, 1986), although this language, as we noted earlier, is constrained by the fact that it does not readily incorporate the reflective aspects of cognition that are very likely to be involved in developmental change. Klahr and Wallace (1976) were the first to attempt such a model. They described a self-modifying production system with features such as consistency detectors, which lead strategies to become more efficient. Case (1984, 1985) likewise has described a process whereby a set of strategies becomes modified during the course of their own functioning. Such efforts, however, have tended only to describe such a process, in a language very different from Piaget's. What is most important now are models that can generate new, testable hypotheses about how the process operates.

Summary: New Approaches to Studying Change

Two major factors have been discussed that have limited progress in understanding the mechanisms of developmental change. One is the lack of satisfactory methods of empirical investigation. The other is the scarcity of specific hypotheses amenable to empirical testing. On the positive side is the fact that we now have a considerably more sophisticated conception of what it is that is developing and, as a result, of the mechanism—or, more likely, *mechanisms*—that will be necessary to account for this development.

Also on the positive side is the fact that in recent years, after being diverted by a number of subsidiary issues such as the existence of stages, current developmentalists of virtually every theoretical orientation have identified a better understanding of the process of change as their primary objective; and a great many of them have begun to focus their research efforts on investigating the mechanisms of developmental change. In particular, researchers interested in both learning and development have begun to explore the use of new "microgenetic" methods as means of obtaining detailed observations of the process as it occurs. These methods differ markedly from the classical training study methodology discussed earlier in that the focus is on the change process itself, rather than on pretest and post-test performance.

Microgenetic methods show promise in affording insight into the change process, although the approaches used do not fit into traditional categories of research methods. Lawler (1985), for example, observed a single subject over several months during the course of which the child mastered some elementary mathematical concepts. His observations led him to emphasize as a central feature of the process the integration of strategic knowledge that initially functions within isolated, unintegrated domains. Similarly, Kuhn and Phelps (1982) observed preadolescent subjects in repeated encounters with a problem-solving task over a period of months. Most subjects' progress, they found, occurred only very gradually and involved prolonged use of both less and more advanced strategies in conjunction with one another. It was during this period of observation, Kuhn and Phelps proposed, that the subject was gaining metacognitive understanding of which strategies were effective and why, as well as gaining practice in the execution of the more advanced strategies. Their observations also pointed to an aspect of the change process that has been largely ignored. The most formidable problem for subjects appeared to be not the acquisition and consolidation of new strategies but rather the ability to abandon old, less adequate strategies, which is a reversal of the way development has typically been conceived. Other current approaches to the microgenetic study of developmental change are reflected in work by Karmiloff-Smith (1984) within a constructivist framework, and in work by Paris and his colleagues (Paris, Newman, & McVey, 1982) within an information-processing framework; the work by Paris also points to the importance of metacognitive regulation of strategy usage.

COGNITIVE DEVELOPMENT IN CONTEXT

The evolution in methods for studying mechanisms of change that has been described arose out of recognition of the need to study processes of development in contexts as similar as possible to those contexts in which they occur naturally, if the inferences made on the basis of such study are to be valid. In a similar way, the field of cognitive development regarded more broadly has in the last few years moved in a direction that reflects this concern.

In part this movement reflects a reaction to the shortcomings that have been perceived in theories and methods that have not concerned themselves with context. These shortcomings have been noted in the preceding sections of this chapter—the futility of the search for context-free processes of learning and memory; the vulnerability of assessments of Piagetian stage level to task effects; the indifference of constructivist accounts of development to children's specific experiences; and the task-boundedness of information-processing models of cognitive performance. In a more positive vein, however, the increasing attention given to context is attributable as well to the influence of two disparate schools of thought and research, one focused on the relation of culture and cognition and the other on cognitive development across the life span. Although the two can be regarded as possessing common roots in the philosophical school of contextualism (Dixon & Lerner this volume), they are both relatively new to developmental psychology and thus far have existed largely independent of one another. They both, however, have contributed to what has been termed the new functionalism in cognitive development theory and research (Beilin, 1984).

Culture and Cognition

Populations containing large numbers of unschooled children, adolescents, and adults seemed to provide an ideal means for investigating the effects of schooling on cognitive development. A number of large-scale cross-cultural studies of cognition that were undertaken had as their major purpose the identification of these effects. These studies, however, turned out to be much less decisive than had been hoped. Sharp, Cole, and Lave (1979) reported the inferior performance of unschooled subjects from a non-Western culture on a wide range of cognitive tasks. These authors, however, were quick to realize the limited interpretability of their findings. The kinds of tasks administered to their unschooled subjects were by and large identical or related to the kinds of tasks and activities that schooled individuals engage in at school (activities such as categorization and memorization). Little could be inferred on the basis of such findings, then, beyond the conclusion that experience in performing school-related skills enhances the performance of those skills. The nature of cognition among unschooled individuals remained an embarrassingly open question.

Exactly the same dilemma was recognized as applying within as well as across cultures (Rogoff, 1982). A Soviet study by Istomina (1977), for example, has been widely cited as demonstrating the critical importance of assessing cognitive performance in contexts that are familiar and meaningful to the subjects being assessed. In Istomina's study, preschoolers asked to memorize a list of items remembered, on the average, only half as many items as they remembered when asked to retrieve the same set of items from a make-believe grocery store. Istomina's study has subsequently been criticized as reflecting an over-simplified conception of the role of context and as being perhaps itself only replicable under a limited range of cultural and contextual conditions (Weissberg & Paris, 1986). A number of different contextual and motivational features of the two conditions no doubt influence subjects' performance in each of these conditions. The important point remains, however, that cognition and cognitive development must be examined in the context of cognitive activities that are meaningful and salient in the lives of the individuals being investigated, if valid conclusions are to be drawn. The appropriate unit of investigation, it has been suggested, should become cultural (and subcultural) practices, not psychological tests and experiments (Laboratory of Comparative Human Cognition, 1983).

Researchers working within this contextualist perspective have been attracted to the theories of the Soviet psychologists Vygotsky (1962, 1978) and Luria (1976) because of their emphasis on the effects of the culture on the individual. It is the child's first social relations, and in particular the resulting exposure to a language system, that give rise to mental development, according to the Soviet view. The mode of such transmission is social interaction: What starts out as interpersonal regulation—for example, a mother guiding her child in performing a task the child is unable to do alone—gradually becomes intrapersonal regulation: The child becomes capable of regulating his or her own actions to produce the performance, without external guidance. Wertsch (1979, 1984) has conducted interesting observational studies of this process as it occurs during the course of a mother assisting her child in a task. The influence of the Vygotsky/Luria perspective in recent developmental work has been an important one, as it balances Piaget's emphasis on the role of individuals in producing their own development. In emphasizing the external influences stemming from social interaction, however, the Soviet view neglects the complementary part of the individual–environment interaction; that is, the role of the individual. Little attention is given to how children attribute meaning to the social interactions they are involved in, and how this attributed meaning mediates the process by which society affects mind. Descriptions of the shift from interpersonal to intrapersonal regulation in parent–child interaction provide an insightful conceptualization of how parents structure their behavior in efforts to aid the child, but they provide less insight into the cognitive processes that enable the child to make use of the adult's input.

Cognition and Adulthood

The situation confronting the researcher interested in cognitive development during the 80% of the life span that remains after childhood is in many ways similar to that of the cross-cultural researcher. For a number of converging reasons, studies of cognitive development have traditionally stopped at roughly the point in the life cycle when both biological maturation and universal schooling cease. For most individuals beyond this point, school-related tasks are no longer a significant part of their everyday activities, yet such tasks are the only tools researchers have to assess their cognitive functioning. In contrast to the study of child development, studies of adult cognition and cognitive development lack the advantage of a meaningful anchor in either biology or the cultural universal of schooling. Nor is there any other readily apparent anchor or unifying concept with respect to the intellectual life of adults that could serve as a point of departure for such studies.

Developmentalists who first undertook to study the course of cognitive functioning across the life span understandably did not wish to add the burden of new, unvalidated measures to the already considerable set of methodological challenges they faced. As a result, the bulk of our present knowledge about cognitive development in adulthood is based on adult performance on the measures of cognitive functioning that have received the most extensive examination by psychologists, those associated with the psychometric assessment of intelligence. These also, of course, happen to be measures whose origins lie in the prediction of school performance. Some of the findings from these developmental studies have led to increasing uneasiness about the measures themselves.

Life-span developmental psychology (Baltes, Reese, & Lipsitt, 1980; Dixon, Kramer, & Baltes, 1985) undertook as one of its initial missions the seemingly straightforward task of assessing whether, during the course of adulthood, normative age-related changes in intellectual performance occur that are not attributable to sampling, testing, or historical (cohort) factors. Not only does this seemingly fundamental question remain unanswered but most life-span developmental psychologists have come to the view that it is not the right question to ask. Several consistent findings from the life-span study of performance on psychometric tasks have led to this conclusion. The major such finding is one regarding the substantial effects of cohort. In other words, the accumulated historical experience common to members of a particular cohort makes that cohort membership an equally or more powerful predictor of performance than is the predictor of chronological age. These results have led theorists in the life-span movement to postulate a model that includes several sources of influence on life-span development, age-graded influences, history-graded influences (unique to cohorts), and nonnormative influences (unique to individuals).

A second major finding has been that of substantial plasticity in the performance of adults, especially older adults, on psychometric tasks. Simple practice over an interval of time is often sufficient to improve the performance of older adults dramatically (Blieszner, Willis, & Baltes, 1981; Schaie & Willis, in press). This finding has led to serious questioning of the validity of these measures in providing accurate or meaningful assessments of normative intellectual functioning across the adult years of the life span. Specifically, psychometric assessment measures have been criticized as youth-centered (Baltes & Willis, 1979; Schaie, 1978)—that is, developed for the purpose of measuring intelligence in the early part of the life cycle and, subsequently, applied to the testing of intellectual functioning in older persons regardless of their appropriateness for those age groups.

These two major findings from life span research on intellectual functioning have led to two related developments in the life-span research program. One development is a recognition of the need to base assessment instruments for adult populations on the kinds of intellectual tasks that are salient in adult life (Willis & Schaie, 1986). In reality we have very little knowledge of the cognitive activities that are part of the everyday lives of the majority of adults who do not pursue scholarly careers. What are these activities and how well or poorly do average adults carry them out? Without such an "ecology of adulthood cognition," we do not have the knowledge that would allow us to evaluate the appropriateness of traditional laboratory tasks in the assessment of adult cognition across the life span.

The second development is a shift away from questions of normative age-graded intellectual functioning toward questions of range, modifiability, plasticity, and process with respect to intellectual functioning during the adult years (Dixon & Baltes, 1986). This shift reflects an acknowledgment of the substantial role of specific experiential factors (in contrast to inevitable, biologically governed aging) in intellectual functioning during the adult years of the life span. It is also closely linked to the shift toward more ecologically relevant measures. If specific experiences particular to individuals are accorded a major role, it becomes more essential than ever to attempt to assess their impact with respect to specific intellectual activities and functions that are significant in these individuals' lives.

Other psychologists not associated with the life-span group turned initially to Piaget—in particular to his stage of formal operations—as the most promising gateway to the study of adult cognitive development. Formal operations held the promise of a qualitative rather than quantitative approach to the assessment of cognitive functioning, and the reasoning strategies described by Inhelder and Piaget (1958) as reflecting formal operations appeared to possess the broad generality that made it likely they would be successful in characterizing an individual's reasoning across a wide range of everyday contexts. Moreover, all of the available data pointed to the conclusion that the stage of formal operations, unlike the earlier Piagetian stages, is not attained universally. This finding suggested both that significant variability in the use of formal operational reasoning exists within adult populations, and that a developmental perspective may be useful in understanding adult cognition. It seemed a simple matter to remedy the problem that Inhelder and Piaget's assessment tasks were drawn largely from the domain of physics, unfamiliar to most adolescents and adults. Familiar, everyday content could easily be substituted without altering the more general forms of the problems posed to subjects.

It soon became apparent, however, that the problem was a deeper one that would not be solved simply by recasting Piaget's tasks into "everyday" content

(Kuhn, Pennington, & Leadbeater, 1983). Doing so still leaves painfully open the question of the extent to which the *form* of reasoning that subjects are asked to engage in (irrespective of the content) is anything like the forms of reasoning they normally have occasion to engage in. To the extent this question remains unresolved, so does the significance of subjects' proficient or inferior performance. Thus we remain unable to say whether poor performance on such tasks reflects important deficits in adult reasoning, or whether it reflects the inappropriateness of the measures used to evaluate the cognitive competence that subjects possess. More broadly, it has come to be recognized that, both theoretically and methodologically, it is important to look beyond competence in formal logic to understand cognitive functioning in adulthood. Logic may play a quite different role in adult thinking than it plays in the thought of adolescents. As one researcher has put it, "Playful exercise of cognitive schemes, endless generating of 'ifs' and 'whens', no longer may be adaptive; the task becomes instead to attempt to utilize best one's knowledge toward the management of concrete life situations" (Labouvie-Vief, 1980, p. 153).

A case can be made for the value of a developmental framework in investigating the ecology of adult cognition. Some of the most interesting recent work that undertakes to examine the cognitive functioning of adults in ecologically valid contexts (Scribner, 1986; Wagner & Sternberg, 1986) has not been undertaken explicitly within a developmental framework. If a major goal is to understand the range, the modifiability, the plasticity of adult cognitive functioning, a developmental framework may be, if not essential, at least extremely illuminating: In what directions and toward what ends might adults' cognitive functioning be modified? The age relations in youthful samples can serve as a basis for ordering response patterns into an ordinal hierarchy of developmental levels. Often, a second criterion for such ordinal ranking exists: the adequacy, power, or validity of the reasoning reflected by different response patterns, on logical/rational grounds. To the extent the two orderings match, they reinforce one another in a bootstrapping fashion, even though neither one alone nor even both together "prove" the correctness or the validity of the ordering. A third is longitudinal data indicating sequential order of attainment. A fourth form of evidence is the predictive power of the ordered levels—that is, the extent to which knowledge of an individual's position in the ordering can predict performance in some external criterion domain—in the way, for example, that aptitude test scores predict school performance.

To the extent a particular sequential ordering receives validation by any combination of these means, it then can serve as a framework in terms of which performance variability in adult samples (which typically is not age-linked to any appreciable extent) can be conceptualized. In other words, administering the same set of measures to a combination of youthful and mature samples of subjects provides a framework for interpreting the performance of the latter. To be sure, such an approach provides not a set of answers with respect to understanding adult cognition but rather a set of questions—an investigative framework—in terms of which the cognitive functioning of adults can be examined.

PAST PROGRESS AND FUTURE DIRECTIONS

In this chapter I have described how the study of cognitive development has been conceived and conducted in American psychology over a period of almost half a century, culminating in the current emphasis on studying cognitive development and the mechanisms underlying it in ways that are sensitive to the contexts in which this development occurs, and to their effects on the developmental process. How might we summarize the progress that the evolution we have described reflects?

Evolution in Theory

One way to summarize this evolution is as the successive rejection of a series of explanatory mechanisms on the grounds of their being too simple to explain what a theory of cognitive development must account for—in other words, too simple to answer the question posed at the outset as underlying the study of cognitive development: How do mind and reality come to be coordinated with one another?

A biologically governed unfolding of developmental forms without regard to environmental influence is no longer taken seriously as a model of psychological development. The more recent hypothesis of a biologically governed, quantitatively increasing processing capacity has similarly been criticized as inadequate by itself to explain how and why cognition develops.

Similarly rejected as too simple to account for the complexity of cognitive functioning and its development are explanatory mechanisms that bypass the internal functioning that takes place within the organism. Influences of external variables on the developmental process are now widely accepted as mediated by characteristics internal to the individual.

Likewise rejected are simple acquisition mechanisms purported to function in an identical manner irrespective of the material being acquired and its relation to what is already known by the acquirer, and to the capabilities of his or her cognitive system. Put another way, it is now widely accepted that mechanisms of learning and retention do not function independently of the individual's intellect as a whole.

While the individual's intelligence, or active structuring of experience, is thus recognized, there also have been criticism and widespread rejection of explanatory mechanisms that attribute cognitive development to the progressive restructuring of this intelligence, as an activity of the individual that takes place isolated from social contexts that might influence it. Individuals develop in a social context of other individuals, and the interdependence of cognitive and social processes must therefore be acknowledged and investigated.

Parallel with this evolution in concepts of an adequate explanation of developmental process has been an evolution in concepts of what it is that is developing. The concept of isolated competencies that accumulate independently has been rejected as ignoring the crucial organizational features of behavior and knowledge. But likewise largely rejected has been the concept of a single structured whole that develops as an integrated entity and mediates all more specific components of cognitive functioning. A major contribution of the information-processing approach has been to highlight the fact that there exist a number of distinct cognitive functions each of which may undergo developmental change. A unique contribution of the constructivist perspective, on the other hand, and one difficult for the information-processing approach to encompass, is its focus on the reflective aspects of cognition and its development—and the "meaning-making" endeavor that such reflection is a part of.

The preceding summary conversely serves to prescribe the features a fully satisfactory explanatory account of cognitive development would need to possess:

1. It would need to refer to mental processes that take place within the organism, including those aspects of such processes referred to as reflective, or metacognitive.
2. It would need to characterize development as a gradual coordination of individual mind and external physical and social reality, in which neither internal nor external forces predominate over the other.
3. It would need to address the social contexts in which development occurs and the ways in which those contexts relate to individual development.
4. It would need to account for context specificity of cognitive attainments as well as trans-situational commonalities in cognitive functioning.
5. It would need to specify mechanisms by means of which developmental change occurs.

During the next several decades, theories that are proposed to account for cognitive development are likely to possess at least the preceding characteristics, as well as others not yet clear. That this is so serves as an indication that the field has progressed, despite the absence of an accumulation of the "hard facts" a reader of this chapter might have anticipated.

Evolution in Method

Not surprisingly, as the field of cognitive development has evolved in its theoretical sophistication, so has it evolved with respect to its methods, and this latter evolution also gives reason for optimism regarding the field's future. Just a decade or so ago researchers in the field of cognitive development could be portrayed, with some justification, as preoccupied with a narrow range of cognitive phenomena investigated in experimental laboratory contexts, where both phenomenon and context were of uncertain relevance to children's cognitive functioning and development in natural settings. Meanwhile, crucial practical decisions as to how children might be reared and educated so as to maximize their cognitive potential, and their productivity and fulfillment as adults, were left to others outside the academic enterprise.

Today such characterizations of the field of cognitive development are much less accurate than they were. As we have indicated, recognition has grown that context and meaning have a profound effect on performance, and increasingly researchers are undertaking to examine cognitive functioning within the natural contexts of meaningful activities engaged in by children—in school as well as in nonschool environments. Cognitive abilities such as reading are currently of great interest to cognitive and developmental psychologists to a large extent because of, rather than despite, their practical importance. The study of cognitive development in contexts not clearly linked to contexts in which that cognitive development occurs naturally constrains significantly the insight such study can yield. There are signs that developmentalists are beginning to take this admonition seriously and that the academic study of cognitive development in the future will not be as divorced from practical or "applied" concerns as it has been.

This issue of ecological validity has been highlighted even further by another trend of the last decade: The study of cognitive development is no longer limited to an exclusive focus on the childhood years. There are indications that it may be fruitful to conceptualize cognitive functioning in adulthood, and particularly the substantial individual variation in cognitive functioning among adults, from a developmental perspective. Parallel to what has been recognized to be the case in cross-cultural work, however, it has been apparent that it will be essential to study cognitive functioning among subjects other than children and in contexts that are meaningful and salient to the individuals studied, if our interpretations are to be valid.

This expansion of the traditional child-focused study of cognitive development to encompass the latter 80% of the life span promises benefits not only for our understanding of adult cognition but for our understanding of cognition and cognitive development during childhood as well. The process of cognitive development during childhood can be fully appreciated only to the extent that we understand the end points toward which it is evolving. The study of cognitive development as a process that takes place throughout life, then, will most likely enrich the conceptual perspectives that over the next several decades will succeed those that have been described in this chapter.

ACKNOWLEDGMENT

Preparation of this chapter was supported by the Redward Foundation.

REFERENCES

Acredolo, C. (1981). Acquisition of conservation. A clarification of Piagetian terminology, some recent findings, and an alternative formulation. *Human Development, 24,* 120–137.

Anderson, N., & Cuneo, D. (1978). The height and width rule in children's judgments of quantity. *Journal of Experimental Psychology: General, 107,* 335–378.

Baltes, P. B., Reese, H. W., & Lipsitt, L. P. (1980). Life-span developmental psychology. *Annual Review of Psychology, 31,* 65–110.

Baltes, P. B., & Willis, S. L. (1979). The critical importance of appropriate methodology in the study of aging: The same case of psychometric intelligence. In F. Hoffmeister & C. Muller (Eds.), *Brain function in old age.* Heidelberg: Springer.

Beilin, H. (1984). Functionalist and structuralist research program in developmental psychology: Incommensurability or synthesis? In H. W. Reese (Ed.), *Advances in child development & behavior* (Vol. 18). New York: Academic Press.

Bijou, S. (1976). *Child development: The basic stage of early childhood.* Englewood Cliffs, NJ: Prentice-Hall.

Bijou, S., & Baer, D. (1961). *Child development: A systematic and empirical theory.* New York: Appleton-Century-Crofts.

Blieszner, R., Willis, S. L., & Baltes, P. B. (1981). Training research in aging on the fluid ability of inductive reasoning. *Journal of Applied Developmental Psychology, 2,* 247–266.

Brainerd, C. (1978). The stage question in cognitive-developmental theory. *Behavioral and Brain Sciences, 1,* 173–213.

Brainerd, C. (1979). Markovian interpretations of conservation learning. *Psychological Review, 86,* 181–213.

Breslow, L. (1981). Reevaluation of the literature on the development of transitive inferences. *Psychological Bulletin, 89,* 325–351.

Brown, A., Bransford, J., Ferrara, R., & Campione, J. (1983). Learning, remembering, and understanding. In P. Mussen (Ed.), *Carmichael's manual of child psychology* (4th ed.). New York: Wiley.

Brown, A., & DeLoache, J. (1978). Skills, plans, and self-regulation. In R. Siegler (Ed.), *Children's thinking: What develops?* Hillsdale, NJ: Lawrence Erlbaum Associates.

Bryant, P., & Trabasso, T. (1971). Transitive inference and memory in young children. *Nature, 232,* 456–458.

Carey, S. (1985). Are children fundamentally different kinds of thinkers and learners than adults? In S. Chipman, J. Segal, & R. Glaser (Eds.), *Thinking and learning skills* (Vol. 2). Hillsdale, NJ: Lawrence Erlbaum Associates.

Case, R. (1974). Structures and strictures: Some functional limitations on the course of cognitive growth. *Cognitive Psychology, 6,* 544–573.

Case, R. (1978a). Intellectual development from birth to adulthood: A neo-Piagetian interpretation. In R. Siegler (Ed.), *Children's thinking: What develops?* Hillsdale, NJ: Lawrence Erlbaum Associates.

Case, R. (1978b). Piaget and beyond: Toward a developmentally based theory and technology of instruction. In R. Glaser (Ed.), *Advances in instructional psychology* (Vol. 1). Hillsdale, NJ: Lawrence Erlbaum Associates.

Case, R. (1984). The process of stage transition: A neo-Piagetian view. In R. Sternberg (Ed.), *Mechanisms of cognitive development.* New York: Freeman.

Case, R. (1985). *Intellectual development: Birth to adulthood.* New York: Academic.

Case, R., Kurland, D. M., & Goldberg, J. (1982). Operational efficiency and the growth of short-term memory span. *Journal of Experimental Child Psychology, 33,* 386–404.

Chi, M. 1978). Knowledge structures and memory development. In R. Siegler (Ed.), *Children's thinking: What develops?* Hillsdale, NJ: Lawrence Erlbaum Associates.

Chi, M. (1985). Interactive roles of knowledge and strategies in the development of organized sorting and recall. In S. Chipman, J. Segal, & R. Glaser (Eds.), *Thinking and learning skills* (Vol. 2). Hillsdale, NJ: Lawrence Erlbaum Associates.

Chi, M. (in press). Representing knowledge and metaknowledge: Implications for interpreting metamemory research. In R. Kluwe & F. Weinert (Eds.), *Metacognition, motivation, and understanding*. Hillsdale, NJ: Lawrence Erlbaum Associates.

Chi, M., & Koeske, R. (1983). Network representation of a child's dinosaur knowledge. *Developmental Psychology, 19*, 29–39.

Dixon, R., & Baltes, P. (1986). Toward life-span research on the functions and pragmatics of intelligence. In R. Sternberg & R. Wagner (Eds.), *Practical intelligence*. Cambridge: Cambridge University Press.

Dixon, R., Kramer, D., & Baltes, P. (1985). Intelligence: A life-span developmental perspective. In B. Wolman (Ed.), *Handbook of intelligence: Theories, measurements, and applications*. New York: Wiley.

Ferrara, R., Brown, A., & Campione, J. (1986). Children's learning and transfer of inductive reasoning rules: Studies of proximal development. *Child Development, 57*, 1087–1099.

Fischer, K. (1980). A theory of cognitive development: The control and construction of hierarchies of skills. *Psychological Review, 87*, 477–531.

Fischer, K., & Pipp, S. (1984). Processes of cognitive development: Optimal level and skill acquisition. In R. Sternberg (Ed.), *Mechanisms of cognitive development*. New York: Freeman.

Flavell, J. (1982). On cognitive development. *Child Development, 53*, 1–10.

Flavell, J., Beach, D., & Chinsky, J. (1966). Spontaneous verbal rehearsal in a memory task as a function of age. *Child Development, 37*, 283–299.

Forrest-Pressley, D., MacKinnon, G., & Waller, T. G. (1985). *Metacognition, cognition, and human performance*. Orlando, FL: Academic.

Gagné, R. (1978). Contributions of learning to human development. *Psychological Review, 75*, 177–191.

Gelman, R. (1969). Conservation acquisition: A problem of learning to attend to relevant attributes. *Journal of Experimental Child Psychology, 7*, 167–187.

Gelman, R. (1985). The developmental perspective on the problem of knowledge acquisition: A discussion. In S. Chipman, J. Segal, & R. Glaser (Eds.), *Thinking and learning skills* (Vol. 2). Hillsdale, NJ: Lawrence Erlbaum Associates.

Gesell, A. (1929). Maturation and infant behavior pattern. *Psychological Review, 36*, 307–319.

Gholson, B. (1980). *The cognitive-developmental basis of human learning: Studies in hypothesis testing*. New York: Academic.

Glaser, R. (1984). Education and thinking. *American Psychologist, 39*, 93–104.

Inhelder, B. (1969). Memory and intelligence in the child. In D. Elkind & J. Flavell (Eds.), *Studies in cognitive development*. London: Oxford.

Inhelder, B., & Piaget, J. (1958). *The growth of logical thinking from childhood to adolescence*. New York: Basic.

Istomina, Z. (1977). The development of voluntary memory in preschool-age children. In M. Cole (Ed.), *Soviet developmental psychology*. White Plains, NY: Sharpe.

James, W. (1890). *The principles of psychology* (Vol. 1). New York: Dover.

Karmiloff-Smith, A. (1984). Children's problem solving. In A. Brown & B. Rogoff (Eds.), *Advances in developmental psychology* (Vol. 3). Hillsdale, NJ: Lawrence Erlbaum Associates.

Keil, F. (1981). Constraints on knowledge and cognitive development. *Psychological Review, 88*, 197–227.

Keil, F. (1984). Mechanisms in cognitive development and the structure of knowledge. In R. Sternberg (Ed.), *Mechanisms of cognitive development*. New York: Freeman.

Keil, F. (1986). Conceptual domains and the acquisition of metaphor. *Cognitive Development, 1*, 73–96.

Kendler, H., & Kendler, T. (1975). From discrimination learning to cognitive development: A neobehavioristic odyssey. In W. K. Estes (Ed.), *Handbook of learning and cognitive processes* (Vol. 1). Hillsdale, NJ: Lawrence Erlbaum Associates.

Klahr, D., & Wallace, J. (1976). *Cognitive development: An information-processing view.* Hillsdale, NJ: Lawrence Erlbaum Associates.

Klahr, D., Langley, P., & Neches, R. (Eds.) (1986). *Production system models of learning and development.* Cambridge, MA: MIT Press.

Kuhn, D., Amsel, E., & O'Loughlin, M. (in press). *The development of scientific thinking skills.* Orlando, FL: Academic.

Kuhn, D. (1983). On the dual executive and its significance in the development of developmental psychology. In D. Kuhn & J. Meacham (Eds.), *On the development of developmental psychology.* Basel: Karger.

Kuhn, D., Pennington, N., & Leadbeater, B. (1983). Adult thinking in developmental perspective. In P. Baltes & O. Brim (Eds.), *Life-span development and behavior* (Vol. 5). New York: Academic.

Kuhn, D., & Phelps, E. (1982). The development of problem-solving strategies. In H. Reese (Ed.), *Advances in child development and behavior* (Vol. 17). New York: Academic.

Laboratory of Comparative Human Cognition. (1983). Culture and cognitive development. In P. Mussen (Ed.), *Carmichael's manual of child psychology* (4th ed.). New York: Wiley.

Labouvie-Vief, G. (1980). Beyond formal operations: Uses and limits of pure logic in life-span development. *Human Development, 23,* 141–161.

Lawler, R. (1985). *Computer experience and cognitive development: A child's learning in a computer culture.* New York: Halsted.

Lerner, R. (1982). Children and adolescents as producers of their own development. *Developmental Review, 2,* 342–370.

Levin, I. (1986). *Stage and structure: Reopening the debate.* Norwood, NJ: Ablex.

Liben, L. (1977). Memory in the context of cognitive development: The Piagetian approach. In R. Kail and J. Hagen (Eds.), *Perspective on the development of memory and cognition.* Hillsdale, NJ: Lawrence Erlbaum Associates.

Luria, A. (1976). *Cognitive development: Its cultural and social foundations.* Cambridge, MA: Harvard University Press.

Martin, S. (1959/60). Rediscovering the mind of the child. *Merrill-Palmer Quarterly, 6,* 67–76.

Morrison, H., & Kuhn, D. (1983). Cognitive aspects of preschoolers' peer imitation in a play situation. *Child Development, 54,* 1041–1053.

Newman, D., Riel, M., Martin, L. (1983). Cultural practices and Piagetian theory: The impact of a cross-cultural research program. In D. Kuhn & J. Meachum (Eds.), *On the development of developmental psychology.* Basel: Karger.

Paris, S., & Carter, A. (1973). Semantic and constructive aspects of sentence memory in children. *Developmental Psychology, 9,* 109–113.

Paris, S., & Lindauer, B. (1976). The role of inference in children's comprehension and memory for sentences. *Cognitive Psychology, 8,* 217–227.

Paris, S., & Lindauer, B. (1982). The development of cognitive skills during childhood. In B. Wolman (Ed.), *Handbook of developmental psychology.* Englewood Cliffs, NJ: Prentice-Hall.

Paris, S., Newman, D., & Jacobs, J. (1985). Social contexts and functions of children's remembering. In C. Brainerd & M. Pressley (Eds.), *The cognitive side of memory development.* New York: Springer-Verlag.

Paris, S., Newman, R., & McVey, K. (1982). Learning the functional significance of mnemonic actions: A microgenetic study of strategic acquisition. *Journal of Experimental Child Psychology, 34,* 490–509.

Paris, S., & Oka, E. (1986). Children's reading strategies, metacognition, and motivation. *Developmental Review, 6,* 25–56.

Pascual-Leone, J. (1970). A mathematical model for transition in Piaget's developmental stages. *Acta Psychologica, 32,* 301–345.

Piaget, J. (1970). Piaget's theory. In P. Mussen (Ed.), *Carmichael's manual of child psychology* (3rd ed.). New York: Wiley.

Piaget, J. (1971). *Biology and knowledge.* Chicago: University of Chicago Press.

Pinard, A. (1981). *The conservation of conservation: The child's acquisition of a fundamental concept.* Chicago: University of Chicago Press.

Pressley, M., Borkowski, J., & O'Sullivan, J. (1984). Memory strategy instruction is made of this: Metamemory and durable strategy use. *Educational Psychologist, 19,* 94–107.

Riegel, K. (1978). *Psychology Mon Amour: A countertext.* Boston: Houghton Mifflin.

Rogoff, B. (1982). Integrating context and cognitive development. In M. Lamb & A. Brown (Eds.), *Advances in developmental psychology* (Vol. 2). Hillsdale, NJ: Lawrence Erlbaum Associates.

Rosenthal, T., & Zimmerman, B. (1978). *Social learning and cognition.* New York: Academic.

Schaie, K. W. (1978). External validity in the assessment of intellectual performance in adulthood. *Journal of Geronotology, 33,* 695–701.

Schaie, K. W., & Willis, S. (in press). Can decline in adult intellectual functioning be reversed? *Developmental Psychology.*

Scribner, S. (1986). Thinking in action: Some characteristics of practical thought. In R. Sternberg & R. Wagner (Eds.), *Practical intelligence.* Cambridge: Cambridge University Press.

Sharp, D., Cole, M., & Lave, J. (1979). Education and cognitive development: The evidence from experimental research. *Monographs of the Society for Research in Child Development, 44* (Serial No. 178).

Shultz, T., Dover, A., & Amsel, E. (1979). The logical and empirical bases of conservation judgments. *Cognition, 7,* 99–123.

Siegler, R. (1976). Three aspects of cognitive development. *Cognitive Psychology, 4,* 481–520.

Siegler, R. (1983). Information processing approaches to development. In P. Mussen (Ed.), *Carmichael's manual of child psychology* (4th ed.). New York: Wiley.

Siegler, R. (1981). Developmental sequences within and between concepts. *Monographs of the Society for Research in Child Development, 46* (Serial No. 189).

Siegler, R. (in press). Unities in strategy choice across domains. In M. Perlmutter (Ed.), *Minnesota symposium on child psychology* (Vol. 21). Minneapolis: University of Minnesota Press.

Siegler, R., & Klahr, D. (1982). When do children learn? The relationship between existing knowledge and the acquisition of new knowledge. In R. Glaser (Ed.), *Advances in instructional psychology* (Vol. 2). Hillsdale, NJ: Lawrence Erlbaum Associates.

Siegler, R., & Shrager, J. (1984). A model of strategy choice. In C. Sophian (Ed.), *Origins of cognitive skills.* Hillsdale, NJ: Lawrence Erlbaum Associates.

Sternberg, R. (1984). Mechanisms of cognitive development: A componential approach. In R. Sternberg (Ed.), *Mechanisms of cognitive development.* New York: Freeman.

Sternberg, R. (1985). All's well that ends well, but it's a sad tale that begins at the end: A reply to Glaser. *American Psychologist, 40,* 571–573.

Sternberg, R., & Powell, J. (1983). The development of intelligence. In P. Mussen (Ed.), *Carmichael's manual of child psychology* (4th ed.). New York: Wiley.

Trabasso, T. (1975). Representation, memory, and reasoning: How do we make transitive inferences? In A. D. Pick (Ed.), *Minnesota symposia on child psychology* (Vol. 9). Minneapolis: University of Minnesota Press.

Trabasso, T., Isen, A., Dolecki, P., McLanahan, A., Riley, C., & Tucker, T. (1978). How do children solve class-inclusion problems? In R. Siegler (Ed.), *Children's thinking: What develops?* Hillsdale, NJ: Lawrence Erlbaum Associates.

Vygotsky, L. (1962). *Thought and language.* Cambridge, MA: MIT Press.

Vygotsky, L. (1978). *Mind in society: The development of higher psychological processes.* Cambridge, MA: Harvard University Press.

Wagner, R., & Sternberg, R. (1986). Tacit knowledge and intelligence in the everyday world. In R. Sternberg & R. Wagner (Eds.), *Practical intelligence*. Cambridge: Cambridge University Press.

Weissberg, J., & Paris, S. (1986). Young children's remembering in different contexts: A reinterpretation of Istomina's study. *Child Development, 57*, 1123–1129.

Werner, H. (1948). *Comparative psychology of mental development*. New York: International Universities Press.

Wertsch, J. (1979). From social interaction to higher psychological processes. *Human Development, 22*, 1–22.

Wertsch, J. (1984). The zone of proximal development: Some conceptual issues. In B. Rogoff & J. Wertsch (Eds.), *Children's learning in the "zone of proximal development."* San Francisco: Jossey-Bass.

Willis, S., & Schaie, K. W. (1986). Practical intelligence in later adulthood. In R. Sternberg & R. Wagner (Eds.), *Practical intelligence*. Cambridge: Cambridge University Press.

Wozniak, R. (1982). Metaphysics and science, reason and reality: The intellectual origins of genetic epistemology. In J. Broughton & D. J. Freeman-Moir (Eds.), *The cognitive-developmental psychology of James Mark Baldwin: Current theory and research in genetic epistemology.* Norwood, NJ: Ablex.

6 Intellectual Development: Psychometric and Information-Processing Approaches

Robert J. Sternberg
Yale University

What is intelligence and how does it develop? As shown by Deanna Kuhn in the previous chapter, psychologists have tried to answer this question in many different ways. In this chapter, the focus narrows to a special concern for psychometric and information-processing approaches to intellectual development. The goal of this chapter is to describe these approaches and to summarize what we have learned from them.

THE PSYCHOMETRIC APPROACH

Psychometric conceptions of intelligence and its development have in common their reliance upon individual-differences data as a means of testing theories, and, in some cases, as a heuristic aiding the formulation of the theories. Psychometric researchers use techniques of data analysis to discover common patterns of individual differences across tests. These patterns are then hypothesized to emanate from latent sources of individual differences, namely, mental abilities.

Psychometric theory and research seem to have evolved along three interrelated but, nevertheless, distinguishable lines. These traditions have conveyed rather different impressions of what aspects of intelligence develop. The three traditions can be traced back to Sir Francis Galton, Alfred Binet, and Charles Spearman.

In his theory of the human faculty and its development, Galton (1883) proposed two general qualities that distinguished the more from the less gifted. The first was energy or the *capacity for labor*. The second was *sensitivity to physical stimuli*. James McKean Cattell brought many of Galton's ideas from England to the United States. Cattell (1890) proposed a series of 50 psychophysical tests, such as dynamometer pressure (the greatest possible squeeze of one's hand), rate of arm movement over a distance of 50 cm, the distance on the skin by which two points need to be separated for them to be felt separately, and letter span in memory. Underlying all of these tests was the assumption that physical tests measure mental ability.

Binet's conception of intelligence and of how to measure it differed substantially from that of Galton and Cattell, whose tests he referred to as "wasted time." To Binet, the core of intelligence was *judgment* (Binet & Simon, 1916a, 1916b). Binet and Simon measured judgment by tasks such as recognizing (a) verbal and pictorial absurdities; (b) similarities and differences; and (c) analogies and other inductive relations. Binet cited the example of Helen Keller as someone of known extraordinary intelligence whose scores on psychophysical tests would be notably inferior, yet who could nonetheless be expected to perform at a very high level on tests of judgment.

An alternative psychometric tradition—a more statistically based one—originated with Charles Spearman. Substance and method have rarely been as closely intertwined as in the investigation of intelligence in the tradition of Spearman. Indeed, use of the most widely accepted method of data analysis in differential psychology, factor analysis, has become almost synonymous with use of the psychometric (or differential) approach to intelligence. In factor analysis, one starts with a correlation matrix, and seeks to discover the latent structure underlying the matrix. The end products are factors. Factors are "categories for classifying mental or behavioral performances" (Vernon, 1971, p. 8). Factors provide one of a number of alternative descriptive systems for understanding the structure of mental abilities (R.J. Sternberg, 1980b). They give us a useful way of identifying constellations of individual differences that in some sense go together, whether because of commonalities in process, structure, content, or whatever.

Spearman's (1904) mislabeled psychometric theory of intelligence—the *two-factor theory*—proposes two kinds of factors of human intelligence (not just two factors). According to this theory, there are (a) a general factor, which pervades all intellectual performances; and (b) a set of specific factors, each of which is relevant to one particular task. Spearman believed the general factor arose from individual differences in levels of mental energy.

Louis L. Thurstone (1938), unlike Spearman, eschewed the notion of a general factor. He proposed a theory that tentatively included seven primary mental abilities. The abilities were verbal comprehension, number facility, memory, perceptual speed, spatial visualization, verbal fluency, and inductive reasoning.

J.P. Guilford proposed an extension of Thurstone's theory that incorporates Thurstone's factors (Guilford, 1967; Guilford & Hoepfner, 1971). It splits the primary mental abilities, however, and adds new abilities so that the number of factors is increased from 7 to 120. According to Guilford, every mental task requires three elements: an operation, a content, and a product. Guilford pictured the relation among these three elements as that of a cube, with each of the elements—operations, contents, and products—representing a dimension of the cube. There are five kinds of operations: cognition, memory, divergent production, convergent production, and evaluation. There are six kinds of product: units, classes, relations, systems, transformations, and implications. And there are four kinds of content: figural, symbolic, semantic, and behavioral. Because the subcategories are independently defined, they are multiplicative, yielding 5 × 6 × 4 = 120 different mental abilities. Each of these 120 abilities is represented by Guilford as a small cube embedded in the larger cube. The theory of 120 independent factors might seem implausible to some; indeed, the methodology Guilford (1967) has used to confirm his theory has been shown to be problematical in many respects when used in the way that Guilford used it (see Horn, 1967; Horn & Knapp, 1973).

A hierarchical model has been proposed by Vernon (1971). At the top of the hierarchy is *g* or general ability. At the second level are two major group factors, verbal–educational ability and practical–mechanical ability; at the third level are minor group factors; and at the fourth level are specific factors.

Psychometric Conceptions and Intellectual Development

Substantial literatures exist regarding the nature of intelligence and the development of intelligence as perceived from a psychometric point of view. Yet the two literatures are surprisingly autonomous: On the one hand, few of the major factor theorists of intelligence have given serious and detailed consideration to the place of intellectual development in their theories. On the other hand, few of the major developmental students of intelligence have given serious and detailed consideration, in their research, to the place of theories of the nature of intelligence. Despite notable exceptions (e.g., Horn, 1970; Stott & Ball, 1965), the literature on the development of intelligence has been very largely empirical in its orientation (see, for example, Bayley's 1970 review of the literature on the development of mental abilities); and some of the work has been almost entirely atheoretical (see, for example, Broman, Nichols, & Kennedy, 1975). Theory and data have thus been separated in the developmental literature, and the goal here is to provide a framework for interrelating work on the nature of intelligence with work on the development of intelligence. The basis for this integration is an enumeration of some of the possible loci of intellectual development in the factorial theories. The various loci are not mutually exclusive: To the contrary, it seems highly likely that multiple loci exist.

Changes in Number of Factors with Age. One possible locus of intellectual development is in the number of abilities and, hence, of factors that constitute measured intelligence at different ages. Arguments in favor of change in number of factors as a locus of intellectual development usually take the form of differentiation theories. Although it is conceivable that intelligence could become either more or less differentiated with advancing age, the former position has been by far the more popular, and certainly more plausible, one. Perhaps the most noted proponent of this point of view has been Henry E. Garrett (1938, 1946). Garrett (1946) defined intelligence as comprising the abilities demanded in the solution of problems that require the comprehension and use of symbols. According to his developmental theory of intelligence, "abstract or symbol intelligence changes in its organization as age increases from a fairly unified and general ability to a loosely organized group of abilities or factors" (Garrett, 1946, p. 373). This theory has obvious implications for how various psychometric theories of intelligence might be interrelated. Again, according to Garret (1946):

> It seems to effect a rapprochement between the Spearman General Factor and the Group Factor theories [e.g., that of Thurstone, 1938]. Over the elementary school years we find a functional generality among tests at the symbol level. Later on this general factor of "g" breaks down into the quasi-independent factors reported by many investigators. (p. 376)

Several sources of evidence provide at least tentative support for the differentiation theory. Garrett, Bryan, and Perl (1935), for example, administered 10 tests of memory, verbal ability, and number ability to children of ages 9, 12, and 15 years. With one exception, intercorrelations among the three kinds of tests showed a monotone decrease between the ages of 9 and 12, and between 12 and 15, suggesting increasing independence of the abilities with age. A factor analysis of the correlations showed a decrease in the proportion of variance accounted for by a general factor with increasing age. Similar results were found by Asch (1936), who discovered a decrease in the correlation between verbal and numerical tests from age 9 to age 12. M. P. Clark (1944) administered an early version of the Primary Mental Abilities Test to boys of ages 11, 13, and 15 years and found that scores on tests of verbal, number, spatial, memory, and reasoning abilities showed decreasing correlations with increasing age. Other studies considered together (e.g., Schiller, 1934) also tend to support the hypothesis of a decrease in correlations with age. Reviewing the literature on changes in the organization of mental abilities with age, Bayley (1955) concluded that there was fairly substantial support for the differentiation notion.

In summary, one possible reconciliation among the various theories of the nature of intelligence is in terms of increasing differentiation of abilities with age. Theories postulating small numbers of important factors, such as Spearman's, may be relevant for younger children; theories postulating large numbers of factors, such as Thurstone's or conceivably Guilford's, may be relevant for older children and adults.

Changes in the Relevance or Weights of Factors with Age. A second possible locus of intellectual development is in the relevance or weights of factors as contributors to individual-differences variance in intelligence at different age levels. For example, a perceptual–motor factor may decrease in weight with age, whereas a verbal factor may increase in weight. Thus, it is not the total number of factors, but the importance of individual factors that changes with age. From this perspective, what makes one person more intelligent than another can be quite different across ages because the abilities that constitute intelligence can shift dramatically in their importance. Variants of this viewpoint have been very popular in the literature on the development of intelligence (e.g., Hofstaetter, 1954). Despite their differences, these variants have virtually all been consistent with the notion that abilities of the kind proposed by Galton, and by successors in his tradition, to constitute intelligence seem most relevant for infants and very young children; abilities of the kind proposed by Binet and successors in his tradition seem most relevant for older children and adults. These views, then, like the differentiation views, seem to point the way toward a developmental reconciliation of the theoretical positions. An interesting ramification of these views is that developmental theorizing becomes essential rather than adjunct to understanding theories of intelligence originally proposed for adults.

One of the most well-known data sets supporting the notion that factors change in relevance with age is that of Hofstaetter (1954). Hofstaetter factor-analyzed data from Bayley's (1933, 1943, 1949, 1951) Berkeley Growth Study, which assessed intellectual performance from infancy through adulthood. Hofstaetter found that up to 20 months of age, a first factor, which he named sensorimotor alertness, accounted for most of the individual-differences variance in children's performance on intelligence tests. From the age of 40 months onward, this factor accounted for practically none of the variance in mental-age scores. Between 20 and 40 months, the dominant source of individual-differences variance could be accounted for by a third factor that tapped manipulation of symbols or simply abstract behavior. Hofstaetter suggested that this factor corresponds to Spearman's (1927) *g*, but he further noted that it was only because of limitations in the data that the factor appeared to be unitary in nature. Hofstaetter concluded from his data that the nature of intelligence changes somewhat from one age to another. Semantic use of the term *intelligence* thus reflects the factors that show the highest weights at a given age level.

Bayley's own view of her data is very similar to that of Hofstaetter (1954). Like Piaget (1972), however, Bayley (1955) has emphasized how the abilities of greater importance in later life build upon the abilities of greater importance in earlier life:

> Intelligence appears to me . . . to be a dynamic succession of developing functions, with the more advanced and complex functions in the hierarchy depending on the prior maturing of earlier simpler ones (given, of course, normal conditions of care). (p. 807)

For example, verbal tasks require perceptual processing for their completion.

Bayley (1933) identified six factors in the correlational data from her First-Year Scale, and six factors in the data from her Preschool Scale. Like Hofstaetter (1954), she found that the factors that contributed substantially to individual differences in measured intelligence varied with age (see, especially, Bayley, 1970, Fig. 4). She found a general tendency for the more complex factors of thought to become of greater importance to individual differences in intelligence with increasing age.

Stott and Ball (1965) factor-analyzed data from intelligence tests administered to children in the age range from 3 to 60 months. They used Guilford's (1956, 1957) structure-of-intellect model as the theoretical framework within which to interpret their results. Although they found significant loadings for 31 of Guilford's factors at one age or another, and although many factors appeared at multiple age levels, results for the younger age levels (especially below 1 year) included important other factors—such as gross psychomotor skills, locomotor skills, and hand dexterity—that did not fit into the Guilford model and that did not apply at the upper age levels. Thus, the Guilford factors appeared not to be relevant at all ages.

Changes in the Content (Names) of Factors Within a Given Factor Structure. Whereas the point of view discussed above suggests that the structure of mental abilities (or at least the factor structure important for generating individual differences) changes with age, the point of view considered here suggests that, for a given theory, structure stays essentially the same across age groups but the content that fills in this structure changes. For example, g, or general ability, might be conceived as perceptual–motor in nature at the infant level but as cognitive in nature later on. In each case, the factorial structure could be the same; that is, there is a single general factor, but the content of that factor differs across ages. The difference between structure and content is not always clear-cut, and we doubt that theorists propounding each of these positions differ; support for the preceding position requires a different factor structure at each age level, whereas support for the present position requires a different content filling in the structure at each level. Historically, proponents of this present position have tended to be most interested in the changing composition of Spearman's general factor at each level, but have found that what is general changes with age.

McCall, Hogarty, and Hurlburt (1972) factor-analyzed data from the Gesell Developmental Schedule administered to children participating in the Fels Longitudinal Study. Children were studied at 6, 12, 18, and 24 months of age. The authors were interested primarily in the first principal component (general factor) at each age level. They found that, at 6 months of age, items loading on this factor tended to measure visually guided exploration of perceptual contingencies. At 12 months, the factor reflected a mixture of sensorimotor and social imitation as well as rudimentary vocal–verbal behavior. The joint presence of sensorimotor and social imitation was interpreted as consistent with Piaget's (1972) notion that imitation mediates the transition between egocentric sensorimotor behaviors, on the one hand, and more decentered verbal and social behaviors, on the other hand. At 18 months, items loading on the first principal component reflected verbal and motor imitation, verbal production, and verbal comprehension. By 24 months, highly loading items measured verbal labeling, comprehension, fluency, and grammatical maturity. Again we see a transition between the types of behaviors studied by Galton (1883) at the lower levels and the types of behaviors studied by Binet and Simon (1916a, 1916b) at the upper levels. It is important to note that the items loading on the first principal component are factorially but not behaviorally unitary: Multiple behaviors are general across the tests that McCall et al. (1972) studied at each age level. Thus, they load on a single general factor. The authors interpreted their data as supporting what they and Kagan (1971) before them had called a "heterotypic" model of mental development. In such a model, there is a discontinuity in the overt developmental function (i.e., in people's rank orders at different ages, despite the differences in the behaviors of consequence). This model was contrasted with five other models that were not as well supported. One such model, for example, was a "homotypic" model, in which individual differences are purported to remain stable, as are the behaviors that generate the individual differences.

McCall, Eichorn, and Hogarty (1977) studied "transitions in early mental development" in much the same ways as had McCall and his colleagues in an earlier study (1972). In this study, however, the investigators used the developmental data from the Berkeley Growth Study, as had Hofstaetter before them. Whereas Hofstaetter factor-analyzed data across age levels, McCall et al. factor-analyzed data within age levels. The investigators interpreted their data (for infants) as supporting a five-stage model of intellectual development: During Stage 1 (birth to 2 months), the infant is responsive primarily to selected stimulus dimensions that in some sense match the structural predispositions of the infant's sensory–perceptual systems. Stage 2 (3 to 7 months) is characterized by more active exploration of the environment, although the infant's view of the world is alleged still to be completely subjective. At Stage 3 (8 to 13 months), means for doing things begin to be differentiated from ends. The separation is complete by Stage 4 (14 to 18 months), by which time the child is able to associate two objects in the environment without acting on either of them. Symbolic relationships emerge during Stage 5 (21+ months).

Changes in Factor Scores of Fixed Factors with Age. The views expressed in the previous discussions are all ones of qualitative changes in the nature of intelligence with age. However, most of the voluminous literature reflecting the psychometric approach to the development of intelligence has dealt with quantitative changes and how to account for them. The preponderance of studies has been atheoretical, although the emphasis here is on theoretically motivated research.

Two basic findings in the literature that have needed to be accounted for are, first, that absolute level of intelligence (as measured, say, by mental age or a comparable construct) increases with age; and, second, that correlations between measurements of intelligence decrease with increasing intervals of time between measurements (see, e.g., Bayley, 1933, 1970; Dearborn & Rothney, 1941; Honzik, 1938; Sontag, Baker, & Nelson, 1958). An elegant attempt to account for these findings was made by J.E. Anderson (1940), who proposed that correlations of IQ at various ages with terminal IQ (perhaps at about the age of 16) increase because "the prediction of final status is based upon a larger proportion of that which is included in the total: that is, scores at 10 years include more of that which is present at 16 years than do scores at 3 years" (p. 388). Anderson suggested that the increase in overlap between final scores and successively later scores would be predicted by a model in which increments to intelligence are additive over the age span, and uncorrelated (or only modestly correlated) with each other and with the current level of intelligence. Anderson tested this simple model by reanalyzing data from the Harvard Growth Study (Dearborn, Rothney, & Shuttleworth, 1938) and the Honzik (1938) study. He compared mental growth curves from these data to Monte Carlo curves generated by cumulating the first to the sixteenth random numbers (where each number represented a "year" of mental growth) in a table of random numbers of 300 artificial subjects. In the random-number table, of course, successive increments in the accumulated sum are uncorrelated both with each other and with the current value of the sum. According to Anderson's model, the closer in time two measurements are made, the less time there has been for intervening changes to take place and, hence, the more highly related those two measurements will be. Fits of the data to the model were quite good, providing at least tentative support for the model.

Most of the research that has been conducted on quantitative development of intelligence has been consistent with Anderson's assumption that intelligence increases in absolute amount over age, and that one's goal should be to plot the form of this function and to account in some way for why the function takes this form. Bayley (1966, 1968), for example, plotted mental growth curves from infancy to 36 years on the basis of her data from the Berkeley Growth Study. Her findings were typical of this literature: Absolute level of intelligence increased fairly rapidly until early adolescence, showed some decrease in the rate of increase from early to middle adolescence, and then pretty much leveled off in middle to late adolescence. However, the assumption of a monotonic growth curve throughout the life span has been challenged as representing a composite of two different component functions, each of which is purported to show a different pattern of growth throughout the life span. The two component functions, in this view, represent what R. B. Cattell (1963, 1971) and Horn (1968) have referred to as *fluid* and *crystallized intelligence*.

Fluid and crystallized intelligence are proposed by R. B. Cattell (1963, 1971) and Horn (1968) to be subfactors of general intelligence (g). Fluid ability is best measured by tests that require mental manipulation of abstract symbols such as, for example, figural analogies, series completions, and classification problems. Crystallized ability is best measured by tests that require knowledge of the cultural milieu in which one lives such as, for example, vocabulary, general information, and reading comprehension. Horn and Cattell (1966) reported that although the mean level of fluid intelligence was systematically higher for younger adults than for older adults, the mean level of crystallized intelligence was systematically higher for older than for younger adults. In general, crystallized ability seemed to increase throughout the life span, whereas fluid intelligence seemed to increase up until the 20s and to decrease slowly thereafter.

Schaie (1974) questioned what he called the myth of intellectual decline, namely, that some or all intellectual functions decline after some point in adulthood. Schaie noted that the evidence on the question of decline is mixed. Cross-sectional studies have tended to support the notion of a decline (e.g., Jones & Conrad, 1933; Wechsler, 1939), whereas longitudinal studies have not (e.g., Bayley & Oden, 1955; Owens, 1953). Mixed designs suggest that the decline may be relatively small, on the average, with significant individual differences in just how large it is.

Conclusions

To conclude, developmental theories are of particular interest because they provide one kind of reconciliation between alternative psychometric theories of intelligence. For example, some abilities theorized by Galton to be important in intelligence do indeed appear to be so in infancy and perhaps for a few years thereafter. As infancy draws to a close, however, these abilities seem to become less important, and the abilities theorized by Binet and Simon (1916a) to be of consequence in intelligence seem to acquire greater importance. By adulthood, the latter kinds of abilities seem to be of much greater importance in measured intelligence, and probably in general adaptation to most adult environments, than do the former kinds of abilities. A reconciliation of sorts among some of the factor theories is also possible on the differentiation view, according to which the number and fineness of factors increase with age. The information-processing work described here elaborates on and provides a more complete account of just what aspects of intelligence develop.

THE INFORMATION-PROCESSING APPROACH

Information-processing conceptions of intelligence and its development have in common their reliance on stimulus (rather than subject) variation as their primary means for testing theories of intelligent functioning. Underlying all of these conceptions is a view of intelligence as deriving from the ways in which people mentally represent and process information. Information-processing researchers use techniques of data analysis, such as computer simulation and mathematical modeling, to discover patterns of stimulus variation that suggest strategies of information processing in tasks requiring the exercise of one's intelligence.

Information-processing research has used the computer program as a metaphor and a heuristic for understanding how humans process information. The major distinguishing feature of the approach, however, is not its reliance on computational notions but rather its concern with how information is processed during the performance of various kinds of tasks.

One of the earliest and most important articles propounding the information-processing approach was that of Donders (1868). Donders proposed that the time between a stimulus and a response can be decomposed into a sequence of successive processes, with each process beginning as soon as the previous one ends. The durations of these processes can be ascertained through the use of a subtraction method; that is, subjects solve each of two tasks proposed by the experimenter to differ only in that the more difficult task requires one more component process for its solution than does the simpler task. The duration of this process can then be computed by subtracting the time taken to solve the easier task from the time taken to solve the harder task. The subtraction method was popular for several decades (Jastrow, 1892) but then came into disfavor (Kulpe, 1895) because of the method's assumption of strict additivity: One had to assume that one could insert into, or delete from, a task a given process without somehow affecting the execution of other processes. This assumption seemed so unreasonable at the time (and still does to many people) that the method went into hibernation for about a century, until it was reactivated in modified form.

Almost 100 years later, two works (Miller, Galanter, & Pribram, 1960; Newell, Shaw, & Simon, 1960) appeared in a single year that revived the information-processing approach. The goal of both programs of research was, as Miller et al. put it, "to discover whether the cybernetic [computer-based] ideas have any relevance for psychology" (p. 3). Both groups of investigators concluded that they did have relevance, and, moreover, that the computer could be a highly useful tool in psychological theorizing. Miller et al. sought to understand human behavior in terms of Plans, wherein a Plan was defined as "any hierarchical process in the organism that can control the order in which a sequence of operations is to be performed" (p. 16). Critical for the information-processing approach was the authors' view that "a Plan is, for an organism, essentially the same as a program for a computer" (p. 16). The authors did not wish to confuse matters, however, by failing to distinguish altogether between computer and human information processing:

> We are reasonably confident that "program" could be substituted everywhere for "Plan" in the following pages. However, the reduction of Plans to nothing but programs is still a scientific hypothesis and is still in need of further validation. For

the present, therefore, it should be less confusing if we regard a computer program that simulates certain features of an organism's behavior as a theory about the organismic Plan that generated the behavior. (p. 16)

The Miller et al. (1960) and Newell et al. (1960) works proposed both theories of information processing and a methodology (computer simulation) for implementing and testing information-processing theories. Newell et al. (1960) proposed a General Problem Solver (GPS) computer program that could actually solve complex problems of the sort that give people considerable diffculty. Subsequent versions of the program (e.g., Ernst & Newell, 1969) could solve large numbers of problems (e.g., Missionaries and Cannibals, Tower of Hanoi, Water Jugs) by using just a small set of routines that were applicable across the entire range of problems. In summary, the computer simulation method allowed experimental psychologists to test theories of human information-processing by comparing predictions generated by computer simulation to actual data collected from human subjects. Some investigators have preferred to test their theories by using quantitative models with parameters estimated directly from the human data.

The Unit of Behavior

Whereas many psychometric theorists of intelligence have agreed on the factor as the fundamental unit in terms of which intellectual behavior should be analyzed, many information-processing theorists have agreed on the elementary information process as the fundamental unit of behavior (Newell & Simon, 1972). It is assumed that all behavior of a human information-processing system is the result of combinations of these elementary processes. The processes are elementary in the sense that they are not further broken down into simpler processes by the theory under consideration. The level of analysis that is considered to be "elementary" will depend on the type of behavior under consideration and the level at which the theory attempts to account for the behavior. The processes must be well defined, and the collection of them must be sufficiently general and powerful to compose all macroscopic performances of the human information-processing system (Newell & Simon, 1972).

R. J. Sternberg (1979, 1980b) has expanded the notion of the elementary information process by proposing that elementary information processes, or what he calls components, can be subdivided by function. Components can be distinguished on the basis of function into two basic and different kinds: *metacomponents* and *performance components*. Metacomponents are higher order control processes that are used for executive planning and decision making in problem solving. Metacomponents (a) decide just what the problem is that needs to be solved; (b) select lower order components to effect solution of the problem; (c) select a strategy for combining lower order components; (d) select one or more representations or organizations of information upon which the lower order components and strategies can act; (e) decide upon a rate of problem solving that will permit the desired level of accuracy or solution quality; and (f) monitor progress toward a solution. Performance components may be viewed as executing the plans and implementing the decisions laid down by the metacomponents. Performance components in a variety of tasks tend to organize themselves into four stages of strategy execution (R. J. Sternberg, 1981). One or more of these components are usually needed to (a) encode the elements of a problem; (b) combine these elements in the execution of a working strategy; (c) compare the solution obtained to available answer options; and (d) respond.

Intellectual development occurs through interactions of the components. The various kinds of components are thought to be interrelated in four basic ways. First, one kind of component can directly activate another. Second, one kind of component can indirectly activate another. Third, one kind of component can provide direct feedback to another kind of component. Fourth, one kind of component can provide indirect feedback to another kind of component. Direct activation (feedback) refers to the immediate passage of control or information from one kind of component to another kind. Indirect activation (feedback) refers to the passage of control or information from one kind of component to another via a third kind of component.

In the proposed system of interrelations, only metacomponents can directly activate and receive feedback from each other kind of component. Thus, all control *to* the system passes directly from the metacomponents, and all information *from* the system passes directly to the metacomponents. The other kinds of components can activate each other only directly, and they receive information from each other only indirectly; in each case, mediation must be supplied by the metacomponents. For example, acquisition of information affects retention of information, as well as various kinds of transformations (performances) on that information, but only via the link of the three kinds of components to the metacomponents. Feedback from the acquisition components can be passed to any other kind of component but only through the filter of the metacomponents.

Consider a typical empirical study of the components of information processing. Keating and Bobbitt (1978) took tasks studied by Hunt, Frost, and Lunneborg (1973) and Hunt, Lunneborg, and Lewis (1975) and studied them in the context of a developmental paradigm. Their self-stated major goal was to "discover whether reliable individual differences in cognitive processing exist in children and, if so, whether these differences are systematically related to age and ability" (Keating & Bobbitt, 1978, p. 157). Like Hunt and his colleagues, their primary interest was in individual differences in the component processes of information-processing activities, rather than in global response times or error rates reflecting a conglomeration of processes.

Keating and Bobbitt's experiments used 20 subjects in each of grades three (average age, 9), seven (average age, 13), and eleven (average age, 17). Half of the subjects at each age level were characterized as being of high mental ability (scores in roughly the 90th to 95th percentile of the Raven Progressive Matrices), and half were characterized as being of average mental ability (scores in roughly the 40th to 45th percentile of the Raven Progressive Matrices).

The authors were interested in the children's performance on three basic sets of information-processing tasks. The first set included simple reaction-time and choice reaction-time tasks. In the simple reaction-time task, subjects were instructed to press a button as soon as a red light appeared; in the choice reaction-time task, subjects were instructed to press a green button whenever a green light appeared or a red button whenever a red light appeared. Subjects did not know, of course, which color of light would appear on a given trial. The second set of tasks involved retrieval and comparison of information in memory. This set included two letter-matching tasks, a physical-match task, and a name-match task, based upon the tasks adopted by Hunt et al. (1975) from Posner, Boies, Eichelman, and Taylor (1969). In the physical-match task, subjects were asked to sort cards that had pairs of letters printed on them that either were or were not physical matches. Examples of the former would be "AA" and "bb"; examples of the latter would be "Aa" and "Ba." In the name-match task, subjects were presented with cards to sort that had pairs of letters printed on them that either were or were not name matches. Examples of the former would be "Aa," "BB," and "bB"; examples of the latter would be "Ab," "ba," and "bA." In the first task, the subject had to sort the cards by the physical appearance of the stimuli; in the second task, the subject had to sort by the names of the stimuli. The third set of tasks involved scanning sets of either one, three, or five digits held in working memory. In this task, which Hunt et al. (1973) adopted from the varied-set procedure of S. Sternberg (1969b), subjects are asked to store the short list of items in memory. This list thus becomes a memory set. Subjects are then presented with a target item and are asked to indicate as quickly as possible whether the target is one of the items in the memory set. For example, if the memory set were "3, 9, 6," an affirmative response would be required for "9," but a negative response would be required for "2."

The results of the experiments on the three sets of tasks generally confirmed Keating and Bobbitt's (1978) hypothesis of developmental differences. In the simple reaction-time and choice reaction-time tasks, the investigators found significant main effects of age, ability level, and task (simple or choice reaction time). In each case, means were in the expected direction, with older and brighter children performing the tasks more rapidly and with simple reaction time faster than choice reaction time. Of somewhat greater interest was a significant age-by-task interaction, whereby the difference between choice reaction time and simple reaction time was greater for younger children than for older children. The ability level by task interaction was nonsignificant, but in the expected direction, with lesser ability children showing a greater increment in choice relative to simple reaction time than was shown by higher ability children. Thus, increased task complexity affected the response times of children who were less able (at least as measured by age and possibly as measured by Raven score) more than it affected the response times of those who were more able.

In the letter-retrieval and comparison task, there were significant main effects of age, ability, and task (physical or name match). Again, the results were as expected; older and brighter children were faster in card sorting, and the name-match condition took longer than the physical-match condition. Again, there were significant age-by-task and ability-by-task interactions, with older and brighter children less differentially affected by the added demands of the name-match task than were younger and duller children.

In the memory-scanning task, significant main effects were found for age, ability level, and set size, with all effects in the expected directions. There was also a significant interaction between set size and ability, with children who were less able showing a greater effect of set size than was shown by those who were more able. To understand this interaction and the main effects fully, subjects' performance on this task was decomposed into two parameters, a *slope* and an *intercept*. The former parameter estimated the duration of the comparison process thought to be performed between the target item and each member of the memory set; the latter parameter estimated the duration of all processes that were constant in duration across set sizes, such as target encoding time and time to respond. The linear model used to estimate these parameters accounted for over 98% of the variance in the latency data and, hence, could be expected to yield meaningful parameter estimates. The authors found in the analysis of slopes that only the main effect of ability was significant, although the age by ability interaction approached significance. In contrast, the intercept was only marginally related to ability level, but strongly related to age. The reason for this particular pattern of findings was not clear.

In an effort to put together the results of the various experiments, correlations were computed between component processes from different tasks. These processes were hypothesized either to be highly related psychologically (e.g., intercept from the memory-scanning task and choice reaction time) or to be only poorly related (e.g., intercept from the memory-scanning task and difference between name and physical match times). In general, the parameters hypothesized to be highly related showed higher intercorrelations (median = .72) than did the parameters hypothesized to be only poorly related (median = .28). An attempt was also made to predict Raven Progressive Matrix scores from three hypothesized components of information processing—choice reaction time minus simple reaction time, name minus physical match time, and memory-scanning slope. These three parameters accounted for 62% of the variance in the Raven Progressive Matrix scores across all ages combined. Age alone accounted for 47% of the variance, however, leaving 15% explained by the central-processing variables.

A useful elaboration of the original Newell–Simon view is the production. A production is a condition–action sequence (Newell & Simon, 1972). If a certain condition is met, then a certain action is performed. Sequences of ordered productions are called *production systems*. The executive for a production system is expected to make its way down the ordered list of productions until one of the conditions is met. The action corresponding to that condition is executed and control is returned to the top of the list. The executive then makes its way down the list again, trying to satisfy a condition. When it does so, an action is executed, control returns to the top, and so on. Hunt and Poltrock (1974) have suggested that the productions may be probabilistically ordered so that the exact order in which the list is scanned may differ across subsequent scannings of the list.

Cognitive development is assumed by some to occur through the operation of self-modifying production systems (see Klahr, 1979, 1984, for reviews of the literature on such production systems). The basic idea is that the action in a condition–action sequence is to build a new production. Anderson, Kline, and Beasley (1979) have proposed four transition mechanisms by which modification could occur. A designation production is one that simply has as its action the instructions to build a new production of a certain kind. A strengthening mechanism increases the probability that a production will be activated. A generalization mechanism weakens the specific conditions that activate a production so that the production is more likely to be executed under a broader variety of circumstances. Finally, a discrimination mechanism strengthens the specifications for activation of a production so that the production will be activated only when more specific conditions are met than was originally the case. Notice that a critical assumption underlying the last three mechanisms is that productions have differential strengths that affect the likelihood of being executed if they are reached. A rough analogy would be to the eliciting conditions necessary to fire a neuron in the nervous system. Intellectual development, thus, continues throughout one's lifetime and is largely a matter of learning, which can alter the productions constituting a production system and, as a result, the person's way of going about problem solving of various kinds.

Siegler (1981) has suggested that an important aspect of information processing is adherence to mental *rules*. Rules can be considered to be mini-Plans or ministrategies for solving problems of various kinds. As the child grows older, the complexity of rules increases, generally because earlier rules fail to take into account all of the relevant information in a given problem. Siegler has used rules most often to translate Piaget's stages of performance on various tasks into information-processing terms (Siegler, 1976, 1977, 1978, 1981; Siegler & Vago, 1978). He has carried this form of analysis further, however, in devising Piagetian types of tasks that are also susceptible to analysis by the rule-assessment approach.[1] Consider, as Siegler (1981) does, Piaget's (1952) description of

---

[1]See also the chapter by Kuhn (this volume) for further information on Siegler's use of Piagetian tasks.

the developmental sequence of the conservation of liquid quantity. In this task, typically, subjects are shown water being poured from a tall thin jar (or beaker) into a short thick jar (or beaker), or vice versa, and they are asked which jar (or beaker) is holding more water; nonconservers will state that the tall thin jar is holding more water. The rule-assessment approach seeks to explain the difference in the ways information is processed by conservers and nonconservers, as well as to explain intermediate stages of processing.

In Piaget's Stage 1, a child is said to be "unable to reckon simultaneously with the height and cross-section of the liquids . . . he takes into account only the heights" (Piaget, 1952, p. 12). Siegler's Rule I, corresponding to Piaget's Stage 1, begins with the child asking him or herself whether the values of the dominant dimension (usually the height of a column of water in each of two jars) are equal. If the heights (or values on some other dominant dimension) are judged to be equal, the child responds that the alternatives are equal (even though the widths of the jars may be grossly unequal). If the heights (or other dominant values) are judged to be unequal, the child responds that the jar or beaker with the water at greater height (or other dominant dimension) has more water in it. Thus, Piaget's concept of nonconservation has been translated into information-processing terms as a rule (or Plan) actualized through self-interrogation.

In Piaget's Stage 2, "a second relation, that of the width, is explicitly brought into the picture . . . [but] when he is concerned with the unequal levels he forgets the width, and when he notices the difference in width he forgets what he has just said about the relation between the levels" (Piaget, 1952, p. 16). In Siegler's Rule II, the child asks himself or herself whether the values of the dominant dimension are equal. If they are, the child asks whether the values of the subordinate dimension are equal. If so, the child responds that the alternatives are equal; if not, the child responds that the jar or beaker with the greater value on the subordinate dimension has more water in it. Suppose, though, that the values of the dominant dimension are perceived as unequal. In this case, the subject responds that the jar or beaker with the greater value on the dominant dimension has more water in it. Note that, in using this rule, the child will respond correctly if the values of the dominant dimension are equal (say, two beakers of equal height). In this case, the child attends to both the dominant and subordinate dimensions (usually height and width). The child will respond incorrectly, however, if the values on the dominant dimension are unequal, unless the values on the subordinate dimension are equal. When the values on the dominant dimension are unequal, the child ignores the subordinate dimension and gets the problem correct only if it so happens that for the particular problem, the value of the subordinate dimension does not affect the answer to the problem (as when the widths of the two jars are equal). Siegler has proposed a Rule III (not considered here) that corresponds to a slightly more advanced substage of Piaget's Stage 2.

In Piaget's Stage 3, "children state immediately, or almost immediately that the quantities of liquid are conserved, and this irrespective of the number and nature of the changes made" (Piaget, 1952, p. 17). In Siegler's Rule IV, corresponding to Piaget's Stage 3, all information about both dimensions is taken into account. The child first asks whether the values of the dominant dimension are equal. If they are, the child asks whether the values of the subordinate dimension are equal. If so, the alternatives are judged to be equal; if not, the jar with the greater value of the subordinate dimension is said to hold more water. Suppose the values of the dominant dimension are unequal: The child still asks whether the values of the subordinate dimension are equal (unlike in Rule II, where this question was not asked in this case). If the answer is yes, the jar with the greater value of the dominant dimension is judged to hold more water; if the answer is no, the values of the dominant and subordinate dimensions are appropriately combined.

Gelman and Gallistel (1978), like Siegler, have used rules—or, as they have called them, *principles*—as units of cognitive development. They have proposed five principles that they believe govern and define the act of counting. Three of these principles deal with how to count, one with what to count, and a final one with a combination of both. These principles seem roughly analogous in the domain of number to Siegler's rules in the domain of problem solving. There are two important differences, however. First, in Siegler's (1981) formulation, more sophisticated rules are believed to replace simpler rules; in Gelman and Gallistel's (1978) formulation, later principles are added onto (rather than replacing) earlier ones. Second, Gelman and Gallistel's rules are more content-based than are Siegler's, dwelling as they do on counting in particular rather than on cognitive processing in general.

Conclusions

From an information-processing point of view, there are a number of different loci of intellectual development. Some of the most important ones include:

1. *Knowledge base.* Obviously, the knowledge base on which one operates increases in extent with age. The knowledge base includes the external world as well as one's internal cognitions. Metacognitive theorists. in particular, have claimed (although the evidence is still weak) that the latter kind of knowledge plays a major role in one's ability to acquire knowledge about the world.

To understand how the knowledge base increases in extent, one has to understand the processes that operate on it; however, the highly process-oriented approach to research during the early and mid-1970s sometimes failed to take into account the bidirectionality of spheres of influence. Processes need a knowledge base on which to operate, and the extent of the knowledge base in large part determines what processes can operate under which circumstances, as well as how effectively they can operate. Sometimes the distinction between knowledge and process is not clear. In part, this reflects semantic confusions. In the literature on metacognition, for example, the term metacognition has sometimes been used to refer to a kind of *knowledge* (knowledge about cognition) and other times to a kind of *process* (control processes, i.e., processes that control other processes). The understandable tendency to blame metacognitive theorists for this and other semantic confusions has sometimes obscured the more important issue—namely, the presumably close but poorly understood relation between knowledge and processes. This lack of understanding has often led to a tendency to attempt to study knowledge in isolation from process, or vice versa. This tendency has been unfortunate because the close relation between the two means that one cannot be fully understood without a full understanding of the other (see J. R. Anderson, 1976).

Some of the most interesting research in contemporary cognitive developmental psychology has looked at the development of level and structure of knowledge (see R. J. Sternberg, 1984). For example, Keil (1979, 1984) has shown that conceptual development can be understood in part in terms of the growth of knowledge about the structure of ontological catagories—that is, knowledge about what can be predicated of what. Chi and Koeske (1983) showed that young dinosaur experts can show better recall than adult nonexperts when the topic is dinosaurs, but not otherwise (see also Chi, 1978).

2. *Processes.* An important source of intellectual development resides in the new availability and increased accessibility of processes with increasing age. The early and mid-1970s saw a perhaps necessary initial tendency to undertake task analyses that isolated processes involved in particular tasks, but that did not attempt to relate these processes either to each other (within and across tasks) or to external referents. Now that we know how to decompose performance on a fairly large class of tasks, as well as what the outcomes of these task analyses look like, researchers must attempt to understand the interrelations of processes and the relations of processes to other variables. This understanding would permit them to start with cognitive theories that specify processes used in the solution of fairly large numbers of tasks, rather than to start with tasks, specify the processes used in their solution, and then trace the development of what may in many cases be task-specific processes (e.g., R. J. Sternberg, 1980a, 1981, 1985).

3. *Memory.* Despite the enormous amount of research that has been conducted on memory development (see, e.g., Kail & Hagen, 1977), our understanding of exactly what develops in memory is still surprisingly meager. Psychologists still do not even agree with the theory that memory capacity (expressed in terms of some kind of slot notion) increases with age, as demonstrated by Osherson (1974) and by Case (1978, 1984). The importance of studying memory development is illustrated by the finding of Trabasso et al. that what had seemed to be a process limitation of sorts, in the ability of preoperational children to perform transitive inferences, is actually a memory limitation which can be overcome with appropriate training (e.g., Bryant & Trabasso, 1971).

4. *Strategies*. Many tasks (e.g., analogies and balance-scale problems) show changes in the strategies applied to them with increased intellectual development. Moreover, these strategy changes reflect increasingly intelligent ways of solving problems. Indeed, it is not the strategy change per se that is of interest, but what it tells us about the developing mind. For example, in both analogy and balance-scale problems, as children grow older they have an increased tendency to use more of the information given in the problem in a more integrative way. In the study of strategies as in the study of processes, investigators should not become bogged down in task-specific aspects of strategy development, but rather focus on what it is about strategy development that reflects generally increasing cognitive competence. Researchers should also continue to study strategy formation and implementation in real-world as well as in laboratory tasks.

5. *Representations of information*. Processes and strategies act on a knowledge base, and this knowledge base must be represented in some form. One thing that may develop with age is the ability to represent information in a way that renders the information easily accessible and highly relatable to other kinds of information. In pictorial analogies, for example, a tendency was observed on the part of children to move from more separable to more integral representations of attribute information; and Kail, Pellegrino, and Carter (1980) suggested the possibility that in spatial tasks also, older subjects may represent forms to be rotated mentally in a more holistic way. On the other hand, the developmental trend sometimes involves moving from more integral to more separable representations of information (see van Daalen-Kapteijns & Elshout-Moher, 1981; Shepp, 1978; Smith & Kemler, 1978; Werner & Kaplan, 1952). Thus, we need to learn a lot more about the circumstances under which children of different ages represent information in different ways. It appears that changes in representation can be understood only in terms of the sense they make in the context of particular task environments or, at least, classes of task environments.

6. *Process latencies, difficulties, and probabilities*. Many recent studies, such as those of analogical and linear syllogistic reasoning as well as of spatial visualization, have sought to isolate component processes and to assign values of some kind (e.g., duration) to these processes. This is a necessary ingredient in information-processing research, although process values (such as latencies or difficulties) are not so much of interest in their own right as they are of interest in comparison to other process values. Thus, it is important to know what it is, for example, that makes one analogy more difficult than another, one kind of balance-scale problem more difficult than another, or one addition problem more difficult than another. Moreover, it is essential to be able to isolate these values at the level of individual as well as group data because sources of difficulty in intelligent performance may differ widely across different individuals. In order eventually to attempt remediation, we need to know what it is that needs remediation in each individual rather than what it is that needs remediation on the average.

7. *Executive control.* Although this item could be incorporated as a kind of process, I separate it here from processes to distinguish it from the kinds of processes that are used merely in the execution of one kind of problem or another. During the past several years, there has been an increasing tendency to study the executive in human functioning (e.g., Brown, 1982; Brown & De-Loache, 1978; R. J. Sternberg, 1985; Sternberg & Ketron, 1982). The core of intelligence is in the allocation and adaptation of one's mental resources to a given task environment: Future research on intellectual development should give high priority to this aspect of functioning.

TRANSPARADIGMATIC PRINCIPLES OF INTELLECTUAL DEVELOPMENT

In this review of two approaches often found in the study of intellectual development, certain prospective loci of intellectual development emerge. These loci are of particular interest because they suggest that it is possible to pose a fairly small set of transparadigmatic principles of intellectual development that emerge from research almost without regard to the kind of research (see Sternberg & Powell, 1983). Some significant ones are described in the following pages.

More Sophisticated Control Strategies (Metacomponents) Develop with Age

Traditional psychometric analyses of intelligence and its development have, largely for historical reasons, tended not to emphasize *executive processes:* Most factor-analytic investigations of intelligence were done at a time when concern with executive processes had not yet arisen. Some more recent factor-analytic work reflects developing emphases in psychological theorizing on executive functions. Das, Kirby, and Jarman (1975), for example, sought to confirm and extend factor-analytically Luria's (1966a, 1966b, 1973) theory of cognitive information processing. In this theory, information may be processed as some kind of unitary or holistic composite that is primarily spatial in character; or it may be processed in a way that is primarily sequential in nature, following a set temporal order. Das et al. refer to the two kinds of processing as *simultaneous* and *successive syntheses.* Each kind of synthesis may be viewed as representing a different mode of executive decision making, as well as action upon the information about which decisions have been made (see Jarman & Das, 1977). Carroll (1980) has conducted the largest scale set of factor analyses on information-processing tasks ever to be undertaken. He has used this set of factor analyses to provide guidance in proposing a set of basic processes used in information-processing tasks. One of the processes Carroll identified is the Monitor process, whereby subjects utilize instructions, rules, and guidelines for task performance.

"Usually, the process has a hierarchical structure in the sense that it has one or a very small number of major goals, each of these having one or a small number of minor goals or 'subgoals' " (Carroll, 1980, p. 34), and so on, down to the finest possible level of analysis. Development of the Monitor process occurs as the quantity and quality of instructions, rules, and guidelines increase.

All of the information-processing units—components, productions, and rules—make allowances for executive processing in development and for the development of executive processing. Executive processing is handled by higher order metacomponents, productions that drive productions, or high-level rules. R. J. Sternberg's (1985) analysis of the development of intellect has led to the postulation of six metacomponential loci of intellectual development. Brown's (1978, 1982) analysis of memory and metamemory development has led to four metacognitive operations driving cognitive processing. Flavell (1981) has proposed a model of cognitive monitoring that includes four basic components. Markman (1981) has also proposed four signals that people use in monitoring their comprehension. Butterfield and Belmont (1977) have shown that a key aspect of developmentally advanced functioning is the ability to select and apply optimal mnemonic strategies in learning. Almost no matter where one looks in the information-processing literature, executive processes (by whatever name) are seen as critical to intellectual development. R. J. Sternberg's (1980b) list of metacomponents is fairly typical of the kinds of executive processes believed by information-processing researchers to develop with age.

Information Processing Becomes More Nearly Exhaustive with Increasing Age

The psychometric tradition has generally not emphasized process modeling so that there are not many places to look for discussions of how information is encoded. Guilford's (1967) factor-analytically based theory is probably the most exhaustive collection of abilities that has been compiled, and it also takes the greatest account of information-processing abilities. Tests used to measure Guilford's factor of cognition—"immediate discovery, awareness, rediscovery, or recognition of information in its various forms; comprehension or understanding" (Guilford & Hoepfner, 1971, p. 20)—measure, in part, thoroughness with which information is encoded and processed. This is also true of some of the tests measuring Guilford's evaluation ability—"comparison of items of information in terms of variables and making judgments concerning criterion satisfaction (correctness, identity, consistency, etc.)" (Guilford & Hoepfner, 1971, p. 20). In one of Guilford's cognition tests (measuring cognition of symbolic units), for example, subjects must identify words with their vowels replaced by blanks, such as *m g c*. Obviously, one skill that will improve performance on this task is the ability and willingness to try out large numbers of vowel combinations. In solving syllogisms (an evaluation test), performance will be improved to the extent that subjects can generate all possible set relations that derive from the encoding and combination of the two syllogistic premises. Some of the Binet and Wechsler tests that measure recognition of absurdities and incongruities in pictures also test in part the subject's ability to encode the pictures fully enough to detect what is wrong with them. Performance on a number of Carroll's (1980) factor-analytically derived components can also be improved by more thorough processing—apprehension, perceptual integration, encoding, and comparison.

Brown and DeLoache (1978) reviewed the information-processing literatures on extracting the main idea of a passage, visual scanning, and retrieval processes, and they concluded that in all of these kinds of tasks a characteristic of intellectual development was the *increase in the number of exhaustive attempts at information processing* that were made. In visual scanning, for example, Vurpillot (1968) found that young children (e.g., age 4) almost never exhaustively scanned pictures of two houses to determine whether they were identical, whereas older children (e.g., age 9) frequently did. In retrieval, Kobasigawa (1974) found that in recalling categories of words, first graders who spontaneously used an available category cue recalled fewer items than did third graders—the younger children failed to scan exhaustively and, hence, to recall the items listed under each category in their memories. Istomina (1948/1975) also noted the tendency of younger children not to scan their memories exhaustively—when trying to recall a list of words from memory, 4- and 5-year-olds rarely tried to retrieve words not immediately recalled. Siegler (1978) found that a major cause of failure of younger children to solve balance-scale problems was in their failure to encode information relevant to all of the dimensions that affected the way in which the scale balanced. Kogan, Connor, Gross, and Fava (1980) found that younger children's failure to pair pictures metaphorically was due in part to their failure to make all possible comparisons between pictures. Both Siegler (1978) and Kogan et al. (1980) found that training of children to use exhaustive information processing could improve their performance on the tasks investigated. Sternberg and Nigro (1980) and Sternberg and Rifkin (1979) found that in analogical reasoning, there was a tendency for information processing to become more nearly exhaustive with age, both in encoding of stimuli and in comparisons made on the stimuli that have been encoded. In summary, the information processing of children seems to become more nearly complete with increasing age.

The Ability to Comprehend Relations of Successively Higher Orders Develops with Age

We have essentially no idea of when the ability to comprehend first-order relations between given terms of a problem initially develops. Evidence suggests (a) that the ability to comprehend second-order relations, at least of the kind used in analogical reasoning (as in the connections between two halves of an analogy), develops around the age of 12 years (Sternberg & Rifkin, 1979; see also Fischer

& Pipp, 1984); and (b) that the ability to comprehend third-order relations (as in analogies between analogies) develops during adolescence (Sternberg & Downing, 1982). The ability to use these kinds of relations may develop before the ability to discover them.

One of the most explicit statements of the role of *higher order relations* in intelligent performance was made by Raymond B. Cattell, the noted psychometrician. Cattell, like Terman, viewed intelligence as comprising in part the ability to think abstractly (R. B. Cattell, 1971; Cattell & Cattell, 1963). In particular, R. B. Cattell saw abstract thinking as critical to "fluid intelligence," which he and others identified in numerous factor-analytic investigations of intelligence. Because for Cattell (1971), "abstraction . . . is intrinsically a building up of relations among relations" (pp. 185–186), he would presumably be sympathetic to the notion that part of what develops in intelligence is the ability to perceive relations of a successively higher order. Indeed, in his and others' intelligence tests, difficulty of abstract-reasoning items is largely a function of the order of relations one needs to perceive. In the most difficult items in the Cattell Culture Fair Scale (Level 3) and in the Raven Progressive Matrices, it is necessary to see higher order relations to be able to solve the problems. For example, in a series problem, one may not only have a change in the angular rotation of a series of figures but also a change in the rate at which the degree of angular rotation changes.

Spearman's (1927) theory of general intelligence posited eduction of relations as one of three qualitative principles that constituted intelligent cognition. Eduction of relations is inference of the relation between two terms, such as the first two terms of the analogy A:B::C:D. Spearman (1927) showed how the difficulty of transitive-inference problems could be understood in terms of the order of relations necessary in order to comprehend them. Consider, for example, the problem "A is larger than B, B is larger than C, and C is larger than D." On Spearman's (1927) analysis (which is probably not wholly correct), one can educe the relation between A and D by comprehending first the first-order relations between A-B, B-C, and C-D; then the second-order relation (not given explicitly in the problem) between A-B and B-C; and so on. Thus, the fact that A is larger than D is recognized by hierarchical solution of the problem.

In the information-processing domain, Case (1978) has proposed that "the search for 'development beyond formal operations' should . . . concentrate on clarifying the nature of second-order intellectual operations and on searching for third-order operations" (p. 63); and a number of information-processing investigations of analogical reasoning have discovered that the ability to map second-order relations appears around the transition between childhood and adolescence (e.g., Gallagher & Wright, 1979; Levinson & Carpenter, 1974; Lunzer, 1965; Piaget with Montangero & Billeter, 1977; Sternberg & Rifkin, 1979). None of these investigations has found further strategy development during adolescence, however, perhaps because by this time the most conceptually difficult aspect of analogical reasoning, mapping of second-order relations, is already expeditiously accomplished. Sternberg and Downing (1982) tested students of junior high school, high school, and college levels in their ability to perceive analogies between analogies—subjects would be presented with two analogies of the form A:B::C:D and asked how analogous they were. We were particularly interested in the degree to which higher order mapping between the domain (first analogy) and range (second analogy) of this higher order analogy problem would affect judgments of higher order analogy. Analogies were rated by other subjects not involved in the primary task for a number of attributes, including goodness of the higher order mapping. We discovered that there was a monotonic increase in the use of higher order mapping with increasing age. Thus, older children seemed better able than younger children to comprehend relations of a third order, a finding consistent with the principle of intellectual development proposed here.

Flexibility in Use of Strategy or Information Develops with Age

Flexibility in strategy or information utilization means that an individual knows when to change strategy or transfer information and when not to do so. One often associates intellectual immaturity with inflexibility in strategy change and in information transfer. But changing strategy when it is unnecessary or harmful to do so, or transferring information when the information is inappropriate to the use to which one puts it, can be just as dangerous as failing to change or transfer. The locus of development, then, is not so much the ability to change as the ability to know when to change.

Flexible thinking is measured in a number of different ways by a number of different psychometric tests of intellectual ability. In the Guilford (1967) tests of divergent thinking, it is measured by items such as those requiring subjects to think of unusual uses for ordinary objects, like coat hangers or fishing rods. In some forms of the Miller Analogies Test, flexibility is measured by set-breaker items that require the test taker to perceive nonsemantic analogical relations: for example, relations based on the sounds rather than on the meanings of the words constituting the analogy item. Even in less exotic types of test items, flexibility may be measured by one's ability to perceive relations that are out of the ordinary or to solve what seem to be difficult problems in simple ways. On the mathematical aptitude section of the Scholastic Aptitude Test, for example, so-called insight problems are ones that can be solved laboriously by a time-consuming algorithm that is usually immediately obvious, or that can be solved simply and quickly by a shortcut procedure whose applicability will generally not be immediately obvious. One of the more interesting, if indirect, measurements of flexibility is provided by tests such as the *in-basket* (Frederiksen, Saunders, & Ward, 1957), which requires an individual to stimulate important functions of the job of a person in some occupation, usually a business executive. The individual is presented with more tasks to accomplish than can possibly be accomplished in the time allotted, and the individual must allocate the time flexibly to fulfill as well as possible the most important tasks. The importance of flexibility in psychometric thinking about intelligence can be seen in theoretical as well as in practical work. R. B. Cattell's (1935a, 1935b) research led him to believe that flexibility is defined as a switch-over from some old, accustomed, over-learned activity to a new way of effecting the same end. R. B. Cattell contrasted this view of flexibility with Spearman's (1927) notion as the degree of impedance from interference in switching from one mental process to another. Thurstone (1944) also believed flexibility to be an important aspect of the perceptual aspects of intelligence. Flexibility in various forms thus seems to enter into a large number of psychometric conceptions of intellectual functioning and its development.

Flexible thinking of various kinds has played an important role in information-processing investigations of intelligence and their antecedents. The importance of flexibility as a psychological construct in such investigations can be traced back at least to Luchins' (1942) famous water jug problems. In these problems, subjects solved a number of items requiring them to state an algorithm by which water could be poured from one jug to another via a third jug. A number of problems were presented that could be solved by one formula; then, problems were presented that could be solved by this formula or a much simpler one. Strong effects of "set" were found whereby subjects failed to recognize that they could change their strategy to the much simpler one. Later, Atwood and Polson (1976) proposed an information-processing model of performance on this task. In literature on loci of deficiency in the retarded, the ability to transfer information flexibly has been identified by a number of investigators as a major source of difference in performance with normals (see, for example, Butterfield & Belmont, 1977; Campione & Brown, 1974; Feuerstein, 1979, 1980). Recently, Brown and Campione (1982) have proposed that inducing flexible thinking is one of the major needs of any program for training intelligent performance, whether in retarded or normal individuals. It was stated earlier that flexible thinking includes knowing when not to change strategy or transfer information as well as knowing when to do so—a consistent characteristic of more intelligent people both within and between age levels is their ability to settle on a strategy that is generalizable across a large class of problems, rather than to settle on very specific strategies that need to be changed as a result of slight variations in problem type (Bloom & Broder, 1950; Jensen, 1982; Sternberg & Nigro, 1980; Sternberg & Rifkin, 1979). Flexibility in a variety of forms seems to be an essential ingredient of intelligent behavior.

CONTINUITY OF INTELLECTUAL DEVELOPMENT

One of the fundamental questions in the study of intellectual development is whether such development is continuous or discontinuous, and—if it is either fully or partly continuous—in what ways it is so. This question has become a particularly "hot" one in recent years because of a changing perspective on the question's answer.

For most of this century, the accepted view was that intellectual development was discontinuous. Intelligence in infancy—inclusive of at least the first two years of life—seemed to be an entity differing in kind from intelligence in the subsequent years of life. What kinds of evidence led to this conclusion?

First, the nature of the developmental tasks for infants has seemed different from the nature of developmental tasks for older children and adults. For the most part, the infant's tasks seem to be perceptual–motor ones—grasping, crawling, walking, and so on. In Piaget's (1972) theory, these tasks are mastered as part of the "sensorimotor" period, a period that differs greatly from the subsequent ones in terms of the lesser cognitive load, compared with that required in other periods, that seems to be required for task performance.

Second, individual differences in these perceptual–motor tasks seem to be qualitatively different from individual differences in later periods. The crucial difference is perhaps that the perceptual–motor tasks are all mastered by almost all children, with the main source of difference among children residing in when the tasks are mastered. Thus, differences are not so much in degree as in age of mastery: Almost all children (except the physically handicapped and the profoundly retarded) eventually walk, for example. But not all children become, say, adept analogical reasoners or spatial visualizers.

Third, correlations of traditional infant intelligence test scores with later intelligence test scores are usually close to negligible (Bayley, 1970). Of course, such trivial correlations may seem unsurprising in view of the differences in task content between the earlier and the later tests. Nevertheless, the data suggest that the perceptual–motor program that unfolds during the first couple of years of life is truly different in kind from the type of cognitive program that unfolds later.

In the face of what seemed to be overwhelming statistical as well as conceptual evidence, researchers generally concluded that earlier and later intelligence had little, if any, overlap. More recent evidence suggests that such a conclusion was wrong, however. Evidence reviewed by Berg and Sternberg (1985a) and by Bornstein and Sigman (1986) suggests one and possibly two or more sources of continuity in intelligence over the life span (see also Fagan & McGrath, 1981; Lewis & Brooks-Gunn, 1981; McCall, 1979; Sternberg, 1981). One source of continuity is in what might be called "coping with novelty."

Coping with novelty refers to a person's ability to adjust to relatively unfamiliar tasks and situations in life. According to Berg and Sternberg (1985a), at least two constellations of attributes underlie this set of skills: *cognitive* and *motivational*. The former refer to information-processing components used to explore and solve novel kinds of problem domains; the latter refer to relative preferences for dealing with relatively novel as opposed to non-novel domains. Both constellations of attributes are important in coping with novelty, as an individual with the cognitive ability but not the motivation to cope with novel situations may simply confront few such situations in which to exercise cognitive abilities, whereas an individual with the motivation but not the cognition may seek out novelty and then be frustrated by an inability to cope with it.

How are abilities to cope with novelty measured? Several paradigms have been used, but for infants, two stand out: decrement of attention to familiar stimuli and recovery of attention to unfamiliar stimuli.

In the "decrement of attention" paradigm, a stimulus is presented to an infant either for a fixed number of trials (in one variant), or for a variable number of trials, until the infant reaches some predetermined level of habituation (i.e., until the infant is looking at the stimulus for only a proportion of the original time). Amount of decrement of attention to the stimulus can be measured in several ways, such as slope of the decay function for looking at the stimulus, or relative amount of time spent looking at the stimulus on later trials versus amount of time spent looking on earlier trials. The basic finding in study after study is that amount (or rapidity) of habituation is moderately correlated with later intelligence test scores. Typical correlations are in the .40s to .60s, which represents a relatively high level of prediction for this kind of task.

In the "recovery of attention" paradigm, subjects are measured in terms of their preference for looking at novel versus familiar stimuli. Typically, an infant is first familiarized with one particular stimulus. The infant is then given the option to look at a new stimulus or the old one. Greater recovery of attention is a function of the relative amount of time spent looking at the new versus the old stimulus. Correlations between performance on this task and later IQ are typically in the .50–.70 range. Performance on the recovery task correlates only moderately with performance on the decrement task, suggesting that the two tasks measure related but nonidentical abilities. Of course, motivational factors are confounded with cognitive ones on both these tasks, in that later preference and cognitive ability can come into play. It is not clear at present whether these two attributes of performance can ever be fully unconfounded.

In sum, there is now evidence suggesting that coping with novelty, an important part of intelligence (see Sternberg, 1985), shows some degree of continuity from infancy through later childhood. An important lesson from this research is that whether or not we discover continuity depends at least as much on what we measure as on anything else. The work also shows the need for a developmentally based theory of intellectual development that recognizes the importance of coping with novelty in the growth of intellectual skill.

Coping with novelty may not be the only source of lifelong continuity in intellectual development, although it is the best documented. Berg and Sternberg (1985b) have applied Sternberg's (1985) "triarchic" theory of intelligence to the question of continuity over the life span, and have suggested at least two other possible sources of continuity, neither of which has yet been fully operationalized for all points in the life span.

A second source of continuity is in certain of the information-processing components of intelligence. Virtually from the day of birth, children have to define problems, set up strategies for coping with those problems, monitor their solutions to these problems, and so on. The need for these skills persists throughout the life span.

There is a growing body of evidence to suggest some decline in these componential abilities in some older adults. In a review of the literature, Papalia and Bielby (1974) concluded that, on the average, older adults conserve substance, weight, and volume less well than do younger adults. Perlmutter (1979) found that in recall tasks, older adults do not encode information as effectively as do younger adults, unless explicitly encouraged to do so. Cerella, Poon, and Williams (1980) reviewed the available literature and concluded that older adults are substantially slower than younger adults in most cognitive as well as motor tasks. However, reviews by Botwinick (1977) and Horn (1970) suggest that whereas decline in performance is evident for "fluid" information-processing tasks, no such decline appears for most verbal, or "crystallized" tasks. To the extent that there is a decline in old age in cognitive task performance, then, it appears to be selective.

The selectivity of the decline in performance with age becomes all the more apparent when one examines a third source of continuity in intellectual development, namely, adaptation to the environment. Individuals of all ages somehow have to adapt to their circumstances in life. A general finding in the research literature is that older adults perform substantially better on tasks that have some contextual relevance to their lives than on tasks that are abstract and essentially meaningless to them (see Baltes, Dittmann-Kohli, & Dixon, 1984; Berg & Sternberg, 1985b; Labouvie-Vief & Chandler, 1978). Moreover, several contemporary theories of intelligence across the adult life span suggest the importance of contextual relevance in assessing intelligence in older adults (Baltes et al., 1984; Berg & Sternberg, 1985b; Pascual-Leone, 1983). Thus, when viewed in terms of adaptation, intelligence probably shows little or no decline for most people in later life.

CONCLUSION

Two conceptions of intelligence and its development have been described and compared in this chapter. The first, a psychometric approach, emphasizes individual differences among children of the same age and of differing ages to specify what it is that develops with time. The second, an information-processing approach, stresses the mental processes and representations that underlie various kinds of cognition, such as perception, learning, and problem solving. Users of this second approach seek to understand how children of differing ages are similar and dissimilar in terms of the information processing the children do when performing various kinds of cognitive tasks. The two approaches are complementary, the first stressing variation among people and the second variation among tasks. Combining the two approaches results in a richer and more integrated understanding of intellectual development than could be had by using either approach in the absence of the other.

REFERENCES

Anderson, J. E. (1940). The prediction of terminal intelligence from infant and preschool tests. In G. M. Whipple (Ed.), *Intelligence: Its nature and nurture* (Thirty-Ninth Yearbook, National Society for the Study of Education). Bloomington, IL: Public School Publishing Co.

Anderson, J. R. (1976). *Language, memory, and thought.* Hillsdale, NJ: Lawrence Erlbaum Associates.

Anderson, J. R., Kline, P. J., & Beasley, C. M., Jr. (1979). A general learning theory and its application to schema abstraction. In G. Bower (Ed.), *The psychology of learning and motivation* (Vol. 13). New York: Academic Press.

Asch, S. (1936). A study of change in mental organization. *Archives of Psychology,* Whole No. 195.

Atwood, M. E., & Polson, P. G. (1976). A process model for water-jug problems. *Cognitive Psychology, 8,* 191–216.

Baltes, P. B., Dittmann-Kohli, F., & Dixon, R. A. (1984). New perspectives on the development of intelligence in adulthood: Toward a dual-process conception and a model of selective optimization with compensation. In P. B. Baltes & O. G. Brim, Jr. (Eds.), *Life-span development and behavior* (Vol. 6, pp. 33–76). New York: Academic Press.

Bayley, N. (1933). Mental growth during the first three years: A developmental study of 61 children by repeated tests. *Genetic Psychology Monographs, 14,* 1–92.

Bayley, N. (1943). Mental growth during the first three years. In R. G. Barker, J. S. Kounin, & H. F. Wright (Eds.), *Child behaviour and development.* New York: McGraw-Hill.

Bayley, N. (1949). Consistency and variability in the growth of intelligence from birth to eighteen years. *Journal of Genetic Psychology, 75,* 165–196.

Bayley, N. (1951). Development and maturation. In H. Helson (Ed.), *Theoretical foundations of psychology.* New York: Van Nostrand.

Bayley, N. (1955). On the growth of intelligence. *American Psychologist, 10,* 805–818.

Bayley, N. (1966). Learning in adulthood: The role of intelligence. In H. J. Klausmeier & C. W. Harris (Eds.), *Analysis of concept learning.* New York: Academic Press.

Bayley, N. (1968). Behavioral correlates of mental growth: Birth to thirty-six years. *American Psychologist, 23,* 1–17.

Bayley, N. (1970). Development of mental abilities. In P. H. Mussen (Ed.), *Carmichael's manual of child psychology* (3rd ed., Vol. 1). New York: Wiley.

Bayley, N., & Oden, M. H. (1955). The maintenance of intellectual ability in gifted adults. *Journal of Gerontology, 10,* 91–107.

Berg, C. A., & Sternberg, R. J. (1985a). Response to novelty: Continuity versus discontinuity in the developmental course of intelligence. In H. Reese (Ed.), *Advances in child development and behavior* (Vol. 19, pp. 2–47). New York: Academic Press.

Berg, C. A. & Sternberg, R. J. (1985b). A triarchic theory of intellectual development during adulthood. *Developmental Review, 5,* 334–370.

Binet, A., & Simon, T. (1916a). *The development of intelligence in children* (E. S. Kite, Trans.). Baltimore: William & Wilkins.

Binet, A., & Simon, T. (1916b). *The intelligence of the feeble-minded* (E. S. Kite, Trans.). Baltimore: Williams & Wilkins.

Bloom, B. S., & Broder, L. (1950). *Problem-solving processes of college students.* Chicago: University of Chicago Press.

Bornstein, M. H., & Sigman, M. D. (1986). Continuity in mental development from infancy. *Child Development, 57,* 251–274.

Botwinick, J. (1977). Intellectual abilities. In J. E. Birren & K. W. Schaie (Eds.), *Handbook of the psychology of aging* (pp. 580–605). New York: Van Nostrand Reinhold.

Broman, S. H., Nichols, P. L., & Kennedy, W. A. (1975). *Preschool IQ: Prenatal and early developmental correlates.* Hillsdale, NJ: Lawrence Erlbaum Associates.

Brown, A. L. (1978). Knowing when, where, and how to remember: A problem of metacognition. In R. Glaser (Ed.), *Advances in instructional psychology* (Vol. 1). Hillsdale, NJ: Lawrence Erlbaum Associates.

Brown, A. L. (1982). Learning and development: The problem of compatability, access and induction. *Human Development, 25,* 89–115.

Brown, A. L., & Campione, J. C. (1982). Discussion: How, and how much, can intelligence be modified? In D. K. Detterman & R. J. Sternberg (Eds.), *How and how much can intelligence be increased?* Norwood, NJ: Ablex.

Brown, A. L., & DeLoache, J. S. (1978). Skills, plans and self-regulation. In R. S. Siegler (Ed.), *Children's thinking: What develops?* Hillsdale, NJ: Lawrence Erlbaum Associates.

Bryant, P. E., & Trabasso, T. (1971). Transitive inferences and memory in young children. *Nature, 232,* 456–458.

Butterfield, E. C., & Belmont, J. M. (1977). Assessing and improving the executive cognitive functions of mentally retarded people. In I. Bialer & M. Sternlicht (Eds.), *Psychological issues in mental retardation.* New York: Psychological Dimensions.

Campione, J. C., & Brown, A. L. (1974). The effects of contextual changes and degree of component mastery on transfer of training. In H. W. Reese (Ed.), *Advances in child development and behavior* (Vol. 9). New York: Academic Press.

Carroll, J. B. (1980). *Individual difference relations in psychometric and experimental cognitive tasks* (NR150-406 ONR Final Report). Chapel Hill, NC: L. L. Thurstone Psychometric Laboratory.

Case, R. (1978). Intellectual development from birth to adolescence: A neo-Piagetian interpretation. In R. Siegler (Ed.), *Children's thinking: What develops?* Hillsdale, NJ: Lawrence Erlbaum Associates.

Case, R. (1984). The process of stage transition: A neo-Piagetian view. In R. J. Sternberg (Ed.), *Mechanisms of cognitive development.* New York: Freeman.

Cattell, J. McK. (1890). Mental tests and measurements. *Mind, 15,* 373.

Cattell, R. B. (1935a). On the measurement of "perseveration." *British Journal of Educational Psychology, 5,* 76–92.

Cattell, R. B. (1935b). Perseveration and personality: Some experiments and a hypothesis. *Journal of Mental Science, 61,* 151–167.

Cattell, R. B. (1963). Theory of fluid and crystallized intelligence: An initial experiment. *Journal of Educational Psychology, 54,* 105–111.

Cattell, R. B. (1971). *Abilities: Their structure, growth, and action.* Boston, MA: Houghton-Mifflin.

Cattell, R. B., & Cattell, A. K. S. (1963). *Test of g: Culture Fair, Scale 3.* Champaign, IL: Institute for Personality and Ability Testing.

Cerella, J., Poon, L. W., & Williams, D. M. (1980). Age and the complexity hypothesis. In L. Poon (Ed.), *Aging in the 1980s: Psychological issues* (pp. 332–340). Washington, DC: American Psychological Association.

Chi, M. T. H. (1978). Konwledge structures and memory development. In R. S. Siegler (Ed.), *Children's thinking: What develops?* Hillsdale, NJ: Lawrence Erlbaum Associates.

Chi, M. T. H., & Koeske, R. D. (1983). Network representations of a child's dinosaur knowledge. *Developmental Psychology, 19,* 29–39.

Clark, M. P. (1944). Changes in primary mental abilities with age. *Archives of Psychology, 291*, 30.

Daalen-Kapteijns, M. M., van, & Elshout-Mohr, M. (1981). The acquisition of word meanings as a cognitive learning process. *Journal of Verbal Learning and Verbal Behavior, 20*, 386–399.

Das, J. P., Kirby, J., & Jarman, R. F. (1975). Simultaneous and successive syntheses: An alternative model for cognitive abilities. *Psychological Bulletin, 82*, 87–103.

Dearborn, W. F., & Rothney, J. W. M. (1941). *Predicting the child's development.* Cambridge, MA: Science-Art Publishing.

Dearborn, W. F., Rothney J. W. M., & Shuttleworth, F. K. (1938). Data on the growth of public-school children (from the materials of the Harvard Growth Study). *Monographs of the Society for Research in Child Development, 3*, 1(Serial No. 14).

Donders, F. C. (1868–1869). Over de snelheid van psychoische processen. Onderzoekingen gedaan in het Physiologisch Laboratorium der Utrechtsche Hoogeschool. *Tweede reeks*, II, 92–120.

Ernst, G. W., & Newell, A. (1969). *GPS: A case study in generality and problem-solving.* New York: Academic Press.

Fagan, J. F., III, & McGrath, S. K. (1981). Infant recognition memory and later intelligence. *Intelligence, 5*, 121–130.

Feuerstein, R. (1979). *The dynamic assessment of retarded performers: The learning potential assessment device, theory, instruments, and techniques.* Baltimore, MD: University Park Press.

Feuerstein, R. (1980). *Instrumental enrichment: An intervention program for cognitive modifiability.* Baltimore, MD: University Park Press.

Fischer, K. W., & Pipp, S. L. (1984). Processes of cognitive development: Optimal level and skill acquisition. In R. J. Sternberg (Ed.), *Mechanisms of cognitive development.* New York: Freeman.

Flavell, J. H. (1981). Cognitive monitoring. In W. P. Dickson (Ed.), *Children's oral communication skills.* New York: Academic Press.

Frederiksen, J. R., Saunders, D. R., & Ward, B. (1957). The in-basket test. *Psychological Monographs, 71*(9), Whole No. 438.

Gallagher, J. M., & Wright, R. J. (1979). Piaget and the study of analogy: Structural analysis of items. In J. Magary (Ed.), *Piaget and the helping professions* (Vol. 8). Los Angeles, CA: University of Southern California.

Galton, F. (1983). *Inquiries into human faculty.* London: Macmillan.

Garrett, H. E. (1938). Differentiable mental traits. *Psychological Record, 2*, 259–298.

Garrett, H. E. (1946). A developmental theory of intelligence. *American Psychologist, 1*, 372–378.

Garrett, H. E., Bryan, A. I., & Perl R. (1935). The age factor in mental organization. *Archives of Psychology, 176*, 1–31.

Gelman, R., & Gallistel, C. R. (1978). *The child's understanding of number.* Cambridge, MA: Harvard University Press.

Guilford, J. P. (1956). The structure of intellect. *Psychological Bulletin, 53*, 267–293.

Guilford, J. P. (1957). A revised structure of intellect (Reprint No. 19). Los Angeles, CA: University of Southern California, Psychological Laboratory.

Guilford, J. P. (1967). *The nature of human intelligence.* New York: McGraw-Hill.

Guilford, J. P., & Hoepfner, R. (1971). *The analysis of intelligence.* New York: McGraw-Hill.

Hofstaetter, P. R. (1954). The changing composition of intelligence: A study of the t-technique. *Journal of Genetic Psychology, 85*, 159–164.

Honzik, M. P. (1938). The constancy of mental test performance during the preschool period. *Journal of Genetic Psychology, 52*, 285–302.

Horn, J. L. (1967). On subjectivity in factor analysis. *Educational and Psychological Measurement, 27*, 811–820.

Horn, J. L. (1968). Organization of abilities and the development of intelligence. *Psychological Review, 75*, 242–259.

Horn, J. L. (1970). Organization of data on life-span development of human abilities. In L. R. Goulet & P. B. Baltes (Eds.), *Life-span developmental psychology: Research and theory*. New York: Academic Press.

Horn, J. L., & Cattell, R. B. (1966). Refinement and test of the theory of fluid and crystallized general intelligences. *Journal of Educational Psychology, 51*, 253–270.

Horn, J. L., & Knapp, J. R. (1973). On the subjective character of the empirical base of Guilford's structure-of-intellect model. *Psychological Bulletin, 80*, 33–43.

Hunt, E. B., Frost, N., & Lunneborg, C. (1973). Individual differences in cognition. In G. Bower (Ed.), *The psychology of learning and motivation* (Vol. 7). New York: Academic Press.

Hunt, E. B., Lunneborg, C., & Lewis, J. (1975). What does it mean to be high verbal? *Cognitive Psychology, 7*, 194–227.

Hunt, E. B., & Poltrock, S. (1974). Mechanics of thought. In B. Kantowitz (Ed.), *Human information processing: Tutorials in performance and cognition*. Hillsdale, NJ: Lawrence Erlbaum Associates.

Istomina, Z. M. (1975). (Originally published, 1948). The development of voluntary memory in preschool-age children. *Soviet Psychology, 13*, 5–64.

Jarman, R. F., & Das, J. P. (1977). Simultaneous and successive syntheses and intelligence. *Intelligence, 1*, 151–169.

Jastrow, J. (1892). Some anthropological and psychological tests on college students—a preliminary survey. *American Journal of Psychology, 4*, 420.

Jensen, A. R. (1982). The chronometry of intelligence. In R. J. Sternberg (Ed.), *Advances in the psychology of human intelligence* (Vol. 1). Hillsdale, NJ: Lawrence Erlbaum Associates.

Jones, H. E., & Conrad, H. S. (1933). The growth and decline of intelligence: A study of a homogeneous group between the ages of ten and sixty. *Genetic Psychology Monographs, 13*, 223–298.

Kagan, J. (1971). *Change and continuity in infancy*. New York: Wiley.

Kail, R. V., & Hagen, J. W. (Eds.). (1977). *Perspectives on the development of memory and cognition*. Hillsdale, NJ: Lawrence Erlbaum Associates.

Kail, R. V., Pellegrino, J., & Carter, P. (1980). Developmental changes in mental rotation. *Journal of Experimental Child Psychology, 29*, 102–116.

Keating, D. P., & Bobbitt, B. L. (1978). Individual and developmental differences in cognitive-processing components of mental ability. *Child Development, 49* 155–167.

Keil, F. G. (1979). *Semantic and conceptual development: An ontological perspective*. Cambridge, MA: Harvard University Press.

Keil, F. G. (1984). Mechanisms in cognitive development and the structure of knowledge. In R. J. Sternberg (Ed.), *Mechanisms of cognitive development*. New York: Freeman.

Klahr, D. (1979). *Self-modifying production systems as models of cognitive development*. Unpublished manuscript.

Klahr, D. (1984). Transition processes in quantitative development. In R. J. Sternberg (Ed.), *Mechanisms of cognitive development*. New York: Freeman.

Kobasigawa, A. (1974). Utilization of retrieval cues by children in recall. *Child Development, 45*, 127–134.

Kogan, N., Connor, K., Gross, A., & Fava, D. (1980). Understanding visual metaphor: Developmental and individual differences. *Monographs of the Society for Research in Child Development, 45*(1), Whole No. 183.

Kulpe, O. (1895). *Outlines of psychology*. New York: Macmillan.

Labouvie-Vief, G., & Chandler, M. (1978). Cognitive development and life-span developmental theories: Idealistic vs. contextual perspectives. In P. B. Baltes (Ed.), *Life-span development and behavior* (Vol. 1). New York: Academic Press.

Levinson, P. J., & Carpenter, R. L. (1974). An analysis of analogical reasoning in children. *Child Development, 45*, 857–861.

Lewis, M., & Brooks-Gunn, J. (1981). Visual attention at three months as a predictor of cognitive functioning at two years of age. *Intelligence, 5*, 131–140.

Luchins, A. S. (1942). Mechanization in problem solving. *Psychological Monographs, 54* (6), Whole No. 248.

Lunzer, E. A. (1965). Problems of formal reasoning in test situations. In P. H. Mussen (Ed.), *European research in cognitive development. Monographs of the Society for Research in Child Development, 30* (2, Serial No. 100).

Luria, A. R. (1966a). *Higher cortical functions in man*. New York: Basic Books.

Luria, A. R. (1966b). *Human brain and psychological processes*. New York: Harper & Row.

Luria, A. R. (1973). *The working brain*. London: Penguin.

Markman, E. M. (1981). Comprehension monitoring. In W. P. Dickson (Ed.), *Children's oral communication skills*. New York: Academic Press.

McCall, R. B. (1979). Qualitative transitions in behavioral development in the first two years of life. In M. H. Bornstein & W. Kessen (Eds.), *Psychological development from infancy: Image to intention* (pp. 183–224). Hillsdale, NJ: Lawrence Erlbaum Associates.

McCall, R. B., Eichorn, D. J., & Hogarty, P. S. (1977). Transitions in early mental development. *Monographs of the Society for Research in Child Development*, Whole No. 171.

McCall, R. B., Hogarty, P. S., & Hurlburt, N. (1972). Transitions in infant sensorimotor development and the prediction of childhood IQ. *American Psychologist, 27*, 728–748.

Miller, G. A., Galanter, E., & Pribram, K. H. (1960). *Plans and the structure of behavior*. New York: Holt, Rinehart & Winston.

Newell, A., Shaw, J., & Simon, H. A. (1960). Report on a general problem-solving program. In *Proceedings of the international conference on information processing*. Paris: UNESCO.

Newell, A., & Simon, H. A. (1972). *Human problem solving*. Englewood Cliffs, NJ: Prentice-Hall.

Osherson, D. N. (1974). *Logical abilities in children: Vol. 2. Logical inference: Underlying operations*. Hillsdale, NJ: Lawrence Erlbaum Associates.

Owens, W. A., Jr. (1953). Age and mental abilities: A longitudinal study. *Genetic Psychology Monographs, 48*, 3–54.

Papalia, D. E., & Bielby, D. (1974). Cognitive functioning in middle and old age adults: A review of research based on Piaget's theory. *Human Development, 17*, 424–443.

Pascual-Leone, J. (1983). Growing into human maturity: Toward a metasubjective theory of adulthood stages. In P. B. Baltes & O. G. Brim (Eds.), *Life-span development and behavior* (Vol. 5, pp. 118–156). New York: Academic Press.

Perlmutter, M. (1979). Age differences in adults' free recall, cued recall, and recognition. *Journal of Gerontology, 34*, 533–539.

Piaget, J. (1952). *The child's conception of number*. New York: W. W. Norton.

Piaget, J. (1972). *The psychology of intelligence*. Totowa, NJ: Littlefield, Adams.

Piaget, J. (with Montangero, J., & Billeter, J.). (1977). Les correlats. *L'Abstraction reflechissante*. Paris: Presses Universitaires de France.

Posner, M., Boies, S., Eichelman, W., & Taylor, R. (1969). Retention of visual and name codes of single letters. *Journal of Experimental Psychology Monograph, 79* (1, Pt. 2).

Schaie, K. W. (1974). Translations in gerontology—from lab to life. *American Psychologist, 29*, 802–807.

Schiller, B. (1934). Verbal, numerical and spatial abilities of young children. *Archives of Psychology, 161*, 1–69.

Shepp, B. (1978). From perceived similarity to dimensional structure: A new hypothesis about perspective development. In E. Rosch & B. B. Lloyd (Eds.), *Cognition and categorization*. Hillsdale, NJ: Lawrence Erlbaum Associates.

Siegler, R. S. (1976). Three aspects of cognitive development. *Cognitive Psychology, 4*, 481–520.

Siegler, R. S. (1977). The 20-question game as a form of problem-solving. *Child Development. 48,* 395–403.

Siegler, R. S. (1978). The origins of scientific reasoning. In R. S. Siegler (Ed.), *Children's thinking: What develops?* Hillsdale, NJ: Lawrence Erlbaum Associates.

Siegler, R. S. (1981). Developmental sequences within and between concepts. *Monographs of the Society for Research in Child Development, 46* (2), Whole No. 189.

Siegler, R. S., & Vago, S. (1978). The development of a proportionality concept: Judging relative fullness. *Journal of Experimental Child Psychology, 25,* 371–395.

Smith, L. B., & Kemler, D. G. (1978). Levels of experienced dimensionality in children and adults. *Cognitive Psychology, 10,* 502–537.

Sontag, L. W., Baker, C. T., & Nelson, V. L. (1958). Mental growth and personality development: A longitudinal study. *Monographs of the Society for Research in Child Development, 23,* (2), Whole No. 68.

Spearman, C. (1904). "General intelligence," objectively determined and measured. *American Journal of Psychology, 15,* 201–293.

Spearman, C. (1927). *The abilities of man.* New York: Macmillan.

Sternberg, R. J. (1979). The nature of mental abilities. *American Psychologist, 34,* 214–230.

Sternberg, R. J. (1980a). Componentman as vice-president: A reply to Pellegrino and Lyon's analysis of "The components of a componential analysis." *Intelligence, 4,* 83–95.

Sternberg, R. J. (1980b). Sketch of a componential subtheory of human intelligence. *Behavioral and Brain Sciences, 3,* 573–584.

Sternberg, R. J. (1981). Toward a unified componential theory of human intelligence: I. Fluid abilities. In M. Friedman, J. P. Das, & N. O'Connor (Eds.), *Intelligence and learning.* New York: Plenum.

Sternberg, R. J. (Ed.). (1984). *Mechanisms of cognitive development.* New York: W. H. Freeman.

Sternberg, R. J. (1985). *Beyond IQ: A triarchic theory of human intelligence.* New York: Cambridge University Press.

Sternberg, R. J., & Downing, C. (1982). The development of higher order reasoning in adolescence. *Child Development, 53,* 209–221.

Sternberg, R. J., & Ketron, J. L. (1982). Selection and implementation of strategies in reasoning by analogy. *Journal of Educational Psychology, 74,* 399–413.

Sternberg, R. J., & Nigro, G. (1980). Developmental patterns in the solution of verbal analogies. *Child Development, 51,* 27–38.

Sternberg, R. J., & Powell, J. S. (1983). The development of intelligence. In P. H. Mussen (Series Ed.) & J. Flavell & E. Markman (Volume Eds.), *Handbook of child psychology* (Vol. 3, 3rd ed.). New York: Wiley.

Sternberg, R. J., & Rifkin, B. (1979). The development of analogical reasoning processes. *Journal of Experimental Child Psychology, 27,* 195–232.

Sternberg, S. (1969a). The discovery of processing stages: Extensions of Donder's method. *Acta Psychologica, 30,* 276–315.

Sternberg, S. (1969b). Memory-scanning: Mental processes revealed by reaction-time experiments. *American Scientist, 4,* 421–457.

Stott, L. H., & Ball, R. S. (1965). Infant and preschool mental tests. *Monographs of the Society for Research in Child Development, 30,* (3), Whole No. 101.

Terman, L. M., & Merrill, M. A. (1973). *Stanford-Binet intelligence scale: Manual for the third revision, Form L-M.* Boston, MA: Houghton-Mifflin.

Thurstone, L. L. (1938). *Primary mental abilities.* Chicago, IL: University of Chicago Press.

Thurstone, L. L. (1944). *A factorial study of perception.* Chicago, IL: University of Chicago Press.

Vernon, P. E. (1971). *The structure of human abilities.* London: Methuen.

Vurpillot, E. (1968). The development of scanning strategies and their relation to visual differentiation. *Journal of Experimental Child Psychology, 6,* 632–650.

Wechsler, D. (1939). *The measurement of adult intelligence*. Baltimore, MD: Williams & Wilkins.

Werner, H. (1948). *Comparative psychology of mental development* (Rev. ed.). New York: International Universities Press.

Werner, H., & Kaplan, E. (1952). The acquisition of word meanings: A developmental study. *Monographs of the Society for Research in Child Development, 15* (1, Serial No. 51).

7 Current Issues in Language Learning

Lila R. Gleitman
University of Pennsylvania

Eric Wanner
Alfred P. Sloan Foundation

INTRODUCTION

Language is learned, in the normal course of events, by children bright or dull, pampered or neglected, exposed to Tlingit or to English. In Leonard Bloomfield's words, "This is doubtless the greatest intellectual feat any one of us is ever required to perform" (1933, p. 29). Appreciation of the enormity of this human capacity, given the intricacy and variety of the languages of the world, has motivated an intense exploration of language learning by linguists and psychologists alike. Both in topic and in theoretical orientation, these approaches vary marvelously. If there is an anchoring point for the disparate efforts, it is Chomsky's break with the Bloomfieldian tradition of language study and, as a particular consequence, his analysis of the logic of language learning. In this chapter, we first review this paradigmatic change in the theory of language learning. Thereafter, we organize current findings in the field as they bear on these two opposing theoretical positions.

BLOOMFIELD AND CHOMSKY ON LANGUAGE LEARNING

Leonard Bloomfield and Noam Chomsky, in succession, utterly dominated the field of linguistics for periods extending over three decades. Within these time periods it is small overstatement that investigating language was a matter of agreeing or disagreeing in detail with the programs developed by these thinkers. Such a history is commonplace in science; for example, the study of learning in

American psychology, for five decades, was a series of responses pro and con to a general problem as framed by Thorndike. For language, it is of some interest that Bloomfield and Chomsky appear to have been in close agreement on the essential nature of the problem. Both their most influential works (Bloomfield, 1933; Chomsky, 1965) open with an analysis of language acquisition, supposing that the problem of learning a first language and the problem of language description are at bottom one and the same.

According to both these accounts, language is a pairing of forms to meanings. These pairings differ from language to language, e.g., in English the sound /si/ is paired to the meaning "gaze at with the eyes" while in Spanish the sound /si/ is paired to the meaning "yes." This variability implies that learning must take place by direct exposure to some particular language. But if there were nothing more to language than such associative pairings between sounds and meanings, learning would probably not be hard to describe. For both Bloomfield and Chomsky, the mystery of the learning feat derives from two further crucial facts about the human use of language: It is rule governed, and it is creative. Bloomfield (1933) wrote:

> It is obvious that most speech forms are regular, in the sense that the speaker who knows the constituents and the grammatical patterns can utter them without having heard them; moreover, the observer cannot hope to list them since the possibilities of combination are practically infinite. For instance, the classes of nominative expressions in English are so large that many possible actor–action forms—say, *a red-headed plumber bought six oranges*—may never have been uttered. (p. 275)

Bloomfield's learner came into the world scantily endowed. He could hear. And he had a single principle of data manipulation that allowed him to classify together materials that occurred in the same positions within utterances. For example, the fact that *the* and *a* both occur sentence-initially, before adjectives and nouns, etc., would be the basis for assigning them to the same class. Bloomfield's learning device could also draw inductive generalizations from the distributional properties of the grammatical classes so formed, and so be able to utter new sentences that exhibited the same regularities: "A grammatical pattern (sentence type, construction, or substitution) is often called *an analogy*. A regular analogy permits the speaker to utter speech-forms which he has not heard; we say that he utters them *on the analogy* of similar forms which he has heard" (1933, p. 275).

For Bloomfield, then, a grammar is a description of the analogies that hold for a language, and learning is the set of discovery procedures (the data manipulations) by which the child forms these analogies. The learner first discovers that the continuously varying sound wave can be analyzed into discrete segments (the *phones*), which appear in discoverable recurrent patterns (the *words*), which appear in yet larger recurrent patterns (the *phrases* and *sentences*), all discovered by extracting generalizations about their relative distribution in the corpus presented to the ear (see Harris, 1951, for detailed proposals about discovery procedures at each of these linguistic levels). The child learns to use each sentence appropriately by connecting the learned situation of its use (the stimulus) with its form (the response).[1]

In all fairness to history, Bloomfield was not as explicit as Chomsky in identifying linguistic theory with the problem of language learning, but his position ("The only useful generalizations about language are inductive generalizations," 1933, p. 29) derives coherently from the assumption that child and linguist are in the same position, each required to identify from scratch a linguistic system that potentially might be anything at all: "Features which we think ought to be universal may be absent from the very next language that becomes accessible" (1933, p. 20). If there are no constraints on the form of a natural language, then each child must be endowed with a set of discovery procedures of an entirely unbiased sort to guarantee equally facile learning of any language.

Chomsky's analysis of the learner's problem began in much the same way, with the joint assumptions that the input data are heard sentences (in context) and that the learning procedure must be some sort of inductive generalization from such a corpus. But Chomsky asserted that these assumptions answer the questions about learning only by begging them. After all, how does the child manage to generalize (learn by analogy) always and only from old grammatical sentences to new grammatical sentences? How is the learner to avoid wrong analogies and seize on the right ones? For example, consider a child who has been exposed to the following sentences:

---

[1]Bloomfield (1933) emphasized that the pairing between speech and event must be complex: "Even if we know a great deal about a speaker and about the immediate stimuli which are acting upon him, we usually cannot predict whether he will speak or what he will say." He put this problem down to

the fact that the human body is a very complex system . . . so that a very slight difference in the state of the body may result in a great difference in its response . . . [we could predict] whether a certain stimulus will lead someone to speak, and, if so, the exact words he will utter . . . if we knew the exact structure of his body at the moment or, what comes to the same thing, if we knew the exact makeup of his organism at some early stage—say, at birth or before—and then had a record of every change in that organism including every stimulus that had ever affected the organism. (p. 33)

Thus, Bloomfield had the courage of his materialist convictions. (See Skinner, 1957, for a modern variant of the same position, but keep in mind that Bloomfield was a professional linguist and made a series of exquisite technical contributions to the study of language structure and history.) Probably no avowed mentalist would disagree with this global claim that speech events are ultimately "caused" by a combination of internal structures and states and the external events they confront. But a large disagreement is whether the description of such speech-to-event relations would constitute an appropriate theory of language knowledge or performance. The problem is that only certain states, events, etc., are relevant to language organization. That is, the relations between sentences and events are mediated by the relations between sentences and their meanings. Presumably, the latter relations constitute a theory of language. (For further discussion, see the final section of this chapter.)

1. John painted the barn red.
2. John painted the barn blue.
3. John painted the red barn.
4. John saw the red barn.

By an analogy based on shared relative position, *blue* and *red* can be substituted for one another in Sentences 1 and 2. The child can therefore try the same substitution in Sentences 3 and 4, correctly inducing new sentences such as:

5. John painted the blue barn.
6. John saw the blue barn.

By similar analogy, the child can substitute *saw* for *painted* in Sentences 3 and 4. However, if the child tries this same substitution for Sentences 1 and 2, he or she will make the *false* induction that

7. John saw the barn red.
8. John saw the barn blue.

are acceptable sentences of English. The problem is that some analogies are the right ones and others the wrong ones, but Bloomfield's learner has no means for making these decisions and hence—according to Chomsky—no sure means for acquiring his native tongue.

Chomsky therefore reasoned that the natural languages could not vary arbitrarily from each other, else Bloomfield's claims must hold and language learning would be impossible. Rather, Chomsky argued that the natural languages must share universal properties, and human infants must be biologically disposed to consider only languages embodying these properties. In sum, the problem now becomes one of clothing Bloomfield's learner with a variety of presuppositions about the system to which it is being exposed, narrowing the hypothesis space on which inductions are performed. At the same time, these predispositions must be cast in some very abstract form so as to accommodate the detailed differences among the real languages:

> The real problem is that of developing a hypothesis about initial structure that is sufficiently rich to account for the acquisition of language, yet not so rich as to be inconsistent with the known diversity of language. (Chomsky, 1965, p. 58)

The focal supposition here is that an unbiased problem-solving device, guessing inductively at a grammar from a finite corpus of instances, cannot be guaranteed to arrive at the correct solution. As one more demonstration of this impasse, consider the question of how the learner is to know whether the sample of sentences heard so far come from the language consisting of exactly those sentences, or from some larger corpus. How could the learner know from a sample of English sentences that the correct grammar is not the union of English grammar and Bantu grammar—although, so far, no Bantu sentences are in the corpus (for a discussion, see Fodor, Bever, & Garrett, 1974)? To the retort "Such hypotheses are mad!" comes the counter-retort "But that is the point!" The problem of explaining language learning is essentially the problem of stating which hypotheses are mad and therefore never to be entertained, and which are sane, for a human learner.

One might, of course, propose that children do launch mad hypotheses in the course of learning their native tongues, only to be reined in by parents who correct them. This proposal faces severe problems. The first comes from examining the real interactions of caretakers with young children: Adults rarely correct their fledglings' syntax (Brown & Hanlon, 1970) and even when they do, children rarely pay attention (McNeill, 1966). Still, one could object that negative information might be available to the child in subtle form. A blatantly ungrammatical utterance by the child may fail to elicit the desired response from an adult who might misunderstand it, and this mismatch between childish expectation and adult reaction may be enough to signal the child that something is amiss.

But true as it may be that negative information of this subtle sort could be available to the child, the objection misses two points. One has to do with the complexities in the child's social environment, an environment in which many things other than language learning and teaching are going on. Owing to this complexity, many of the child's utterances are objected to by caretakers on grounds that have nothing to do with syntax, but instead pertain to the truth or social acceptability of what the child says (Brown & Hanlon, 1970). For example, the perfectly grammatical sentence "I'll color the wall red" may be rejected by the mother. How is the child to know that this is a correction of action, not grammar, while the (much rarer) rejection of sentences such as "Me wuvs yer, Mom" is in aid of grammaticality, not social correctness? Woe to the child— both as social being and as speaker of English—who guesses wrong about the basis for these two rejections of what she has said.

Beyond this practical difficulty, the theory that children learn by correction misses a logically prior point: Children hardly ever *require* correction of either direct or subtle varieties. For the overwhelming number of linguistic generalizations the child never errs at all, and therefore no opportunity to correct him or her ever arises. To be sure, as we shall detail later on, children do make some errors, such as saying "foots" for "feet" or "Mail come" instead of "The mail comes." In such cases, it is possible to believe that children acquire the right forms because they are corrected when they say the wrong forms. But such cases of overt error, while very noticeable to parents and to investigators of child language, are really the exception when compared to the huge number of semantic and syntactic generalizations each child learns without committing any overt errors along the way. To continue with an example mentioned earlier, children learning English do sometimes hear noun-phrases in which an adjective follows a noun, as in "I painted the town red" or "That ice is paper thin" or "Her cheeks were rose red" or "I'm dog tired." But they never overgeneralize, e.g., to "I saw the house red." This failure to make a mistake means that the parent never gets the chance to correct such attempts, either overtly or tacitly.

Thus by and large, it is necessary to assume that the child learns from the "good" sentences he or she hears, i.e., learning from *positive examples,* rather than from being corrected for the "bad" sentences he or she utters, i.e., learning from *negative examples.* Thus the job for investigators of language learning is to explain how, among the myriad grammatical generalizations that children might draw from their limited experience with language, somehow they seem to draw the right ones or very nearly the right ones from the start. That they do so is evident even from examples that are sometimes marshaled to argue just the reverse.

For instance, Ervin (1964) has shown that children are good—all too good—at forming inductive generalizations. Children who at two and three years of age spontaneously and appropriately produce both weak (*talked, pushed*) and strong (*brought, sang*) past-tense endings for English verbs, frequently around age four produce weak endings almost exclusively; that is, they now say "*bringed*" and "*singed*" in systematic violation of the input corpus. For the stock of most frequent English verbs (the ones children are likely to hear), the weak tense ending occurs far less than half the time on types and still less on tokens. This is no formal proof, but it is a clear suggestion that young children are inclined to draw grand inductive generalizations even over noisy data. The corpus violates the generalization the majority of the time; still, the learner evidently prefers a bad generalization to none at all. But now the question must be just how many false generalizations are true of English sentences 30 or 40 percent of the time. For example, it has been noted that substantives preceding -*hood* are very predominantly kinship terms (*childhood, motherhood, neighborhood*) and yet no child supposes that *robin* is a kinship term.

To approach these issues, Chomsky (1965) designed a hypothetical language learner who would be spared these never-ending inductive pitfalls. In some ways, Chomsky's model is an odd candidate for the attention it has received in developmental psycholinguistics, since it was never offered as a serious empirical account of how a child acquires a language. In fact, Chomsky's model is really no more (or less!) than a description of the problem of language acquisition, and it is a description framed from a particular point of view—namely, that in acquiring language the child must master the rules of a generative grammar. However, Chomsky was able to develop a number of very strong claims about acquisition simply by stating the problem in this way, and much of the empirical work in the field can be seen as an effort to develop these claims, to test them, or to reject them outright.

Chomsky's analysis begins with the unarguable claim that children receive little or no formal instruction about the rules that presumably underlie adult performance. Rather, or so it would seem, the child is exposed only to some finite sample of utterances, different for each child, in the presence of certain events and circumstances in the world. Sometimes, though surely not always, these utterances will be appropriate to the circumstances in some way. For instance, a lucky learner may hear "A rabbit is running by" as a rabbit runs by. From such exposure to utterance/situation pairs, the learner must induce a finite representation of the language that projects to an infinite set of sound/meaning pairs.[2]

According to Chomsky's idealization, the child has the internal wherewithal to assign a "partial and tentative" structural description to the input utterance, aided by its context (Chomsky, 1965, p. 32). The child is also armed with an innate linguistic theory that includes all the logical apparatus necessary to construct candidate transformational grammars. An innate learning theory tests these grammars against the input, by matching the structural descriptions generated by the candidate grammar with those given in the primary linguistic data. In case more than one grammar survives this test, Chomsky endowed his hypothetical child with an evaluation measure that provides a way of ranking all the empirically successful grammars. If correct, such a ranking would favor just the grammar that the real child actually emerges with from his encounter with the primary linguistic data.

According to Chomsky's idealization, this process of grammar acquisition takes place instantaneously; that is, grammar construction occurs in the presence of a large body of primary linguistic data, and the evaluation procedure will immediately choose the most highly valued grammar appropriate to these data. Although this is clearly counterfactual, it has never been the source of much controversy because Chomsky was more interested in demonstrating the logical prerequisites to language learning than in making claims about the details of the process. In general, those who have accepted Chomsky's instantaneous model have assumed that it could be "slowed down" without changing any of its essential properties (see, e.g., Roeper, 1982). Those who have rejected this model have objected on other grounds.

We organize our discussion of language learning against the backdrop of Bloomfield's and Chomsky's formulations of the task. Such an organization leaks, in part, for some work in this field verges on issues outside these idealizations. Granting this, we adopt a historical method that is unblushingly Thucydidean, interpreting the varying research efforts in a way that maximizes their joint

---

[2]Note that, although the environment could pair only utterances to situations, the character of learning must be more general than this: To a remarkable degree, adults can assign a compositional meaning to sentences on request, in the absence of external context. And they can comprehend books about ancient history. The theoretical task then becomes: asking how the child recruits information of a certain sort (primary linguistic data, or utterance/situation pairs) and constructs a system of a different sort (sound/meaning, or deep-structure/surface-structure pairs).

coherence. This coherence resides, we believe, in their relation to the logic expressed by these two great linguists, even though some investigators will deny, quite correctly, that they were explicitly influenced by them.

THE CONTENT AND FORM OF THE PRIMARY LINGUISTIC DATA

As Bloomfield and Chomsky would agree, the nature of learning crucially depends on how the learner naturally organizes what he hears; how he represents the input to himself. On Bloomfield's story, the organizing principles must be very general and subject to revision all along the line, for what is to be learned varies arbitrarily. On Chomsky's story, the languages "out there" are of an antecedently well-defined type, so innate knowledge about them is useful; in fact, to the extent that the forms and categories of language are distinct from the forms and categories of cognition in general, innate knowledge of the language principles is the requirement for learning. In detail, the specification of a learning procedure requires the answer to two prior questions having to do with the state of the organism as learning begins: (a) How does the child make a relevant semantic analysis of the situation while listening to adults talk about it; and (b) How does the child analyze the sound wave that results from the adult talk? We address these two issues here. Afterward, in the presence of a tentative specification of the initial state, we address the learning problem: How does the child develop a system that maps between the sounds and the meanings?

Extracting Meaning from the Situation

On Chomsky's formulation, the child is assumed to hear utterances in situations from which she can recover partial and tentative structural descriptions including, of course, some characterization of meaning. No matter the theoretical stance, the same assumption seems to be made by all investigators. For Bloomfield, each "situation" was that extralinguistic event (stimulus) connected by temporal contiguity to a particular linguistic event (response). That all parties agree to the requirement for extralinguistic sources of information is not surprising, for this follows from prior agreement about the analysis of the task: Since a language is a pairing of sounds (linguistic forms) to meanings, and since languages *vary* in these pairings, learning logically requires that samples of the forms be presented, paired with samples of the meanings; the main source for discovering these meanings seems to be in the situations accompanying the speech events. It follows that the prerequisite ability to interpret the real world in a linguistically relevant fashion must exist *ab initio*, if the child is to acquire her native tongue (for an informative discussion, see Wexler, 1982).

It is sometimes assumed that these claims for a learner are quite innocent, that language learning is easy to explain because the child can "rely on meaning from the context." However, it is hard to conceive how such claims could be brought to ground at all. The difficulty is that neither words nor sentences, nor even propositions, are in any direct way encodings of scenes or situations in the world.

As a simplest instance of problems here, consider the fact that a child observing a cat is observing, *a fortiori,* an animal, an object, the nose of a cat, Felix the cat, and the nose-plus-ear of a cat at the same time. Should someone now say "cat," this is presumably the situational context from which the child is to learn that "cat" means 'cat.' But what is to prevent the child from assuming that the meaning is *nose-ear-complex of a cat,* instead? If a (currently unknown) representational principle of mind automatically excludes this as a possible human concept, it is still the case that the child must learn *nose* and *Felix,* as well as *cat,* under these frightful circumstances (Quine, 1960).

These problems re-arise at every level of the linguistic hierarchy, reaching their ultimate exacerbation for the case of the sentence unit. A child who observes a cat sitting on a mat also observes, *a fortiori,* a mat supporting a cat, a mat under a cat, a floor supporting a cat and a mat, and so on. If the adult now says, "The cat is on the mat," even while pointing to the cat on the mat, how is the child to choose among these interpretations of the situation? Especially as the less probable (whatever this means) choices are sometimes made: The adult sometimes does say "What a good bed that mat makes for the cat." Such problems are materially worsened by the fact that the adult may speak of one thing while the child attends to another. The adult may say "Time for your nap" as the child regards the cat on the mat. Worst of all, certain structures in a language, among them those most frequently used with children, are specifically reserved for mismatches with the world: The felicitous occasion for positive imperatives such as "Eat your peas!" or "Go next door to Granny and borrow an egg!" is the absence of pea eating, Grannys, and eggs.

In sum, there is no innocence to the claim that the child learns language by relying on "meaning" or "the world." Nevertheless, it seems impossible to avoid the posit that the child will, in some crucially exploited cases, feel justified in assuming that a sound wave that enters his ear refers in some particular way, from some particular point of view, to a situation he is currently observing, as, for example, cat-on-mat rather than mat-under-cat. Three kinds of evidence bear on (though they do not explain) ways children solve this puzzle: As learning begins, children naturally represent concepts (1) lexically and (2) propositionally; and (3) caretaker and child conspire to converse in ways that map as transparently as possible from these initial lexical and propositional representations to the contexts in which they occur.

The Word Is the Natural Domain of Simple Concepts

Theories of the Lexicon.   The classical view of word meaning (Locke, 1690/1965) holds that most words are not simple, but rather are cover labels for a bundle of simpler meaning-atoms, usually called elements, features, or attributes. These basic elements are taken to be those that sensory (or low-level perceptual) experience yields *directly*. Consider a hue experience such as 'red,' assumed (at least for present expository purposes) to be an automatic neural response to specifiable light stimulation. According to the classical theory of word meaning, when a child hears the speech sound "red" while having this experience, he associates the sound with that experience; that association is the meaning of the word *red*.

But on the classical view, the number of basic elements (such as *red*) is rather small, certainly much smaller than the number of words eventually acquired by children. The complex words are built up by combining the simple elements. The basis for combination is generally taken to be the co-occurrence of more than one of the simple elements in experience, and the mechanism for combination is again taken to be association. For example, suppose that *round* and *object*, like *red*, are among the basic elements of experience. If some object that is red and round is usually seen while hearing some speech sound, say, "blitso," then the child will *compose* a new category: the category *blitso* with the meaning 'red round object.' To repeat, the category is constructed because of the co-occurrence of simple elements in experience with each other and with that word.

Compositional theories usually invoke the simple elements for more than learning: The basic elements are taken to be involved in comprehension performances, even those of adults. Pursuing the example above, the learner stores with the sound *blitso*, as its meaning, the list of its elements; i.e., the meaning entry for *blitso* is 'red and round and object.' To speak, the user pulls out *blitso* whenever he wishes to mean 'red and round and object.' To understand the heard word "blitso," the listener looks up this word in his mental dictionary, but does not understand this word directly. Rather, he pulls out its components (red, round, object) and understands these instead. In short, to comprehend words, the listener *de*composes them into their primitive atoms.

A potential problem for such theories is that not all associates of a word, say, *ball*, could be permanently stored in the head as parts of the meaning of that word. This would be an embarrassment of representational riches, and would sometimes do more harm than good for speaking and understanding. For example, sometimes *ball* is heard in the presence of a red thing, and sometimes in the presence of a green thing. Presumably the learner could not and would not want to store all these color associates as part of the meaning of *ball*. On the contrary: English speakers come to know that *ball* can be used appropriately in total disregard of the color of the object observed. To model this fact, compositional theories of meaning limit the number of elements stored as a word's meaning. In the best-known variant, words are semantically represented by their *definitions*, a smallish subset of the basic elements: just those that are individually necessary and jointly sufficient to determine category membership (Locke, 1690/1965; for recent discussions see, e.g., Katz, 1972). The color of a ball is irrelevant to its category membership and so is not chosen as one of the elements stored as its meaning.[3]

In some more recent variants of compositional semantic theory, the necessary and sufficient conditions of the classical view are dropped, and instead the words are semantically represented as a cluster of elements (Wittgenstein, 1953; for recent discussions, see Rosch, 1975; Rosch & Mervis, 1975). In this variant, there is no criterial (necessary and sufficient) list of the features. Rather, there is a set of features associated with each lexical concept, but an individual falls into the class by partaking of some of them. For example, perhaps a bird is characterizable in terms of such attributes as flying, having feathers, being two-legged, and laying eggs. If these features were jointly necessary for 'birdness,' then neither an ostrich nor a bird amputee could be considered a bird. But according to the cluster theories, it will often be sufficient, for an entity to be identified properly as a bird, simply to have feathers and to lay eggs.

Details aside, the two positions just sketched agree in supposing that most words do not represent elementary concepts, but represent certain combinations of those elementary concepts. Whenever the listener hears a word spoken, she identifies it by the sound of its cover label (e.g., "blitso," in our example) but then extracts its meaning elements (*red, round, object*) as a step in the comprehension process.

A radically different position denies the compositional character of word meaning (for discussion, see Fodor, 1975; Fodor, Garrett, Walker, & Parkes, 1980; Armstrong, Gleitman, & Gleitman, 1983). According to this third kind of theory, both the learning and use of words is *holistic*. The bulk of vocabulary items in a language directly encode the elementary categories of experience rather than being constructs out of some very limited, covert, mental vocabulary of "features." To understand the implications of this view, it is easiest to consider a concrete example of how compositional and holistic theories would describe early word learning.

Consider how the word *cat* is to be acquired. Both approaches agree in assuming that the required condition for learning is that someone says "cat" in

---

[3]The machinery by which these choices are to be made is not easy to describe. Presumably, successive exposures will reveal to the learner that balls are not limited to any particular color. Yet it is logically possible to envisage a machine that would represent such facts by adding to a disjunctive definition, i.e., "a ball is a round thing that is red, or green, or violet, or blue and red striped, or . . ." Further machinery would be necessary to conclude that "any color" is closer to the facts about items standardly called balls. But a further problem is that "any color" is sensibly excluded from the definition too, despite the fact that each observed ball is some color. Redundancy rules are often invoked to handle this problem. All physical objects must be some color—whether they be balls, giraffes, pebbles, or sofas. An efficient dictionary would filter the specification *colored* up to the highest level at which it obtains. That is, balls would be described as colored only insofar as balls are described as being physical objects. Since physical objects are described as colored, balls would inherit this property, but *colored* would not be among the necessary and sufficient features specified for *ball*.

the presence of a cat. But the compositional learner has no way of *directly* perceiving 'catness.' Rather, she is able to experience (out there in the world), say, a shape, whiskers, fur, movement, a sinuous tail (or whatever the elementary experiences really are). Her entry for *cat* is a list of such features—and that list may be modified by subsequent events in which someone says "cat" in the presence of some new cat, e.g., a tailless cat. In contrast, the holistic learner is postulated to be able to observe a cat out in the world, under the same conditions, so he directly learns that "cat" means 'cat.' This means that, in advance of any learning, the holistic learner is assumed to have the internal (innate) wherewithal sufficient to represent 'catness' and to recognize an instance of that category in the world. Of course this learner, just like the compositional learner, may make errors during learning. Since by hypothesis he can experience animals, giraffes, statues, etc., as well as cats, he may on occasion misidentify and form a wrong meaning for *cat*. Subsequent exposures may cause him to change his entry for the sound "cat," therefore, but that change is not an addition or subtraction of more elementary features.

Lexical Concept Attainment by the Young Child.   Empirical study of the child word learner has some relevance to the issues just addressed. According to the compositional views, it would be reasonable to suppose that the child's innate equipment, that allows him to interpret the world, consists of the elementary features. Moreover, learning word meanings would consist of learning feature by feature. It has been demonstrated that this position can make sense of some of the child's early word use. Specifically, the young child often overgeneralizes the use of a word; for example, he or she may use the word *ball* to refer to all round things, including faces and the moon as well as balls (things perceptually close to balls, see Clark; 1973), or all things she plays with, including dolls and blocks (things functionally close to balls; see Nelson, 1973).

A number of further investigations appeared to offer more detailed support for the compositional approach to lexical learning. For example, one set of experiments seemed to show that children first learned only one or two features of the meaning of *more* and *less,* those sufficient to establish that these words are *comparative* and have to do with *numerosity* (Donaldson & Balfour, 1968; Palermo, 1973): Two- and three-year-old children will change the number of apples on a magnetic tree if told either to "Make it so there are *more* apples" or "Make it so there are *less* apples." But to perform this task correctly, i.e., to *add* apples in response to *more* and to *subtract* apples in response to *less,* the children would also have to know that *more* represents the positive pole (greater than some standard numerosity) and that *less* represents the negative pole (smaller than the standard numerosity). The investigators showed that the children did not seem to have this additional information. When asked to "Make it so there are less apples," they *added* apples, just as they did for "Make it so there are more apples." The compositional theory of meaning handles this outcome by claiming that the young learners had acquired the features *comparative* and *numerosity,* that these words share, but not the features that distinguish them from each other, *positive pole* and *negative pole.*

Unfortunately, this apparent success of compositional theories in describing word learning has turned out to be largely illusory. Carey (1977) asked young children who made the errors on *less* one more question, involving a nonsense syllable: "Make it so there are *tiv* apples on the tree." The children who had added apples for *less* added them for *tiv* as well. This begins to suggest that a partial meaning for *less* is not what led the children astray in the original demonstrations. They stray in just the same way when they have no lexical entry at all. The simplest answer seems to be that children err on *less* (and *tiv!*) just when they have no idea of what the word means. Given the situation of movable apples, their response bias is to add apples rather than to remove them, but this does not imply that they have "partial knowledge" of words like *less.* Thus the original findings cannot be interpreted as supporting a compositional theory any more than they support a holistic theory.

Carey and Bartlett (1978) subsequently studied word learning in a more direct way, by introducing new words to young children in settings that seem natural. For example, they introduced the unknown word *chromium* (to be assigned the meaning 'olive green') to two- and three-year-olds during play in the following way: Interrupting the ongoing activity, the experimenter pointed toward two trays (one red, one olive green) and said to the child "Get me the chromium tray; not the red one, the chromium one." The contrast color (here, *red*) was always one that pretests had established was known to the child. The children were tested about a week later for what they had learned from this single introducing circumstance. That half the children failed to remember anything about *chromium* is no surprise. But fully half of them had made an initial mapping between *chromium* and color concepts. To be sure, they differed in what they had learned; some children knew that *chromium* meant 'olive green,' others knew only that it was a color word, others that it was a synonym for *green,* and so on. Two properties of this learning are of special interest for evaluating the feature-by-feature learning hypothesis. The first is the rapidity of mapping—learning a meaning from a single introducing event. This is inconsistent with the idea that word meaning always is built up through repeated exposures, that dissociate necessary features from adventitious properties of a single event. The second is that the children's entries for *chromium,* while sometimes "wrong," could rarely be characterized as wrong in the sense of being incomplete. The results seem best characterized by saying the children learned a whole word concept, sometimes the one intended by the experimenter ('olive green') and sometimes some other one (e.g., 'green').

The Carey and Bartlett experiments thus provide a first evidentiary basis for a holistic theory of early word learning. Examination of the lexicons of very young children gives further support to this position, though only in a negative way: by displaying more of the difficulties of the feature-by-feature view. If children were initially sensitive to a very small set of properties that were constitutive of word meanings, it is plausible to suppose that the (relatively few) words that encoded only these elementary properties would be among the first vocabulary items acquired. For example, if a bird is, notionally, a two-legged, feathered, flying, animal, we would expect items such as *feather(ed)*, *fly(ing)* and *animal* to appear earlier than *bird* in the child's lexicon. But the facts seem to be otherwise, with these terms usually appearing in just the opposite order to that predicted: Property terms and superordinate terms are late, compared to basic object terms, in the vocabularies of child learners (cf., Nelson, 1973; Rosch, 1973; Rosch, Mervis, Gray, Johnson, & Boyes-Braem, 1976). Similarly, children learn verbs with many features (if they have features) as easily as verbs with few (if they have features). *Walk* and *run* must have *move* as one of their features; and yet the former words are usually learned before *move*, and there is no obvious stage of learning at which *run* means only *move* (Gentner, 1978, 1982; see Carey, 1982, for an important general discussion of lexical concept attainment).

Despite the descriptive difficulties of compositional theories that we just reviewed, there is good reason to be cautious about accepting the holistic theory of lexical concept attainment as the correct position. For one thing, componential theories of word meaning and word learning are hardly dead in the water. Various rescue operations are very much alive, often proceeding by increasing the power of the logical combinatorial machinery that organizes featural descriptions (Katz, 1972). Moreover, the underlying implications of the holistic view are so awesome as to dictate a wary stance. To embrace it, one must be prepared to suppose that there are as many *simple* categories of experience as there are, say, easy vocabulary items in a language, i.e., that the learner's innate conceptual furnishings are much more extensive and various than are supposed by compositional theories (Fodor, 1975, 1983). In the light of this implication and the fragmentary nature of currently available evidence, a certain agnosticism on these matters may be the best stance to adopt. We do accept as a tentative state-of-the-art generalization that the child selects the linguistic formative *word* as the repository for his elementary experiences with the world. This is the framework principle according to the holistic approach, but at present it is best interpreted more as a program for research than as a theoretical conclusion. Appropriately, Carey's and related early work just cited have been the basis for a burgeoning exploration designed to discover the conditions of learning, the kinds of words learned under varying exposure conditions, the organization of words in the lexicon as a whole, and so on (for further discussion, see Keil, 1979; Markman, Horton, & McLanahan, 1980; Waxman & Gelman, unpublished manuscript).

Before leaving this topic, it is important to note that in present guises neither of the approaches just discussed really touches the problem with which we began: How, when, and why does the learner who can putatively observe Felix, a cat, an animal, a thing (or elements constitutive of these), decide which such representation of the world is apposite to a particular external event? This problem area is certainly being addressed, e.g., in the work of Eleanor Rosch and her collaborators on the child's bias toward so-called "basic-level" concepts (Rosch et al., 1976). But general solutions are not likely to be just around the corner.

The Three Bears Description: Formatives Higher and Lower Than the Word Are Learned Late

Details aside, we have organized the literature as suggesting that single words encode single concepts for very young children. But many words are morphologically complex and encode more than one concept at a time. One case is the word *walked,* which encodes tense as well as the lexical content 'walk.' How is the child to treat such items, if he or she associates the linguistic notion *word* with a single conceptual notion? We believe that early speech is consistent with the idea that the child rejects such complexity within the word. Moreover, the child seems to take a very strict view of the way words function as components of propositions; namely, that *each word must code exactly one of the arguments of a predicate, the predicate itself, or a logical word* (such as *and* or *or*). Let us term this The Three Bears description of the roles words play in earliest sentences: To the extent a received word codes more than one of the countenanced functions, it is too big; less than one, it is too small; exactly one, and it is just right. It is because this equation of propositional functions with single words is untrue of the adult language that the child's interpretation of the scope of a word will often differ from the adult's.

One line of evidence comes from the acquisition of American Sign Language (ASL). This manual communication system has by now been studied sufficiently to determine that it is formally and substantively equivalent to other natural languages, differing from these mainly in the modality (eye and hand, rather than ear and mouth) that carries the information (Klima and Bellugi, 1979). Therefore, the case of ASL is not too far afield to consider here, and for the present issue it is particularly informative. Newport and Ashbrook (1977) have shown an early tendency to map each relational element of this system as a separate lexical (sign) item. Certain ASL predicates morphologically incorporate some of their arguments. For example, the actor of *give* is uniformly expressed in the mature language as a modulation of the *give* sign, not as an independent sign. But child learners, systematically violating these input data, express the agent of *give* as a separate sign. The generalization is to the effect that each argument and the predicate ought to be carried by a separate wordlike item. No single word can be both predicate and argument (that would be "too big"), so *give* is first interpreted as carrying only one of these functions.

Even more common is the young learner's indifference to further meanings and functions (other than predicate, argument, logical vocabulary) coded inside the word unit; for example, tense or number. (They are "too small".) Evidence suggests that complex words such as *knew* (*know* + *ed*) and *don't* (*do* + *not*) are treated as unanalyzed wholes by the youngest learners, and only much later unpacked. Errors such as *knowed* developmentally succeed instances of *knew*, as we mentioned earlier (also see Klima & Bellugi, 1966, for this treatment of first negative words). Newport (1981, 1982) has demonstrated for a range of items that young ASL users acquire holistic "frozen signs," only later analyzing these into a root form with associated derivational and inflectional modulations; Gleitman and Gleitman (1970) offer a similar discussion of children's holistic treatment of English compound nouns. The appropriate generalization seems to be that semantic information within the word (e.g., tense) that is neither argument, predicate, nor logical word simply goes unanalyzed at earliest stages, as our Three Bears description predicts.

Morphological analysis of the word item is not only late: it is variable in the linguistic population. Gleitman and Gleitman (1970) have shown that the bulk of mature speakers have difficulty analyzing the internal morphology of English compound nouns. Freyd and Baron (1982) have shown that vocabulary size for academically average eighth-graders and for precocious fifth-graders is about the same for morphologically simple items, but the talented fifth-grade youngsters have a massive advantage for morphologically complex items. Indeed, certain kinds of creative activities involving productive morphological analysis do eventually appear in the repertory of the developing child. For one such process, see Clark (1982) on the creation of denominative verbs by young speakers of English, French, and German. For another, see Bowerman (1982) on the emerging understanding of English lexical causatives. Although such analyses do take place, the authors just cited agree that these are not among the first developments. In fact, Bowerman tenders the same interpretation of her findings as do we: Each early word is an unopened package; only much later does productive lexical analysis begin to appear.

This formulation of early lexical concept attainment allows us to reapproach a famous incident recorded by McNeill (1966) and to interpret it further. McNeill's 2-year-old subject remarks "Nobody don't like me." His mother corrects him: "No, say 'Nobody likes me'." The child mulishly repeats himself. The mother stubbornly recorrects. This interchange repeats itself seven times. On the eighth correction, the child says "Oh: Nobody don't likes me." McNeill takes this as a very strong indication that overt corrections do not very much affect language learning, and we concur. But perhaps we can say more about what the child is willing to revise (adding the *s*) and what he is not (omitting the negative). He is indifferent to the *s* on the grounds just stated—it is not a predicate, an argument, or a logical word—so he can take it as well as leave it. But he cannot apparently conceive that the logical notion *negative* does not have its own separable lexical reflex. He cannot accept that, in a cranky rule of English, the negative can be incorporated into the subject nominal (and, what is more, still have the verb phrase in its semantic scope).

Summarizing, children seem to approach language learning equipped with conceptual interpretive abilities for categorizing the world. As Slobin (1973) has proposed, learners are biased to map each elementary semantic idea (concept) onto the linguistic unit *word*. We have interpreted Carey's findings of holistic word learning as one explication of this proposal: Internal analysis of the word unit is a late and variable step in cognitive–linguistic development. We have also just examined the word as a functional unit in the sentence, concluding that the lexical items are at first stages the linguistic expressions of predicates, their arguments, and logical items.

The Sentence is the Natural Domain of Propositions

A fascinating line of research, beginning with Bloom's (1970) groundbreaking work on children's spontaneous speech, provides evidence at another level about how children meaningfully interpret the world. From the earliest two-word utterances, the ordering of the component words interpreted against their context of use suggests that they are conceived as playing certain thematic roles, such as *agent, instrument,* and the like, within a predicate–argument (propositional) structure (Bloom, Lightbown, & Hood, 1975; Bowerman, 1973; Braine, 1976; Brown, 1973). Greenfield and Smith (1976) have maintained that even isolated first words betray, by their relation to events, rudiments of this propositional conception. Feldman, Goldin-Meadow and Gleitman (1978) have shown that a similar componential analysis describes a manual system of communication developing in isolated deaf children who received no specifically linguistic input, who neither heard speech nor saw formal signing (for further discussion, see Goldin-Meadow, 1982).

To be sure, as Braine (1976) has pointed out, it is by no means clear precisely what these first relational categories are, whether terms such as *agent* are appropriate in scope and content to describe them (see, for example, Braine & Hardy, 1982, for experimental manipulations designed to extract the detailed content of these categories in young children). But whatever the initial categories, there seems to be little doubt that the child approaches language learning equipped with a propositional interpretation of the scenes and events in the world around him. This is not particularly surprising. After a modest number of observations, Premack's chimpanzee, Sarah, can learn to put a sticky star on the agent and a sticky circle on the patient, as shown in brief video movies (Premack, forthcoming). If Sarah, why not human children?

The question remains how much this tells about learning a language. This depends on whether the categories and forms of natural language sentences are simple with respect to the preexisting meaning structures. From varying perspectives, a number of authors have assumed that linguistic categories and forms map transparently from the meaning structures, and hence that the bulk of explanatory apparatus—for child learner and for developmental psycholinguist—exists when these categories are isolated and described (e.g., Bates & MacWhinney, 1982; Braine & Hardy, 1982; Bloom, 1973, 1983). This view is not unreasonable on the face of it. After all, we previously subscribed to the view that the mapping between words and concepts may be quite direct. The question now on the table is whether the relation between sentences and propositional thought is as straightforward as the relation between words and concepts may be (see also Section 3.1 for further discussion of this issue).

A singularly interesting source for understanding this issue is Slobin (1982). Using evidence from a variety of natural languages, he argues that an explanation of language learning from the cognitive–interpretive basis is strictly limited by the real variation among languages. Partly different aspects of meaning are coded in the syntax of different languages. As one of many examples, the child will have to discover whether his language codes tense or aspect, or both, in the syntax. Moreover, even within a single language, it is obvious that there are many ways to say the same thing. So in this sense, too, it is massively overexuberant to hope that knowing meaning is tantamount to knowing language. As Bowerman (1982) has argued, the learner must eventually transcend his initial semantic-categorial organization of language to acquire certain grammatical categories and functions that crosscut these.

Motherese: Saying the Obvious

It is possible to suppose that caretakers' speech to young children has properties that respond to the problems we have been discussing, properties that enhance the probability that learner and teacher will be referring to the same matters from the same perspectives (for the clearest statement of this hypothesis, see Bruner, 1974/75). When speaking to the youngest learners, mothers use language that is propositionally simple, limited in vocabulary, slowly and carefully enunciated, repetitive, deictic, and usually referring to the here and now (Broen, 1972; Cross, 1977; Newport, 1977; Phillips, 1970; Snow, 1977). These same properties of speech to young children have been reported in various language communities (Blount, 1970; Schieffelin, 1979) and social classes (Snow et al., 1976) and among various caretaker types, even including the 4-year-old playmates of 2-year-old learners (Sachs & Devin, 1976; Shatz & Gelman, 1973). Although the syntactic forms vary considerably both within and across caretakers, topics to the youngest listeners are interestingly narrow in range. They are mostly a matter of focusing the listener's attention on a present scene or thing and getting him or her to act upon, or at least gaze upon, that thing: *action directives* (Newport, Gleitman & Gleitman, 1977; Shatz, 1978).

These descriptive facts about maternal speech cohere on the view that it is a matter of getting together with the young listener on what is meant. The motivation for the caretakers is not hard to find, nor need it be explicitly linguistic-tutorial. We need only suppose that the mother wishes to be understood and obeyed, and these properties will fall out.[4]

---

[4]These properties fall out because, apparently, no matter what you say to a young child, it responds by acting, if it responds at all. Shatz (1978) has shown that there is a good match between what mothers say (mothers' speech consists largely of *action directives;* whatever the syntactic form,

But one's enthusiasm for the explanatory potential of these findings requires a good deal of tempering. They suggest only *that* mother and child endeavor to represent the ongoing scene "in the same way" but do not suggest *how* they manage to do so. The explanation rests on the (unknown) cognitive system that learner and teacher share, such that in some critically exploited cases they will interpret the same scene in the same way. To be sure, contributions to the solution of such problems are currently appearing; an exemplary discussion, based on syntactic analyses, of bridges between linguistic and conceptual categories has been provided by Jackendoff (1983; see also Landau & Gleitman, in press), and we have also mentioned such experimental work as Keil's (1979), which attempts to describe the child's ontological categories. But the question here is how the *caretaker,* by special manipulations, may be helping the child understand the words and sentences she hears. Contributors to the literature on maternal speech assert—both innocuously and probably truly—that mothers say "what is obvious" or "what is salient" to children, but this terminological fiat does not seem to resolve anything. The question is why is what's obvious or salient as obvious or salient as it is. If the caretaker's special manipulations help the child understand what is obvious to the caretaker, what is it that allows the child to understand the special significance of these manipulations?

As an instance of the underlying problems here, it is instructive that children blind from birth learn the same lexical items and thematic relations in about the same order as do sighted children (Landau, 1982; Landau & Gleitman, 1984), though clearly what is "here" or "now" must differ for the blind and the sighted listener. A blind 3-year-old knows, for example, that she is to perform different acts if told to *show* an object or to *give* it to a sighted listener. It is not at all obvious how the mothers of blind children differentially model the here and now so as to secure these surprising competencies.[5] Such findings of course

---

the intent is to get the child to act) and what children are inclined to do. Children "behave" in response to speech acts they even partly understand. They are likely to pick up the blocks if you say "Pick up your blocks" or "Could you pick up your blocks?" but they are just as likely to act even if your intent is merely to get information. For example, if you ask, "Can you jump to the moon?" you are liable to get a little jump from the child listener. If the mother is implicitly aware that this is the child's bias, and her motive is to be obeyed—or, what comes to the same thing, to display for herself and others the child's competence—she will select action directives when she speaks to the child. All descriptive evidence supports the view that action directives occur far more often (proportionally) in speech to younger children than in speech to older children and adults. These joint motivations in tutor and learner probabilistically increase the likelihood that the child's interpretation of the meaning of the maternal speech act will be correct.

[5]The finding here is that the blind child holds up an object for the sighted listener to perceive at a distance when told to "show" but delivers it to that listener when told to "give." Moreover, the child evidently adapts perceptual-cognitive terms to her own requirements, again in ways that are hard to explain as effects of maternal modeling. She distinguishes *touch* (contact manually) from *look* as used of herself (apprehend manually). For example, she touches her back to "Touch behind you"

cannot vitiate the claim that children learn language by "relying on meaning in the world." Rather they suggest that—since language clearly *is* learned by relying on meaning in the world—explaining language learning is more mysterious than ever.

Extracting Form from the Sound Wave

Though children may have their own devices for extracting meaning from situations, they will need other kinds of devices for extracting linguistically functioning units from the sound wave. Recall that Bloomfield's learner (and hence structural linguistics [cf. Bloch, 1941; Harris, 1951]) approached the gloriously confusing, continuously varying sound wave in a spirit of complete open-mindedness. This learner, like any objective physicist, would have no excuse to chop the complex and continuous wave form into discrete, linguistically functioning units, and even less excuse to classify these units as real speakers–listeners do. The problem of discovering the language forms from the sound waves, then, is directly comparable to the problem of discovering the meanings from the situations: What makes the learner digitalize the wave, break it into whole phones rather than halves of phones, whole words and phrases rather than nonintegral sequences of these, and so on? The analyses chosen are not inevitable inductions from the wave forms. We ask here what kinds of evidence are available to a listener with the right capacities and inclinations, to determine the forms of particular languages.

The Unit "Phone"

Chao (1934) demonstrated in a brilliant analysis of Chinese that no unified discovery procedure for a classificational scheme for sound-segments was likely to be discovered, because the criteria sufficient to isolate the phones of a particular language could not simultaneously be met (i.e., they were mutually contradictory). Classical phonemics nevertheless continued for some twenty years more to try, apparently on the plausible assumption that, if babies can do it, why not linguists? But babies could not. Therefore, language learners all over the world must be grateful to the Haskins Laboratory group of researchers who have

---

but feels in the space behind her for "Look behind you," without turning her head. She taps a cup when told to touch it, but explores it all over, manually, when told to look at it. She happily stabs at the air above in response to "Touch up" but is angry (when there's nothing to be found there) when responding to "Look up." She responds by touching when told "Touch it but don't look at it" but with confusion when told "Look at it but don't touch it." What claims about the natural categorial representations of humans account for the fact that blind and sighted children represent perceptual exploration so similarly, despite different sources of exposure to the world? It seems that the developmental literature substitutes semantic categories for syntactic ones successfully only by failing to define the former. For the present instance, we will require a semantic description of a term like *look* that subsumes the blind experience.

saved them the bother: The children need never learn to segment the acoustic wave phonetically just because they perceive such a segmentation "automatically" (see particularly Liberman, 1970; Liberman, Cooper, Shankweiler, & Studdert-Kennedy, 1967; for studies of infant phonetic perception, see Eimas, Siqueland, Jusczyk, & Vigorito, 1971; Jusczyk, 1980).

There is much controversy about the size and specific nature of the phonetic segments (for a summary discussion, see Foss & Hakes, 1978)—about whether they are the unique property of human organisms or belong to chinchillas and macaques as well (Kuhl & Miller, 1975), and about whether they derive from properties of speech perception in particular or auditory perception in general (Cutting & Rosner, 1974; Liberman & Pisoni, 1977; Newport, 1982). But these problems do not mitigate the case for rejoicing among the aspiring language learners. For them, it is enough to note that no learning apparatus is required for an initial segmentation of the acoustic wave into discrete phones. This segmentation has already been provided in the nervous system.

At this level, then, an objective, highly instrumented sequence of empirical investigations shows that the language learner has relevant information in advance about the inventory of possible phonetic elements (see Jakobson, 1941, for a seminal discussion in this context). It is interesting that in light of these findings from the acoustics laboratory, American psychology has felt entirely comfortable in adjusting to the fact of innate prespecification at this level. The curiosity is that findings of this sort seem not at all to suggest to many psychologists that higher-level language units may be prespecified in the same or a related sense. However, further findings from language learning suggest that the child has more in his bag of tricks than the phones, as learning begins.

The Unit "Word"

The learner must recover words, word classes, and phrases from their encoding in the wave form. Distributional properties of the phonetic sequences are inadequate bases for these further discoveries, for the phonetic sequences woefully underdetermine the identification of words (is it *an adult* or *a nuhdult*?), word classes (is *yellow* a noun, verb, or adjective?), and phrase boundaries (e.g., *I saw a man eating fish*). Our question, then, is whether there are units—above and beyond the phonetic distinctive features—that physically are manifest in the wave form and operative in the child's induction of language structure.

In an earlier discussion we claimed that the child selects the word unit and identifies it as the linguistic repository of simple concepts. But how does the child extract this linguistic unit from the utterance-context in which it is embedded? The child is rarely offered single words, so this problem is real. Slobin (1973) rightly conjectured that there must be some "acoustically salient" and "isolable" property of words that children can discover prelinguistically, else these claims about word and concept learning beg the question that is at issue. Here, we organize the known facts about the emergence of speech in a way we believe bears on this problem. We will try to demonstrate that there *is* an acoustically salient property well correlated with the linguistic unit *word*. This property, we argue, is an abstract characterization of the sound wave whose surface manifestation in English and other stress–accent languages is the *stressed syllable*. And we will try to show that early speech is consistent with our claim that the child is especially sensitive to this feature of the incoming property of the wave forms.[6]

The most striking fact about the English speaker's first utterances is that the little "functor" words are approximately absent; hence, the speech sounds "telegraphic" (Brown & Bellugi, 1964). To this extent, the child's early linguistic behavior again deviates systematically from the environmental model. Children have their own ideas about the forms, just as they have their own ideas about the meanings. It is particularly interesting that youngsters learning Russian omit the inflectional affixes that are the main device for marking the thematic roles in that language, adopting instead a word order strategy that has poor support in the input data (i.e., the speech of their Russian mothers; see Slobin, 1966). In light of this finding, it is impossible to suppose that the functors are omitted on the grounds that they are not semantically important. Surely it is important to distinguish between the do-er and the done-to and, as just stated, the youngest Russian learners do make this distinction, but by means of word ordering, not inflections. Given these findings, it is not surprising that some investigators have supposed that word order is easy and inflection is hard for the youngest learners. That is to say, they have described these findings as facts about earliest *syntax* (see, e.g., Feldman et al., 1978). Note, however, that it is not easy to bring this syntactic claim to bear on all the little words that are missing from earliest speech. The personal pronouns, the prepositions, the specifiers, are approximately as absent as the inflectionally functioning auxiliaries (e.g., *will*) and affixes (e.g., *-ed*). A bias toward word ordering rather than inflection does not describe these facts very satisfactorily. But if we claim instead that *the unstressed items* are what are missing, we approximate the real facts about early speech very well (see Kean, 1977, for a related hypothesis and the argument that it is relevant to describing aphasic speech).

One immediate objection to this proposed generalization is that, if the child learner is differentially sensitive to stress in the speech signal, he should not be able to tell—for a language such as English—the difference between an un-

---

[6]The specific acoustic correlates of primary stress in English include longer duration, higher fundamental frequency, and intensity (see Lehiste, 1970, for general discussion and the evidence from analysis of the speech wave and its perception). For the following argument to hold, it would be necessary to show that the same, or definably analogous, acoustic properties are available and exploited to mark phrase boundaries in the nonstress-accent languages, and that these are the properties reproduced in early child utterances. This prediction seems plausible enough, e.g., features such as rhythmicity and prepausal lengthening seem to be universal properties of speech, differing only in the details of how they map onto the phrasal units.

stressed morpheme and the unstressed syllables of monomorphemic words. However, there is good evidence, widely known but rarely mentioned, that young speakers cannot make this distinction very well. For example, it is striking that words are often first pronounced as their stressed syllables, e.g., "raff" for *giraffe* and "e-fant" for *elephant*. Moreover, when the unstressed syllables begin to be uttered, it is often in undifferentiated form (as the syllable schwa, /ə/, for all instances), for example "əportcard" for *report card,* "tape-ə-cor-də" for *tape recorder.*[7] Particularly interesting at this stage is the frequent misanalysis of clitic pronouns as the unstressed syllables of preceding words, e.g., "read-it" and "have-it," yielding such utterances as "Readit ə book, Mommie?" and "Have-it ə cookie." These properties of earliest speech suggest that the child analyzes stressed syllables reasonably well, but is less successful in rendering the unstressed syllables and in segmenting the wave form into words on this basis (see also Blasdell & Jensen, 1970, who have shown that young children are better at repeating stressed syllables than unstressed syllables in words presented for imitation; Spring & Dale, 1977, who demonstrated that young infants can discriminate the acoustic correlates of stress location in di-syllables; and Fernald, 1982, 1983, who has shown that infants prefer to listen to speech with the exaggerated prosodic properties of "motherese" even when this speech is filtered to remove all of its segmental content).

Later stages of speech development lend weight to the same generalization. Bellugi (1967) has demonstrated that when the elements of the English verbal auxiliary make their first appearance in children's speech, the items are in their full, rather than their contracted, form—e.g., "I will go" rather than "I'll go"—for some developmental time. This is in contrast to the input corpus (mothers' speech) in which, as Bellugi has shown, these items are contracted in the overwhelming majority (over 90%) of instances. Evidently, the contracted version of a word fails to be the acoustically salient element the child requires, if we take *stressed syllable* to be the appropriate specification of "salience."

Further evidence comes from investigations of input effects on learning. Newport, Gleitman, and Gleitman (1977) provided correlational evidence that the rate of learning of English verbal auxiliary elements is accelerated for children whose mothers used them proportionally most often in the noncontractable, stressed, sentence-initial position (by asking many yes/no questions, such as "Will you pick up the blocks?"). In contrast, the sheer frequency of auxiliary use (ignoring stress and position) is uncorrelated with learning rate. These results are very reliable. The correlations between yes/no questions and the child's rate

---

[7]These phenomena have not been closely studied, to our knowledge, doubtless because their theoretical interest has not been very clear. Hence, we can give no quantitative evidence about how often errors of this kind occur, though surely they are not rare. Anecdotal evidence favoring the view that the unstressed items are at first undifferentiated is quite persuasive. For example, the child of our acquaintance who said "əportcard" at an early stage of development said "Can we go to grandma's repartment house?" just as she switched to "report card."

of auxiliary growth are in the range of .80 even after partialing to correct for baseline differences among the children studied (see Furrow, Nelson, & Benedict, 1979, for a replication of this effect; and Gleitman, Newport, & Gleitman, 1984, for further discussion). It is reasonable to hypothesize either that initial position favors learning (a prediction that would follow from any theory of learning in which memory is a factor) or that the noncontracted, stressed form favors learning. We consider it likely that both these properties are relevant to the observed learning effects.

Intriguing new evidence for the same generalization comes from Slobin (1982), who has studied comprehension among 2- to 4-year-old learners of English, Italian, Serbo-Croatian, and Turkish. The Turkish children comprehended Turkish inflectional cues to thematic roles earlier in life than the learners of Serbo-Croatian comprehended Serbo-Croatian inflectional cues to thematic roles. This is exactly the prediction we would have to make on the supposition that stressed items are available earlier in development than are unstressed items: According to Slobin, the relevant inflectional items in Turkish are a full syllable long, are stressed, do not deform the surrounding words phonetically, and do not contract or cliticize. In Kean's (1979) terms, these items are phonologically *open class*. The late-comprehended Serbo-Croatian inflectional items are subsyllabic, stressless, and phonetically deformed by adjacent material (phonologically *closed class*). In sum, these two languages differ according to whether the inflectional cues to the thematic roles are encoded onto isolable stressed syllables, or not. This distinction predicts the differences in learning rate.

In the other two languages investigated by Slobin, English and Italian, the thematic roles are cued primarily by word order, not inflection. Thus, as with Turkish, they do not require the young learner to notice stressless grammatical items in order to recover the relational roles. Accordingly, there are no main-effect differences in the rate of the relevant comprehension development between Turkish and these two other languages. Only Serbo-Croatian stands apart, showing a clear delay at each point in development.

Our position is that a single principle, the advantage of stressed materials over unstressed materials, accounts for Slobin's main finding: The one language among the four investigated that requires attention to stressless materials for recovering thematic roles is the one for which comprehension is delayed. Inflection itself poses no severe problem for the learner when it is encoded on stressed materials, as in Turkish, nor does sequence pose a severe problem under the same circumstances. Recent evidence from the acquisition of Quiche Mayan (Pye, 1983) is particularly informative. For many verbs in certain syntactic environments, this language stresses inflectional suffixes, while the verb root is unstressed. Young learners often pronounce only one of these two syllables; that is, they are forced to make the choice between the semantically salient root and the perceptually salient suffix. They very consistently choose perceptual saliency, pronouncing the inflection and omitting the root. In fact, morpheme bound-ary and syllable boundary often do not coincide in this language, providing a good testing ground for what it is the child is actually picking up and reproducing of the verb that he or she hears. According to Pye, these children reproduce the syllable unit rather than the morpheme unit: Often, they pronounce the whole syllable consisting of the final consonant of the unstressed verb root and the whole terminus, the inflectional suffix.

Summarizing, the cross-linguistic evidence strongly supports the view that the unit *stressed syllable* is highly salient perceptually and organizes early speech. Stressed verb roots are pronounced early (English, Turkish, Italian, and Serbo-Croatian) and unstressed verb roots are often omitted (Mayan); symmetrically, stressed inflections are pronounced early (Turkish, Mayan) and unstressed in-flections are often omitted (English, Serbo-Croatian). Insofar as attention to unstressed inflections is crucial to recovering the argument structure, the child will show some delay in comprehension (Serbo-Croatian). Insofar as the pronun-ciation of the verb roots is obviously necessary to the adult's comprehension of the child's message, child messages in those languages that contain unstressed roots will be hard to understand (Mayan, as noted by Pye, 1983).[8]

The generalizations we have been considering are perforce limited to the stress–accent languages. As Chomsky has pointed out (see Section 1), the trick is not to make the learning of some languages easy to describe, if the cost is rendering the learning of others forever mysterious. That is, something more abstract than the notion *stress* in the sound wave may be required to account for

---

[8]Notice that Mayan is the only one of the languages just discussed that does not usually confound inflection with stress. This confound is what makes the extraction of the currect learning variables so difficult. The same confound between inflectional items and unstressed items complicates interpreta-tion of the many studies of related distinctions in adult performance. Thus there is controversy as to whether the phonological or syntactic properties of the closed class account for their different patterning in various tasks with various populations. For example, Kean (1979) has explained certain speech and comprehension impairments in Broca's aphasics on the phonological hypothesis, while Marin, Saffran, and Schwartz (1976) emphasize the syntactic distinctiveness of the items these aphasics cannot manage. Current evidence, for the various task domains, is insufficient to give overwhelming support to one or the other hypothesis, though only the phonological hypothesis can serve as part of the explanation—rather than mere description—of language learning. But for the learning hypothesis to do work, it must be that the acoustic facts correlate with the syntactic facts to be learned, and so either or both properties could account for distinctive adult performance with open and closed class. Whatever the correct analysis, it has recently become clear that the open-class/closed-class distinction has highly reliable effects in a broad range of adult linguistic perfor-mances. For example, speech errors differ for the two classes (Fromkin, 1973; Garrett, 1975); lexical access differs for the two in normals but not in Broca's aphasics (Bradley, Garrett, & Zurif, 1979); intrasentential code-switching constrains the two classes distinctively (Joshi, 1983); and forgetting differs in language death (Dorian, 1978). Reading acquisition also differs for the two classes (Labov, 1970; Rozin & Gleitman, 1977), as does the historical development of writing systems (Gleitman & Rozin, 1977) and the reliability and patterning of judgments of anomaly and paraphrase (Gleitman & Gleitman, 1979).

this aspect of learning, given the real diversity among the natural languages (see fn. 6 to this chapter). The only well studied case we know of, apart from stress–accent languages, are studies of ASL by Newport and her colleagues (Newport & Ashbrook, 1977; Newport, 1981, 1982). We have noted that learners of ASL first treat each sequentially produced sign as an unanalyzed whole, a "frozen form." The extraction of derivational and inflectional substructures within these signs appears only in later developmental steps (see also Klima and Bellugi, 1979). The question is how to describe the physical, visually observable, manifestation called a separable *sign*.

The linguistic analyses by this group seem to us to suggest physically based distinctions between the frozen-form morphological means of ASL (e.g., handshapes) and the inflectionally and derivationally functioning morphology (e.g., certain movement types that modulate form and meaning). The latter, specially formed and specially functioning properties of manual language, are acquired later. That is to say, there seems to be evidence here for "visually salient," "isolable" properties of visible signs that are analogous to the "acoustically salient" isolable properties of speech signals. Whether there is a substantive principle of similarity underlying this analogy remains, of course, a matter for further investigation.

Whatever the ultimate description of the child's predispositions toward linguistic forms, when framed broadly enough to encompass the real languages and narrowly enough to tame induction so that language can be learned, it will almost certainly show that the child does not approach the speech wave or the visible stream of sign like an objective physicist or structural linguist. To the extent that the child must learn language by discovering the distributional properties of the input corpus (as Bloomfield stipulated), the inductive machinery appears to be constrained by the way the organism represents the materials on which induction operates (as Chomsky stipulated). In addition to discrete, featural descriptions at the phonetic level, we have argued that the child has at his or her disposal another analysis of the input. For certain well-studied languages, a physical distinction between stress and nonstress is an interim characterization. For ASL, there seems to be a related physical distinction. Appropriate characterization of the unit awaits investigation of the acquisition of nonstress–accent languages.

Sequence

We have so far determined that the child is sensitive, from earliest developmental moments, to (1) phonetic segments and (2) stressed syllables. There is clear evidence, again from early points in language learning, that the child is sensitive to the ordering both of the phonetic segments and of the stressed syllables. For the phonetic segments, it is enough to say that children seem to know *tap* from *pat* from *apt*. Errors that can be characterized as phone-order confusions are rare (though not altogether absent, e.g., transpositions such as "pǝ-sketti" for *spaghetti*). There is also very good evidence that sensitivity to the order of words in sentences emerges early.

During the period when the unstressed syllables are mostly missing and ill-analyzed, the child starts uttering more than one word at a time. There is massive evidence that at this point the words are sequenced in the rudimentary sentence. To be sure, the child's observance of ordering constraints are less exact than the adult's; moreover, there is controversy about the nature of the units so sequenced. That is, these might be grammatical units such as *subject*, thematic units such as *agent*, discourse units such as *topic*, or *old information*: All of these postulated units make much the same predictions about which noun-phrase (NP) the child will utter first, and which second, in declarative sentences. This overlap, taken together with the fact of the child's inexactness in honoring these ordering constraints, makes it difficult to identify the psychologically functioning units among these choices (see Section 3). But whatever their correct description, these units are sequenced fairly reliably from the first two-word utterances (for analyses of English, see, e.g., Bloom, 1970; Bowerman, 1973; Brown, 1973). As we have seen, sequencing is common even where the data base provides little support for it, as in the Russian cases reported by Slobin. Most remarkably, the sequencing of signs according to their thematic roles arises without any input support among the deaf isolates studied by Goldin-Meadow and her colleagues.

Given these strong and stable findings, it is surprising that some authors, particularly Slobin (1982), seek to discount sequential ordering in children's speech as theoretically uninteresting. Slobin adopts this stance because of his cross-linguistic finding that competence with inflection precedes competence with word order in certain comprehension tasks (encoding of the thematic roles in Turkish seems to be understood earlier than it is for English). However, as Slobin also acknowledges, attention to word order is clear from the earliest moments in speech—an inconvenient fact for the developmental generalization "inflection first, word order second." We have argued that the facts about what comes first, inflection or word order, are artifacts of phonological properties of the particular languages studied (see also Gleitman & Wanner, 1982): Unstressed material is the hardest to learn; hence, if the inflectional resources of a language are unstressed, they will appear relatively late in the child's speech; if they are stressed, they appear earlier. If we are correct, there seems little reason to take comprehension performances more seriously than speech performances—or the reverse—as indicants of the child's language organization. Findings in both domains are adequately handled by acknowledging that the child is first sensitive to stressed syllables, interpreted as words, and to orderings of these.

Nonetheless, it is important to note that a characterization of the child's word order is not really simple with respect to the adult's word order (the real utterances the learner hears from his caretakers). Only a small proportion of the sentences a child hears, in English, are subject first, because well over half the input sentences are questions and imperatives (Newport, 1977). Moreover, there is suggestive evidence that children do not reproduce the subject-first property of the heard language; rather, they may produce something of their own, perhaps agent first (see Section 3). We have already noted that the noncanonical position of the verbal auxiliary (stressed initial position, as in "Could you jump to the moon?") favors the *learning* of these auxiliaries. Still, the child first *utters* auxiliaries in declarative sentences, where they appear medially ("I could jump to the moon"). The learner, then, seems biased toward a notion of canonical word order, a notion that can arise only very abstractly from properties of the input. This is most striking for instances in which the input language *demands* noncanonical order for certain functions: Young English speakers sometimes express questions by intonation ("I could jump to the moon?") but do not invert the order of subject and auxiliary; this phenomenon is very frequent for wh-questions ("Where I could jump?"), although the inversion appears in just about every yes/no and wh-question that children hear (see Slobin & Bever, 1982, for a detailed discussion of the canonical form bias in young learners).

In summary, we must believe that the child learner is sensitive to sequence, for she orders the words in her utterances from the time there are two words to order, and the orderings she chooses conform in general to canonical or preferred orderings in the language to which she is being exposed. But learners preserve this canonical ordering even if it is not present in the input speech (as in English interrogatives); or if the ordering of the input speech is only a nonsyntactic statistical preference (as in Russian); or if there is no input at all (as in the home sign of the deaf isolates studied by Feldman et al., 1978). Hence, though sequence is a property of the wave form that the learner clearly notes and exploits, this property does not explain the character of what is learned.

The Unstressed Subcomponent of the Lexicon

As we will see in the discussion of inductive processes in language learning, the distinction between open and closed class may play a role in the child's discovery of linguistic structure. This is because, though this distinction may be discovered through a physical property (i.e., stress, in the languages we have discussed), it is well correlated with syntactic analyses that the child will have to recognize in order to recover the structure of sentences. We have seen that the closed class is acquired late. The pattern of development within this class is also distinctive. For example, Brown (1973) has shown that the closed class is learned in an item-by-item fashion over a lengthy developmental period, and in a very regular sequence (for instance, *-ing* is almost always learned before *-ed*). Moreover, learning rate is dependent on properties of the input corpus much more clearly for closed class than for open class (Landau & Gleitman, 1984; Newport et al., 1977). In certain cases of linguistic isolation, the closed class may not emerge (Bickerton, 1975; Feldman et al., 1978; Goldin-Meadow, 1982; Newport & Supalla, 1980).

Slobin (1973, 1977, 1982), citing evidence from language learning, language change, and creolization processes, has conjectured that the closed class arises through the fluent user's need to be quick and efficient in language use. In homely terms, the phonological squeezing of closed class items (e.g., in English, the fact that *will* becomes *'ll* and *him* becomes *'əm*) may be an inevitable concomitant of rapid, fluent communication among linguistic experts. There is good evidence in favor of this hypothesis: The phonologically short, stressless forms of closed-class items make their appearance at late stages of acquisition, in the presence of increasing fluency. An independently interesting fact is that these distinctive properties of the closed class are fully achieved only as they are filtered through the learning process by children who are native speakers. Learning a language later in life, even in the presence of adequate fluency and habitual use, does not yield these same properties (Bickerton, 1975; Newport, 1982).

One sample case has been discussed by Sankoff & Laberge (1973). They have made extensive studies of Tok Pisin, an English-based pidgin developed and acquired by linguistically heterogeneous adults in Papua New Guinea. They have shown that, in its historically earliest forms, this language had only impoverished inflectional resources. Notions such as *future* were expressed by optional, sentence-initial adverbs (such as *baimbai,* from the English *by and by*). In a second stage of evolution—a stage at which the learners were still adults acquiring Tok Pisin as a second language—this item moved into the verb-phrase (VP) and became syntactically obligatory as the marker of the future tense. In fluent usage, the item is often shortened to *bai,* thus erasing the residue of its original semantic content. This seems to show that adults are quite capable of expanding the syntactic resources of their language, as it comes into broad use as the ordinary means of communication. But at this point the new inflectionally functioning item (either *baimbai* or *bai*) is still a word with regular stress, not a clitic; that is, it is phonologically open class, even though it performs a syntactic role—tense marking—that is often reserved for the closed class in fully elaborated languages.

Recently, the use of Tok Pisin has become so general that children are acquiring it as their native language. However, the language they are hearing has little closed-class morphology, so there is little for them to omit in the so-called telegraphic stage; in short, as Bickerton has argued, pidgins share interesting properties with early child speech. These learners, approximately in the period from 5 to 8 years of age, make a further move: *Baimbai* or *bai* is shortened and destressed to /bə/, becoming an obligatory verb prefix. This is an intriguing suggestion that, at a late stage of the learning process, the (phonological) closed class makes its appearance even though it is absent from the input language (see also concordant findings from Bickerton for Hawaiian creoles).

Newport (1982) has provided related evidence from the acquisition of ASL. Very often ASL is learned relatively late in life, either because it is not used by the deaf child's hearing parents (in which case ASL may still be the learner's first language, though exposure begins only when she comes into contact with other deaf individuals) or because deafness is acquired (in which case ASL is acquired as a second language). Newport has demonstrated that learners first exposed to

ASL after the age of about 7 years fail to acquire fully the inflectionally and derivationally functioning substructure of the signs (the gestural equivalents of the closed class). Again, the product of late learning is much like the utterances of native speakers at first stages.

In sum, young learners are biased to notice phonetic features, stressed syllables, and the sequences in which these are ordered. Learning a language later in life seems to show sensitivity to these same properties of the wave form. Unlike adults, children in the later stages of language acquisition become sensitive to the unstressed subcomponent of the language. At the limit (i.e., in the absence of such features in the speech heard), children can add to the stock of language resources by inventing the closed class.

The Unit "Phrase"

If we are right, the stressed syllable stands out from the rest of the wave form approximately as figure stands out from ground in the child's innate visual analysis of space (cf., Spelke, 1982). Although the stressed syllable is by no means equivalent to the mature word form, the evidence strongly suggests that its acoustic correlates (i.e., fundamental frequency, intensity, and duration) are available to the child as a bootstrap into the morphological scheme of the language. Evidence from recent studies of adult speech production and perception shows that potential bootstraps exist in the wave form for other linguistic units. For example, speech timing is affected by major syntactic boundaries, by deletion sites, and by lexical category assignment (cf., Klatt, 1975, 1976; Nakatani & Dukes, 1977; Nakatani & Schaffer, 1978; Sorensen, Cooper, & Paccia, 1978; Streeter, 1978; and many other sources). Whether learners exploit these additional acoustic cues is an open question, but recent work in infant speech perception makes this appear likely (for an informative study, see Fernald & Simon, 1984). We discuss here some ingenious advice, from older children, that suggests a continuing reliance on prosodic cues for phrasal classification.

Read and Schreiber (1982) taught 7-year-olds to play a game in which the children must listen to a sentence and then repeat some portion of it that corresponds to one of its major constituents. Children are remarkably successful at this task, learning to pick out such constituents as surface subject NP with impressive accuracy. However, they show one curious weakness: If the subject NP is only a single word (e.g., a pronoun or a generic nominal), children are regularly unable to disentangle it from the rest of the sentence. Read and Schreiber track this clue to its source, showing that, of all the many properties of single word NP's, it seems to be their intonational contour (or lack of one) that accounts for the difficulty that children experience. Unlike longer NP's, single word phrases are not rendered with falling fundamental frequency and lengthened final vowel at the close of the phrase. It is this phonological merging of the single word NP with the following VP that throws the children for a loop. Apparently phrase boundaries are largely a matter of intonation for these children. They do not appear to be able to locate these boundaries by syntax alone.

It would be perilous to reason in a straight line from 7-year-olds to 1-year olds. Simply because a second-grader shows heavy reliance upon the intonational correlates of phrases, it does not necessarily follow that he or she began learning phrases as an infant through their intonational correlates. Neither do the studies of infant sensitivity to these properties settle the case for whether these perceptions play a causal role in the discovery of syntax. Bever (1970) has argued that the mastery of an abstract syntactic rule can precede the development of heuristic perceptual strategies that come to replace the rule in practice, because they are easier to apply in the rapid-fire business of understanding or producing speech. It is not impossible that phrase-structure learning conforms to Bever's developmental sequence. Read and Schreiber's seven-year-olds may have learned the syntactic structure of phrases first and only then have come to appreciate the intonational correlates of phrases—and even if, as is likely, the discrimination of intonation patterns came well before. It is also possible that Read and Schreiber's judgmental task captures metalinguistic knowledge, or "accessible" knowledge that is partly at variance with linguistic knowledge (Gleitman & Gleitman, 1979). But it is also possible that the seven-year-old's heavy reliance on intonation is a remnant of a dependency formed at the earliest stages of acquisition. If this is the case, it would have important consequences for the way we think about the acquisition of syntax. For, as we argue later, an infant who is innately biased to treat intonationally circumscribed utterance segments as potential syntactic constituents would be at considerable advantage in learning the syntactic rules of his or her language.

Before closing, it is worth mentioning one more (indirect) source of evidence that strengthens the case for the prosodic guidance of syntax acquisition. Morgan and Newport (1981) have shown in an artificial language learning task that different physical cues to phrase grouping, such as intonation contour (when "sentences" from the language are presented orally) or physical closeness of within-phrase items (when sentences are presented visually) are sufficient for an adult subject to induce rather complex phrase-structure grammars, whose elements are nonsense phrases comprised of nonsense syllables. When sentences are presented without these phrasal cues (and without alternative semantic cues to the phrases), adults generally fail to learn the language. Again, this is no guarantee that infants are equally disposed to exploit intonational clues. But the Morgan and Newport result adds one more reasonable basis for entertaining this possibility.

Motherese: Saying it Obviously

We have expressed considerable caution about how caretakers could make special adjustments to render "meanings" easier for children to acquire. This is largely because meanings are not the sort of things that are out there in the world, available to be emphasized to one who (presumably) is not in control of the linguistic–semantic facts of the matter in advance. Barring language knowledge itself, there is no obvious way to remove the multiple possibilities of 'animalness' or 'Felixness' from cat-situations. However, we have just implicitly accepted an opposing position about the role caretakers may well play in revealing the language *forms* to their infants, for the sounds of speech *are* out there in the world, and are, in principle, available for exaggeration (of the "important" properties) and suppression (of the less important properties) so as to help the novice learn. Briefly, we now make this hypothesis more explicit.

As Newport and her colleagues (1977) have shown (see pp. 228–231 of the current chapter for further discussion), it is difficult in the extreme to show specific syntactic and semantic adjustments that mothers make, or to show effects on acquisition predicted by those adjustments that seem relatively stable (e.g., the relative shortness of maternal utterances, or their very heavy use of the imperative structure). The few adjustments that seem to work to aid the learner are largely restricted to rate-effects on closed class acquisition, e.g., of the English verbal auxiliary. In contrast, it is easy to point to universal properties that are specific to "motherese," if attention is restricted to prosody. These have been noted by many investigators, but have been systematically investigated by Fernald and her collaborators (Fernald, 1983), who have shown that motherese is special in having higher pitch, wider pitch excursions, shorter utterances, and longer pauses than speech between adults. These prosodic adjustments occur in all language communities that have been studied and, according to Fernald, they may represent a complementary adaptation by mother and child. Adapting remarks from Darwin, Fernald holds that maternal vocalizations are "sweet to the ears of the species," and so facilitate the mother–infant interaction. Specifically, Fernald and other investigators we have cited have demonstrated that infants are sensitive to the prosodic features characteristic of motherese, and prefer hearing motherese to hearing adult-to-adult speech. As stated earlier, such demonstrations do not constitute a knockdown causal argument, but they do lend persuasiveness to the view that prosodic cues help in the discovery of syntactic form. As we will now argue, the wise child should accept such available bootstraps with some alacrity, for the acquisition of syntax is no mean trick. In short, because help is clearly available in the sound wave, the best guess is that the learner is prepared to recruit it.

THE PROJECTION PROBLEM: PAIRING THE MEANINGS AND THE FORMS

In the preceding discussion, we have summarized the information available about the state of the child requisite to language learning; namely, some means for representing input speech signals and some means for representing the real-world context that co-occurs with the signals. We have asserted that input signals are interpreted as ordered phonetic strings bracketed by stress into words and bracketed by intonation into phrases. Acknowledging that some input may be physically too imperfect or indistinct to allow these analyses, we took the findings from the maternal speech literature to suggest that this problem is not greatly damaging to the position; that is, the mother's speech is generally slow, intonationally exaggerated, and almost always grammatical. As for the meaning representations, we have stated that information about these is currently orders of magnitude more fragmentary. The literature does suggest that the child assumes that words represent concepts and function as the markers of predicates and thematic roles in a propositional structure, carried by the sentence. What the concepts are and just how the sentence heard relates to a particular proposition (the cat-on-mat/mat-under-cat problem) is unknown, but we interpreted the maternal speech literature to suggest a caretaker–child conspiracy designed to respond to these problems. Just as for the speech signals, we assume that the child will have to filter out, as unusable data, those utterances whose interpretation is particularly ambiguous or murky. Granting that almost everything is unresolved here, all parties seem to agree that the preconditions for learning are that the child be able to interpret and represent the sound wave to himself in linguistically relevant ways, and also interpret and represent real-world events to himself in linguistically relevant ways. Having granted these prerequisites, we now raise the question: How does a child learn a language? That is, how does the child project from these data a general system that pairs each possible meaning with each possible form?

Directions for an answer proposed by contributors to the field differ radically. Not only do investigators disagree, they do not even seem to be addressing the same topics. Some investigators (e.g., Braine & Hardy, 1982; Schlesinger, 1971) seek to explain how the child connects semantic-relational (thematic) roles to positions in surface strings. Other investigators (e.g., Maratsos & Chalkley, 1980) ask how the child discovers such syntactic categories as noun and verb. Still others (e.g., Roeper, 1982; Wexler & Culicover, 1980) ask how an abstract learning device might acquire transformational rules. Partly, it is possible to understand all these undertakings as attempts to resolve different subparts of the syntax acquisition question. But we believe that in large part the disparity of topics investigated arises from a much deeper disagreement among these investigators about the complexity of the mapping between form and meaning. Believing this mapping to be essentially simple, some authors propose that it can be learned as a direct projection from thematic roles to the surface string. Others view the relation between form and meaning as more complex, but still believe that it can be learned by a direct projection, albeit in quite the opposite direction: from form to meaning. Still other theorists have held that no such direct projection is possible. For them, the relation between form and meaning is so complex that it must be learned through the mediation of another level of representation.

As a result of their differing beliefs about the complexity of the mapping between sound and meaning, child language investigators have offered an embarrassing variety of hypotheses about what is to be learned: case grammar, constituent structure grammar, and transformational (or lexical-functional) grammar, among others. We take up these hypotheses in turn, concentrating discussion on some current major proponents of each view. In each case, the authors are asking about the discovery of sentence structure—the main battleground of linguistic and psycholinguistic theorizing over the last two decades.

Learning a Case Grammar

In 1966, McNeill put forward the claim that children essentially "talk deep structure" at earliest developmental moments. That is, the ordering of words looks much like the left-to-right sequence of terminal nodes in deep-structure descriptions of the Chomsky (1965) variety. The retort from developmental psycholinguists (e.g., Bowerman, 1973; Braine & Hardy, 1982; Schlesinger, 1971) has been that the child's categories are semantic-relational ones, e.g., *theme, source, goal,* or *agent, instrument, patient* (depending on the particular account). It is these categories that explain the patterning of young children's speech, rather than categories such as *subject noun-phrase.*

Although this view seems plausible, the evidence in its favor is not overwhelming. One problem has to do with the analysis itself. It is not easy to define "semantic roles" nor to assign such roles to the nominals in child sentences, so as to determine whether these categories actually organize the facts about early grammars (see Braine, 1976, for a discussion of these issues). As Wexler & Culicover (1980) have pointed out, the lists of children's productions, so analyzed, themselves seem to contain counterexamples, if the definitions of the semantic roles are accepted literally. For instance, among the examples Schlesinger (1971) gives of agent + action constructions is the child utterance "Mail come"; *mail* cannot be an agent according to accepted definitions for it is not the *animate instigator* of an action. Another difficulty is that the semantic-relational analyses of children's speech may be artifacts of another variable. For a large class of English action verbs of special interest to toddlers, the subject is the agent. If the tots are really biased to use action verbs, for cognitive and motivational reasons, then a coding of the child utterances will pretty well identify subjects with agents. But, especially in light of the occasional counterexamples, it does not follow that the children believe *in principle* that subjects must be agents. A final problem with these analyses is their failure to cover the full range of phenomena observed early in the acquisition period. Young children do acquire certain linguistic subsystems that are known not to be semantically organized. For example, in the earliest learning period, German children acquire gender systems in which *masculine, feminine,* and *neuter* as conceptual categories map only very inexactly onto inflectional categories; similar effects have been reported for young Hebrew speakers (Levy, 1980, 1983; Maratsos & Chalkley, 1980).

Despite all these provisos, there is some intuitive appeal and correlational evidence supporting the semantics-based categorial view. Our question is how this supposition helps to explain language learning. It is our impression that many investigators believe they are making this problem easier by pointing to these functional semantic categories as the ones that operate in early child speech, and by supposing that these categories map onto the child's word orderings or inflectional markings in a *simple* and *direct* way. But to the extent that the child really makes these suppositions of simplicity in the mapping of form to meaning, they can only complicate the problem of learning a language. The reason is that the supposition is false for any adult language. And the reason for *that* (among many others) is that so many subtle semantic dimensions are encoded syntactically that it is literally impossible to find a single linearization for them all.

One outcome of this complexity is that the position of semantically definable propositional components (thematic roles) varies with the predicate. John's role, but not his sentential position, differs in *John is easy to please* and *John is eager to please,* as well as in *John sold a book to Mary* (where he is *source*) and *John bought a book from Mary* (where he is *goal*). John's sentential position, but not his role, differs in *John received a tie from Mary* and *Mary gave a tie to John;* in *John collided with Bill* and *Bill collided with John;* and in *Bill resembles John, John resembles Bill,* and *Bill and John resemble each other.* These old saws are no less problematical for being old saws. Moreover, the phenomenon of constructional ambiguity is understandable only if we acknowledge the complexity of relations between surface and logical forms, e.g., *These missionaries are ready to eat* allows two interpretations of the relational role of the missionaries, at least if the listeners are cannibals. Note that none of these examples, nor all of them taken together, argue that the relation between phrase order and sentential meaning is arbitrary—maybe it is arbitrary and then again maybe it is not. The examples show only that these relations cannot be simple or direct; rather, they must be mediated through, and derived from, the interaction of a number of distinct linguistic organizing principles (for discussion, see Chomsky, 1981).

A related problem is that, beyond the puerile sayings of the first 3 years of life, it is difficult indeed to describe sentences as syntactically organized by known or even stateable semantic functions. To understand the descriptive problems here, consider the following first sentence from a recent Letter to the Editor appearing in *TV Guide:*

How Ann Salisbury can suggest that Pam Dauber's anger at not receiving her fair share of acclaim for *Mork and Mindy's* success derives from a fragile ego escapes me.

This writer, whatever his odd preoccupations, displays some formidible syntactic skills. It is hard to state that the first 27 words of his sentence represent some semantic role. What role would that be? Still, the 27 words function together as a linguistic unit; namely, the unit that determines that word 28 is to end with an *s*. Mature language knowledge involves, in addition to many semantically coherent classes, knowledge of such incoherent surface categories as noun-phrase, subject of the clause, and so forth, as the domains of these categorial contingencies. Moreover, if there is anything like an agent or do-er in the sentence above, it would have to be *me*. For its predicate (*escape*), this do-er is the second noun-phrase. But for predicates of quite similar meaning, the do-er is the first noun-phrase. That is, the sentence could be recast:

> I fail to understand how Ann Salisbury can suggest that Pam Dauber's anger at not receiving her fair share of acclaim for *Mork and Mindy's* success derives from a fragile ego.

The point, an old point, is that the grammatical notion *subject* (the NP immediately dominated by S, the NP that agrees in number with the verb) is only complexly related to semantic notions such as the agent or experiencer. Thus, if we claim the child is preprogrammed to construct a semantic representation to match each sentence that he hears, we have arrived only at the beginning of the language learning problem. The rest of the problem involves acquiring the system of rules that relates surface forms to their underlying meanings. Recapitulating, we do not deny the relations between form and meaning, for learner or for user. We only deny that these relations are simple and direct.

Many developmental psycholinguists reject the standard arguments we have just given. Certain investigators suppose, to the contrary, that a grammar based simply on semantic-relational categories can describe the facts about natural language, as used both by children and adults. Such *case grammars* are described below. Another group of investigators accept a more abstract grammar for adults, but postulate that case grammar is the appropriate description for young learners. This latter description implies that the language organization of the child undergoes reorganization sometime during the learning process. We discuss this position in the following section.

Case Grammar as the Outcome of Learning

Some investigators have proposed that case grammar (of roughly the type envisaged by Fillmore, 1968) is the appropriate "psychologically real" descriptive mechanism for human language. In Fillmore's proposal, the combining categories are semantic-relational. The surface configurations of sentences arise by rule from these semantic-categorial (deep case) representations; hence, no separate interpretive device would be required for the semantic interpretation of the syntactic configurations. It has sometimes gone unnoticed that Fillmore postulated a mediating system of rules operating on the initial case representations to account for the complex relations between surface orderings and semantic roles. To our knowledge, Fillmore never argued that these relations would be simple—that is, immediate. In addition, a number of questions have been raised about the descriptive adequacy of this approach. For instance, Chomsky (1972) has pointed out that the same case descriptions would apply to *pinch* and *pull*, accounting for the surface manifestations *John pulled Mary's nose* and *John pinched Mary's nose*. But then it is hard to explain why *John pinched Mary on the nose* is acceptable but *John pulled Mary on the nose* is anomalous, on the relevant reading. Chomsky's approach has been to state the syntactic-categorial facts and, separately, an interpretive system that carries the grammatical structures to the logical structures. Another approach is to list the case relations for each predicate, and surface specifications for that predicate, as lexical information (Bresnan, 1978, 1982). Yet another approach seeks to discover certain limited semantic domains or fields and study the syntactic encodings that apply to predicates within the domain but not to predicates that fall outside it (e.g., Gruber, 1968; Jackendoff, 1983; Landau & Gleitman, 1984). It remains for extensive further research to discover the extent to which semantic fields may constrain syntactic formats. However, in our opinion it is hopeless to suppose that there are a very few semantic-functional categories that transparently determine phrase orders and other syntactic properties. In general, although linguists disagree on *how* to state the relations between semantic roles and grammatical dependencies, none (to our knowledge) assert that these relations will turn out to be simple.

Nevertheless, many developmental psycholinguists have argued for such a view. For example, Braine & Hardy (1982) have conjectured that a sane creator who had the language learning problem in mind would write a case grammar that mapped semantic-relational roles onto surface structures in simple ways. We do not disagree with these directions to a good God, but we have just argued that the real deity has not been so benevolent (probably this is only one of many grounds for questioning the goodness of God). That is, the evidence of natural language design fails to suggest a transparent mapping between meanings and sentence forms. Rather, successful descriptions have had to postulate transformational rules, or lexical rules of a complexity just as great, or rules of like complexity that generate phrase-structure rules recursively, and so on. Though the complexity can be moved, then, from component to component of a grammar, it evidently cannot be *re*moved.

Case Grammar as a Stage in Learning: The Problem of Reorganization

We have argued that the relationships between form and meaning are not simple in adult grammars, i.e., that a very simple case grammar is inadequate to describe the final outcome of learning. Many investigators hold, however, that the youngest learners' grammars are organized by semantic categories, but later change (e.g., Bowerman, 1973). They reject the supposition that the child's early language is just like the adult's—but somewhat less complete—arguing instead that it is different in kind. These differences may be of units (e.g., agents but not subjects) and of combinatorial rules (e.g., serial orderings but not hierarchical arrangements or transformational rules).

The question, then, is whether language acquisition is a relatively seamless progression, characterizable in terms of the steady accretion of knowledge, or whether it involves qualitative changes in organization during the course of growth. Recent investigations seem to support the latter view: Although acquiring more information is surely a part of the learning process, the reorganization of previously acquired information is also a part of the story of language acquisition.

Some of the most interesting empirical investigations of such postulated reorganizations have been carried out by Bowerman (1982). Her primary method is to look at the "errors" a child makes during language learning. With a variety of contents and structures, she has shown that the child uses certain accepted language forms at early stages without error. For example, children will use such known lexical causatives as "I broke the window" (causative of "The window broke") or "I melted the wax." Presumably what is going on here is an item-by-item adoption of heard forms. At a later stage, errors suddenly make their appearance. The child says "Don't eat the baby—she's dirty" (presumably, this is an invented lexical causative corresponding to "The baby eats," i.e., the child means "Don't feed the baby"). As Bowerman argues, through the internal analysis of these late-appearing errors, the novel usages imply that the learner has seen through to a new organization that relates the items that were previously learned separately. This new organization allows the child to project beyond the heard instances in various ways, some of them wrong. (For a related and very interesting example, see Clark, 1982, and Clark & Clark, 1978, on the emergence of denominative verbs in speakers of English, French, and German. And see also Bever, 1970, for an interesting account of reorganization, based on the learning curves for comprehension of English passive voice constructions).

Apparently, there is a significant reorganization of knowledge during the learning period. At the extreme, this makes it reasonable to describe "stages" of language learning that are quite distinct from each other. In particular, an early stage of learning may be well characterized as a simple case grammar. However, if the concept of reorganization is adopted in the language acquisition theory, a new question immediately arises: What causes the child to reorganize his or her grammar—especially to reorganize it in a way that increases the abstractness of the relations between forms and meanings?

One kind of answer is strictly maturational: There may be relevant biological changes in the learner that cause her to revist old linguistic evidence and interpret it differently. Put another way, it could be that there is a succession of learners, each of whom organizes the linguistic data as befits her current mental state. If these learners are really quite separate—if they literally dismantle the old system and substitute a new one—then it becomes quite reasonable to do as many developmental psycholinguists have done: write a (case) grammar for the 2-year-old, and assume no responsibility for that description as a basis for describing the 3-year-old (for discussion, see Gleitman, 1981). But notice that this is a kind of metamorphosis, or tadpole-to-frog, hypothesis. It is not easy to defend, for there is no evidence that we know of to suggest that old principles and categories are literally discarded during the learning period.

The opposing view is that language learning is continuous. One version of this position is that reorganization is motivated by a data-driven process. The learner is presumed first to acquire information about the language essentially one piece at a time, e.g., generalizations that are applicable only to one or a few verbs or nouns (Bowerman, 1982; Braine, 1976). This relatively unorganized method eventually leads to an unmanageable clutter of facts. Organization into general rule systems will both simplify the storage of information and, sometimes, vastly increase the generative capacity of the system.

Another explanation of apparent reorganization has to do with the modular nature of the language system itself. It is possible that language consists of a number of distinct processes and principles that are at least partly autonomous (Chomsky, 1981). The acquisition of some of these modules may be logically contingent on the acquisition of others. If this is the correct view, then the child's usage may look radically different from an adult's, while in reality the underlying knowledge is of a proper subpart of the adult language. For example, suppose that the learner has control of the thematic-role system and some version of a phrase-structure hierarchy (or even a linearization of phrases), but lacks knowledge of a syntactic module that in the adult language stands between these and mediates their relations. By default, the learner may map one-to-one between the modules that he currently controls.

Summary

We have argued against the view that semantic roles in a language map one-to-one onto syntactic configurations. Nonetheless, case grammar may be a useful device for describing the linguistic organization of very young learners. Even if so, as usually stated this hypothesis is at best a data summary for the speech of the youngest learners, giving no hint as to how learning could progress toward the real complexities of the adult language. We have suggested two main ways out of this pickle. The first is biological: The 2-year-old molts linguistically and becomes a 3-year-old, discarding virtually all principles of the prior system. The second also acknowledges that the character of early and late stages of acquisition look very different from each other, but holds that the learning process is at bottom continuous. In one variant, the learner is motivated by the accumulation of information: Groaning under the burden of storing myriad separate facts, he or she tries some higher-order generalizations that subsume more instances. In another variant, the child maintains the original system essentially without change, but adds semiautonomous new modules at the interface between old ones, radically changing the linguistic outcomes at the surface.

PC—M

Learning a Bloomfieldian Grammar

The case grammar approach to language learning takes as certain the child's mastery of a small set of semantic distinctions (agent–patient, possessor–possessed, etc.) and attempts to build the rest of syntax acquisition on this base. In contrast, the neo-Bloomfieldian position, to the extent that one exists, builds in an altogether different direction and begins with an entirely contrary certainty; namely, the unarguable fact that adults control some syntactic categories that have little if any direct correlation with matters semantic. More than anyone else, Maratsos and his colleagues (Maratsos, 1979, 1982; Maratsos & Chalkley, 1980; Maratsos, Kuczaj, Fox, & Chalkley, 1979) have been identified with the renovation of Bloomfieldian ideas. Chief among their labors has been the simple but essential reminder that adult grammatical categories, such as *noun, verb,* and *adjective,* cannot summarily be reduced to the semantic definitions of grade school. It follows that such categories must be acquired on some basis that is at least partly independent of semantics, a fact that is something of a conundrum for any theory of acquisition run exclusively on semantic machinery.

In his most recent paper, Maratsos (1982) makes a new and interesting pass at this argument. He begins with the fact that there are some syntactic distinctions, such as the German gender distinction, that are notorious for their failure to show any semantic correlation. For these categories, there is no alternative but to learn category members word-by-word on the basis of the syntactic contexts in which they appear. For example, upon hearing "das machen," one can unequivocally assign *machen* to the neuter gender (semantics be damned) and predict that *machen* will pronominalize via *es,* take *das* in the accusative, and so forth. It is this correlated set of syntactic effects that, according to Maratsos, makes up the German neuter gender. To learn the neuter gender is to learn that these syntactic phenomena predict each other, and nothing more.

From here, the argument moves to interesting ground. In effect, Maratsos argues, if *some* syntactic categories must be learned as clusters of distributional facts, then why not *all* syntactic categories, including the major grammatical categories such as noun and verb, as well as the major constituent categories, such as noun-phrase and verb-phrase? Why postulate more than one sort of language acquisition unless forced to it? A very good question, one worth some pursuit.

Maratsos' learning device is basically an inductive scheme that is capable, in principle, of classifying words together on the basis of shared contexts. We have argued from the beginning the failure of unbiased induction to account for the fact of language learning. Nonetheless, learning must ultimately be by inductive generalization. This follows from the fact that languages differ from one another and hence must be learned, in the classical sense of the term (just Bloomfield's point, as we stated in our introductory remarks). The problem is to isolate units on which induction takes place, given the capacities and inclinations of a human language learner. Maratsos explicit proposal seems to be for a general distributional analyzer that recognizes associations among *any* morphemes. We believe, however, that to the extent this proposal seems plausible, it is because it really (albeit implicitly) builds upon a quite narrow and interesting hypothesis about the nature of these units; specifically, the distributional analyzer Maratsos sketches seems to be particularly sensitive to the open-class/closed-class distinction that we described earlier. The bulk of Maratsos' *co-predictors* (correlations exploited to determine word-class membership) turn out to be associations between a closed-class item and an open-class position. For instance, "takes plural *-s*" predicts noun status for a stress-bearing word; "takes *-ed* and *will*" predicts verb status for other words. Note that a blind inductive device might focus on quite different, and ultimately useless, potential correlations, such as the correlation of *black* with *coal, night,* and *ink* vs. the correlation of *white* with *swan, milk,* and *snow;* no syntactically functioning units are picked out by these latter correlations. To the extent that Maratsos' distributional analyzer is plausible, then, it is because it has eyes for something like an open-class/closed-class distinction. These eyes rescue Maratsos' analyzer from contemplating the limitless false analogies it might otherwise be forced to consider as potential bases for grammatical categories. But this rescue raises problems of its own.

First, there is serious empirical doubt as to whether the closed-class items are generally available to children to support the initial construction of grammatical categories. The evidence we have presented thus far suggests that the closed-class and relevant distinctions among the closed-class items are beyond the grasp of the youngest learners. If this is so, these items would not be available to the inductive device at the stage—a very early stage, as the literature tells us—when the initial distinction between noun and verb is acquired (as evidenced by ordering). Moreover, nouns and verbs apparently emerge without difficulty in early stages of Turkish, which has few closed-class resources, according to Slobin's analysis, and in the historically early version of Tok Pisin which, according to Sankoff, has virtually no inflectional resources. Hence, whatever the facts for normally circumstanced English speaking learners, it cannot be maintained that the distinction between noun and verb, in general, arises from a distributional analysis of open-class/closed-class relations.

Maratsos tries to resolve these problems, but succeeds only by means of weakening the pure Bloomfieldian strain of his proposal. Following Braine (1976), he acknowledges that in the initial stages of language acquisition, grammatical categories (perhaps they should be called pregrammatical categories) are probably formed on semantic grounds. Subsequently, when the closed-class distinctions have been mastered (at about age three), the child is in a position to renovate these categories on the basis of distributional properties. Postulating such a renovation is necessary to account for the fact that children make so few category errors based on semantic uniformities. Thus the verb *like* and the adjective *fond (of)* mean much the same thing. Yet children are not heard to invent *John was fonded of by Mary* on the analogy of *John was liked by Mary* (note that this is just the kind of issue that case grammars have difficulty explaining). Presumably, it is the child's growing appreciation of the ways in which verbs and adjectives co-vary with closed-class items that prevents over-generalizations of this sort.

All this seems plausible enough, but it leaves rather mysterious the acquisition of the closed class itself. Notice that this is not simply a problem of picking out phonetic segments that seem to have low initial salience in the wave form. The child must also learn the grammatical significance of these phonetic elements. It is not, for instance, the location of a word just prior to the appropriate sounds for an *-ed* ending that predicts verb status. Consider, as evidence, that there are no verbs *to lightheart, to lighthead,* or *to lightfinger,* corresponding to the adjectives *lighthearted, lightheaded,* and *lightfingered.* There *is* a distributional regularity here characteristic of verbs, but it holds only when the *-ed* form has been assigned the morphemic value, *past tense.* It follows that if the child learns the verb category partly by learning about its deployment with respect to *-ed* as a marker of past tense, then she first must have learned that *-ed* marks past tense. This much Maratsos specifically acknowledges. But the unanswered question is just how the child manages to accomplish this crucial prior feat. Put generally, the child's move from categories based on semantic properties to categories based on the syntactic distribution of grammatical morphemes is not just a matter of changing the basis of induction. The child's new syntactic base *presupposes* the analysis of grammatical morphemes, and this analysis requires an explanation of its own.

We have left the child with a problem that neither Maratsos nor Bloomfield has solved: to induce the morphemic values of the closed-class items. We will now try to show that, armed with tentative semantic heuristics and exploiting phonological properties of the input strings, the child can in principle bootstrap from partial information to converge on the correct solution. This involves a bottom-up attempt to parse the string from its physical form, combined with a top-down attempt to establish its semantically functioning lexical and phrasal categories.

So far we have granted the learner the open-class/closed-class distinction, at least roughly (that is, as picked out by associated phonological properties). We have also adduced some of the evidence demonstrating that the child is sensitive to the sequencing of open-class elements from the earliest stages. From this it is reasonable to conclude that the learner has established rough precursors to these basic open-class categories, perhaps partly on primitive semantic grounds, as Maratsos and Braine both suppose (see also Pinker, 1982). Perhaps the child is willing to guess, based on preliminary correlational evidence, that concrete objects are encoded by nouns and actions and states are encoded by verbs, a few counterexamples notwithstanding.

However, even more detailed information about strings is required to solve the problem we have just raised: particularly, to find out that *-ed* in *lighthearted* is participial, but might be a finite verb ending in, say, *hotfooted*. The problem still exists because neither the meaning nor the morphology of *hotfooted* renders it more or less verb-like than *lightfingered* or *lighthearted;* that is, there is no semantic heuristic basis in the contrast between action and thing for establishing the open-class categories of these particular words. And then there is no basis for establishing the closed-class morphemic value either, as we have already shown. To repeat, this is because the value of *-ed* can be assigned as *past* only if the learner has secure knowledge that it is bound to a verb.

It is now clear that knowing something approximate about semantic correlates of open-class lexical categories is not enough information for resolving the *-ed* discovery problem. Most generally, this is because not every verb is an action and not every noun is a person, place, or thing. Thus the discovery procedure cannot be reduced to the class definitions of grade-school grammar courses (ask yourself on what semantic basis, for example, *thunder* is both a noun and a verb, while *lightning* is a noun only). As we will show, further analysis of the global phrase structure of the sentence is required.

As we have already described, there are a variety of cooperating cues in the sound wave—stress, rhythm, prepausal lengthening, etc.—to help the learner group formatives into phrases, and we have presented evidence (Read & Schreiber, 1982; Morgan & Newport, 1981) that learners are probably disposed to exploit these cues. Moreover, recent formal demonstrations suggest that phrase labeling can be derived from the bracketings (Levy and Joshi, 1978). If a child has such a phrase structural analysis in hand, based on such cues, we can at least in principle describe how she or he learns the facts about *ed*.

One traditional way in which the syntactic values of grammatical morphemes have been determined in linguistics is by means of their relative position in the phrase structure of the sentences in which they appear. The advantage of the phrase-structure representation is that it permits global description of the sentence, as divided into an integral sequence of phrases, hierarchically organized together. At the point at which we are now engaging the learner, he or she is in possession of a partial open-class parse, but (a) one that specifically identifies only open-class elements, and among these (b) only items that conform to the semantic heuristic for identifying nouns with objects and verbs with actions. For example, we now are assuming that the child possesses the mental equivalent of grammatical rules that allow her to construct a parse tree like this:

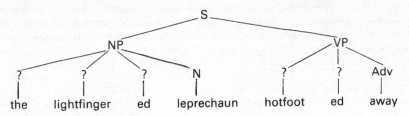

The categorial assignment of *leprechaun* is presumed to be established based on the semantic heuristic, because it is a concrete noun ("a thing"); and differential labeling of the phrasal categories is established by the procedure described by Levy and Joshi (1978). What remain to be specified are the values for *lightfinger* and *hotfoot,* as well as those for the closed-class elements: *the* (determiner), *ed* (participle), and *ed* (finite verb ending). For present purposes, we ignore the solution for *the.* Given the parse tree above, there can be little, if any, uncertainty about the appropriate syntactic categorization of *lightfinger* and *hotfoot,* or the correct assignment of the morphemic value *past* in the second case but not the first. The reasons are straightforward: *Lightfinger* occurs cophrasally before the noun and within the noun-phrase, and hence in a position appropriate to an adjective; that is, before a noun. *Hotfoot* occurs in a verb-phrase, in the position appropriate to the verb. As the first *ed* is bound to an adjective, it cannot be assigned a finite verb interpretation. In contrast, the second *ed* occurs within the verb-phrase and postposed to the verb. Thus, *past* is a possible analysis of *ed.*[9] Assuming that a similar analysis deals with the *the* case, the learner can now construct the final labelings for the parse tree:

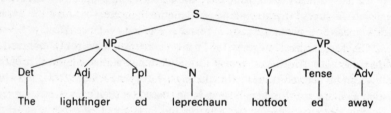

If we accept the moral of this story, the child must learn to parse (though tacitly and unconsciously) and must acquire the syntactic rules on which parsing

---

[9]The fact remains that, given our own prior discussion, the charge can be laid that we have been highhanded (if not lightfingered) in assuming that the learner is disposed to believe properties (adjectives) are of nouns, and times (tenses) are of actions (verbs). We acknowledge that we are assigning such meaningful interpretations of the world, as coded by language, to the child *ab initio,* even though the extent and usefulness of this knowledge is sharply limited by issues mentioned earlier: The interpretation of sentences by reference to scenes is a tricky business; languages vary in the properties of the world that they encode syntactically; and in any case the correlation between form-class and meaning is quite loose. Following Pinker, we here grant only a rough and tentative bias to associate whole concrete objects with the nouns and whole activities with the verbs. Even this, presumably, can be accomplished only in particularly dramatic or compelling circumstances. However the issues here may work out in detail, we submit, without such a rough ability to interpret the world in terms of forms and structures not too distant from the ones used by natural languages, there is simply no account for the acquisition of language (for discussion, see Wexler & Culicover, 1980). As for evidence, it is at least relevant that the creolizing languages we have mentioned (Bickerton, 1975; Sankoff & Laberge, 1973), developed by preliterate societies, move time markers into verb-phrases. And we have mentioned the evidence that even 18-month-olds distinguish actions from objects in their utterances by the order of the words.

depends, to determine the placement and syntactic class values of the closed class. Neither unabetted semantic learning (that *ed* means *past*) nor induction over surface regularities (that *ed* often follows verbs) escapes this conclusion. As we have mentioned in connection with the *thunder/lightning* example, this problem is not specific to such rare items as *hotfooted*, but is a general consequence of the fact that semantic properties are only loosely correlated with the formal lexical classes. To converge on the real richness of the lexical and phrasal properties of any real language, then, the child is forced to consider a deeper and more formal analysis. Detectable clues to the correct analysis can be found in the wave form, by an organism so constructed as to seek them out.

Learning a Transformational Grammar

The question of how syntactic rules are acquired returns us to the first principles of the debate between Chomsky and Bloomfield. Now, however, we can restate the issues in terms of the territory since covered:

1. Given that the child is innately able to "hear" the wave form of parental speech as an ordered string of words, intonationally bracketed into major phrases (possibly, labeled phrases); and
2. Given that the child can, by dint of his own conceptual abilities and through parental efforts to direct his attention (for which, see Bruner 1974/75), achieve an accurate interpretation of some of the sentences he encounters—even before achieving a full grasp of the language he is learning; and
3. Given that the mapping between the semantic interpretation and the surface string is not sufficiently simple to be learned either as a direct projection from semantic representation to the surface string (Braine & Hardy) or vice versa (Maratsos); it follows that
4. We must provide some independent account of how the rules that map between the semantic interpretation and the surface string are acquired.

This task is severely complicated by the fact that there is no single grammatical system now known to be the one psychologically valid statement of these mapping rules. Among the best studied of the alternative grammatical systems are transformational grammar in its several incarnations (Chomsky, 1965, 1975, 1981; Fiengo, 1980); lexical functional grammar (Bresnan, 1982); arc pair grammar (Johnson & Postal, 1980); and relational grammar (Perlmutter, 1980). Given the uncertain choice among these and other alternative descriptions of the adult system, it is difficult to achieve definite results about the process of acquisition. However, it is possible to study some of the boundary conditions under which this acquisition could conceivably take place. It is noteworthy that the study of such conditions can place constraints on the choice among possible grammatical systems because, whatever else is true of adult grammar, it must be learnable by the child. Kenneth Wexler and several colleagues have carried out an extended study of such constraints (see Wexler, 1982, for an overview). Put very simply, Wexler's work is an examination of the compatibility of holding two assumptions: (1) that children learn a mapping between form and meaning (equivalent to our assumption *1* in the preceding list); and (2) that the mapping they learn is, at least in part, a transformational grammar of the so-called "Standard Theory" vintage.

Wexler examined the consistency of these two claims by designing a hypothetical learning device for transformational grammars and determining under what conditions it will converge on the correct transformational grammar for a given language. His earliest result (Wexler & Hamburger, 1973) showed that no such convergence is possible so long as the learner has access only to positive examples of sentences in the target language. This negative result motivated Wexler and his colleagues to examine an altered scenario in which the child is considered able to derive the meaning of adult utterances from extralinguistic circumstances (our assumption *2* in the preceding list) and is also able to derive the deep structures of a transformational grammar from these meanings. On these assumptions, the child is confronted with data consisting of a word string paired with a deep structure for every sentence he or she can interpret in this fashion. Wexler's learning device is extremely simple. Whenever a string/deep-structure pair arrives, it attempts to find a set of transformations in its current grammar that will map from the deep structure to the string. If it is successful, it makes no change in its grammar. If it is unsuccessful, it either deletes one of its current rules at random or attempts to formulate a new transformation (given only its knowledge of elementary transformational operations) that will permit a successful mapping of the current input pair. If such a new rule can be found, it is added to the current grammar.

Hamburger and Wexler (1975) were able to prove that, with this kind of a learning device of this simple type can successfully converge in the limit on the target transformational grammar, but only if the grammar includes certain *new* constraints on the operation of transformational rules. These constraints (for which, see Wexler & Culicover, 1980) are necessary to insure that if the learner makes an error (i.e., infers an incorrect transformation), it will not require a sample sentence of unbounded complexity to reveal that error. A learner requiring examples of unbounded complexity might have to wait an unbounded amount of time to stumble onto even one such example. Hence, convergence could not be guaranteed.

One of the chief thrusts of Wexler's work is linguistic. In collaboration with Culicover, he has attempted to show that the constraints required to guarantee learnability have independent linguistic motivation. Very roughly, the theory imposes constraints on the application of transformational rules under general conditions that would lead to undetectable (from information available in the surface string) errors when deriving a phrase-structure analysis of the sentence derived by the transformation. Wexler and Culicover (1980) have shown that these constraints, put forward to guarantee learning, offer an explanation for certain otherwise mysterious constraints on the applicability of rules that have had to be proposed simply on descriptive grounds: to explain away some nonoccurring structures in adult languages. To the extent that the learnable grammar is also the most successful description of the adult language, it becomes possible to offer learnability as an explanation of descriptive success: The language is as it is just because it must be learned.

No one, incuding Wexler, would propose that his learning device is a full model of how children acquire syntax. It may be that Wexler's current scenario assumes both too much and too little about the input to the child: Too much because it is not known how the child gets from meaning to deep structure without additional learning to supply this mapping, as Wexler acknowledges; too little because, as we have suggested, the child may have intonational access to major phrase boundaries, while Wexler has worked from the assumption that the learner begins by recognizing only the linear string of words. If even partial phrase structure is available to the learning device, certain "undetectable" errors in Wexler's system would become "detectable." Whether the prelinguistic availability of approximate phrase bracketing might have a sufficiently general effect on detectability to render unnecessary any of Wexler and Culicover's transformational constraints is a question that may be worth attention.

Whatever the final details, Wexler's study of learnability is an important move in developmental psycholinguistics. Where much work in the field seems aimed at description for its own sake, Wexler's program serves to refocus attention on explanatory goals. Moreover, it sets exacting standards for the acceptability of explanatory proposals that are a model for future work. How many current notions about how language is learned can offer hard proof that language is, even in principle, learnable in the proposed way? Many arguments in developmental psycholinguistics rest upon unexamined assumptions about learnability that prove to be false once their consequences are examined by more formal techniques. An example of just this sort, and further discussion of Wexler's formal results, will concern us in the following section, describing the "Motherese Hypothesis."

Although the Wexler group's work is surely the most extensive effort to examine the conditions under which a transformational grammar might be acquired, several investigators have taken up the formal approach to studying language learning, sometimes from quite different perspectives about the nature of the learning device and the grammar that is being learned (for further discussion, see Pinker, 1979, 1982, and the collection of learnability studies in Baker & McCarthy, 1981). In fact, as transformational grammar has evolved away from the so-called standard theory, and as the complexity and variety of the transformational rules has steadily diminished, it has become increasingly clear that the learning of transformations is only a small part of the task of learning a generative grammar. Moreover, the very difficulty of establishing rapid convergence for a learning system that proceeds by enumerating grammars has led Chomsky (1981) and others to consider a more restrictive framework in which the child's innate knowledge of universal grammar hypothetically goes well beyond the elementary transformational operations countenanced by Wexler, including instead a rich knowledge of universal rule schemata. In theory, these schemata contain empty slots (where languages vary) that the child needs only to fill in to learn his or her own language. Under this idealization, which is often called "parameter setting" to distinguish it from the hypothesis-testing framework, the child might come pre-armed with schema for core grammar rules informing him that (say) an NP is composed of a head noun plus specifier, but leaving open the problems of determining what order these elements appear in, how specification is marked in this language, and so on. Although some empirical work has recently appeared within this framework (see Roeper, 1982), it is still too early to estimate reliably the value of this alternative way of looking at grammar acquisition.

Saying It Won't Make It So: Caretakers' Role in the Learning Process

As we mentioned earlier, a number of investigators have suggested that the properties of caretaker speech can, in addition to easing the utterance-meaning inductions, contribute causally to solution of the projection problem: relating the forms to the meanings; that is, acquisition of grammar. The idea behind this approach is that the caretaker could order the presentation of syntactic types, so as to narrow the candidate generalizations the child would be in a position to entertain, consistent with his or her data. Certain properties of caretakers' speech to young children give some support to this claim. The caretakers' earliest utterances to children are short and propositionally simple; hence, they are uniclausal. Possibly, mothers say easiest sentences first to littlest ears, successively adding the complications as learning proceeds, and so being responsive at all times to the requirements of an environmentally dependent learning device. This has been called the "fine tuning" hypothesis. (See Cross (1977) and Gleitman et al. (1984) for arguments pro and con.)

There are a number of problems in making good this claim. First, if it is intended to remove requirements for endowments supporting language learning, it could succeed only by transferring this claim from learner to tutor; that is, by placing apparatus in the mother so that she could effectively determine (a) the syntactic simplicity of her potential utterances and (b) the current grammar of the child, plus (c) machinery for rapid implementation of these ideas during her speech planning, so that she could monitor her performance to the child on line, in order to carry out her tutorial aims. It is not obvious why "endowment with linguistic tutorial skills" of this sort should be any more palatable than "endowment with linguistic-learning skills.'' At the very least, this is an empirical question.

Apart from this problem, the evidence of maternal speech does not add plausibility to the view that it would materially aid the acquisition of syntax. For example, the earliest utterances to children are by and large not canonical sentences of the language, and a sizable percentage are not full sentences at all, but are isolated (but well-formed) NP's and interjections. The majority of the full sentences are imperatives and questions. If a transformational grammar is the envisioned end point of learning, it is clear that the child is not selectively receiving simple syntactic structures (i.e., the straightforward, least transformationally deformed outputs of base rules and the obligatory transformations). More generally, it would seem that *any* syntactic theory would have to regard the active, declarative sentences as simplest, but these are not the forms favored by caretakers in their speech to the youngest learners. Moreover, as the child grows older, the percentage of canonical declaratives said to him increases rather than decreases, while the noncanonical forms decrease in proportion. Reliable predictions of the child's growth rate from properties of the maternal speech style that vary among mothers are also limited. In fact, they are limited to the acquisition of the closed-class morphology. Many correlations of other kinds between child's linguistic stage and mother's current usage disappear once these are corrected for baseline differences among child learners. These empirical outcomes limit the extent to which the child's learning of syntax can be assigned to the effects of ''intelligent text presentation'' by the mother (for discussion, see Gleitman et al., 1984; Wexler & Culicover, 1980, ch. 2).

Other problems with this hypothesis are logical. Chomsky (1975) and Wexler (1982) have pointed out that narrowing the learner's data base, although it might do no harm, certainly cannot do good if the outcome of learning is to be a grammar covering the full range of the language. The narrower the range of data, the more hypotheses can describe them. In fact, the difficulty of proving the learnability of language formally would be considerably reduced if it were plausible to suppose that the learner received and could analyze complex input data. This is because the trans-clausal relations within sentences (the transformations, on one formulation) are revealed only in complex sentences, quite obviously.

The major result achieved by the Wexler group thus far has been to devise a set of constraints on transformational operations such that learning is demonstrable from ''degree 2'' input (sentences that are constituted, at maximum, of a clause within a clause within a clause). If the child were assumed able to deal with yet more complex input than this—thus deriving further information about the character of derived phrase structures—fewer constraints (i.e., *less* innate apparatus) would be required, as Wexler and Culicover have shown in detail. To summarize their position, the formal description of learning is *complicated* by the plausible assumption that mothers speak *simply* to their young offspring. Constraints on transformations are required just so that learning can take place, even though the real data are simple (of no more than degree 2 complexity). Why this point has been so hard for developmental psycholinguists to grasp is itself hard to grasp. It seems reasonably obvious that learning should be more difficult from limited and biased ("degenerate," in Chomsky's wording) data than from rich and unbiased data. The degree 2 result, along with the constraints on transformations required to make it work, provides a formal demonstration that would seem to render unassailable the logical point that partial ("simplified") input does not ease the problem of acquiring complex systems.

Despite the logical and empirical difficulties just described, the Motherese Hypothesis continues to be pursued in the developmental psycholinguistic literature (see, for example, the collection of essays in Snow & Ferguson, 1977). This is usually done by claiming that maternal speech aids the young learner in some other and more subtle ways: Perhaps it is the gestures accompanying maternal speech that secure learning; perhaps the mother limits herself, in using a certain form, to a single semantic function for that form. Shatz (1982) has delivered the *coup de grace* to many of these fallback positions by submitting them to a series of observational and experimental tests. She has found that the form–function relations are not materially simplified in maternal speech to young learners, and that these children are quite insensitive to whatever gestural supports to comprehension their parents might be giving (see also Landau, 1982, on language learning in blind children for another kind of support for Shatz's position). It should go almost without saying that the Goldin-Meadow group's demonstrations of the survival of syntax in the absence of formal linguistic input similarly diminish hope that the environment of the learner straightforwardly determines the character of what he or she learns.

There are counterattacks, however, that were not considered by Shatz. One is the conjecture that pragmatics-based theories of language can capture the real richness of human language organization, swallowing what have usually been conceived as syntactic theories (for interesting general discussions, see Clark & Clark, 1978; Searle, 1975; and for a description that specifically attempts to account for the child's acquisition of denominal verbs, see Clark, 1982). How far these approaches, that attempt to incorporate general inferential capacities and richer analyses of situations into the description of language structure, can go is an open question, for understandably there are as yet no well-specified theories of appropriate scope within this framework (at least to our knowledge).

It is worth mentioning that at least one group of investigators has claimed that general social-interactive properties of the mother-child discourse will causally determine the actual form-meaning pairings the child learns. This position has been explicated by Bates and MacWhinney (1982). Their discussion is important, for it recognizes the essentially social nature of language and tries to bring this to bear on the problem of acquisition (see also Fernald & Simon, 1984, for related arguments). This *functionalist* approach to language and its learning is in its infancy, and to this extent the discussion by Bates and MacWhinney is programmatic. At present, it is difficult to say whether social properties of conversations that differ in England and in Germany will account for the fact that English babies put the verb in the middle while German babies put it at the end; that English babies learn to say "I won't put up with that" but not "I won't tolerate with that," and "I painted the wall blue" but not "I painted the wall beautiful"; that they can interpret the *he* in "When he sang, John entranced the audience" anaphorically, but not the one in "He sang, when John entranced the audience"; and all the myriad other facts about how to interpret English sentences meaningfully. On functional grounds, so far as we can see, these issues threaten to require independent explanations, yielding an infinite variety of things that must, and therefore cannot, be learned. Perhaps a functionalist grammar can be written for adults and for children that will bring this approach under control, but for the reasons just stated we must remain pessimistic. However, the descriptive apparatus does not now exist on which to support or falsify the various detailed suggestions about learning that Bates and MacWhinney have proposed.

FINAL THOUGHTS

At the bottom of any scientific paradigm lies a set of beliefs that are usually called metaphysical. It is sometimes claimed that these deep beliefs about the nature of theories and the things they describe cannot be confirmed or disconfirmed by empirical means. It is, however, quite possible to compare different metaphysical beliefs according to the degree of success of the scientific programs they support. Moreover, substantive arguments for one set of metaphysical assumptions over others can be constructed on this basis.

At its deepest level, Chomsky's break with Bloomfield is just this sort of argument. If a grammar can be construed, not as a physical description of linguistic behavior a la Bloomfield, but instead as a description of the linguistic knowledge represented in the human mind, then—so Chomsky argued—it will be possible to construct a more successful and interesting theory of language. Chomsky's familiar commitment to linguistic competence as an object of study is at once a metaphysical decision as to what sort of thing a theory of language is about, and a very practical decision as to what sorts of data the theory will be responsible for and what sorts of constraints on the theory will prove most fruitful. If a grammar describes the speaker's linguistic knowledge, then it is only indirectly revealed in linguistic behavior, and it is not to be held accountable for the physical facts about linguistic behavior for which Bloomfield's grammar must take responsibility. There is a basis (in linguistic judgments) for making an empirical distinction between acceptable and unacceptable sentences, and grammars that aim at describing linguistic knowledge can reasonably restrict themselves to sentences that speakers know to be acceptable. In contrast, attempts, such as Bloomfield's, to construct a grammar that describes behavior directly can at best account for unacceptable sentences (such as slips of the tongue) as improbable utterances, no different qualitatively from the mass of other linguistic-behavioral data.

Although Chomsky's move allows the grammar to escape responsibility for accounting in detail for linguistic behavior, it also imposes a heavy explanatory burden on linguistic theory, and on the theory of language learning in particular. For if a grammar is to be interpreted as a psychological description of human knowledge, then it necessarily raises questions about how this knowledge is acquired. Much of our discussion has attempted to summarize just how well these questions have been answered.

Recently, however, Katz (1981) has mounted an argument against Chomsky's psychologistic interpretation of grammar, one that formally parallels Chomsky's argument against Bloomfield's physicalistic interpretation of grammar. In effect, Katz argues that it is possible to achieve a better theory of language if we drop both the idea that grammar describes human knowledge and the attendant responsibility for showing how such grammatical knowledge is learnable. This can be achieved in Katz's view only if we adopt a Platonic (or realistic) interpretation of the grammar, in which grammatical principles are supposed to describe an abstract reality entirely independent of human knowledge of it, much as the reality of a mathematical relationship (e.g., the Pythagorean Theorem) is sometimes held to be true independent of human appreciation of that truth. According to Katz, this metaphysical interpretation is to be preferred because it permits a full-blooded account of necessary linguistic truths (such as lexical entailments of the "vixen is a fox" variety), which would otherwise have to be held contingent on the nature of the human mind. Moreover, Katz holds that Platonist metaphysics permits simpler solutions to certain thorny problems of grammatical description once the grammar is freed of the requirement that it be rendered in a form learnable by human beings. It may be worth noting that this is exactly the opposite of the views advanced by certain other authors we have discussed (e.g., Wexler, 1982; Newport, 1982), who take the position that the requirement of learnability and its incorporation into linguistic theory explain otherwise mysterious grammatical facts.

Bever (1982) has explored the possible consequences of the Platonist challenge to the Chomskian paradigm for theories of language acquisition. First among these consequences would be the unhooking of linguistic theory and acquisition theory. Linguistic theory describes the set of possible natural languages, and acquisition theory describes the set of languages learnable by humans. According to Platonist assumptions, there is no theoretical reason to expect these two sets to be identical. Thus, Bever argues, the Platonist paradigm remains unembarassed when it turns out that certain cognitive operations never show up in language, just as certain linguistic operations never appear elsewhere in cognition. The Chomskian paradigm can handle such facts by postulating the mental segregation of the linguistic faculty: Language is as it is because of the structure of the human mind, but language is unlike the rest of mind in some respects because the mental organ devoted to language is unlike the rest of mind (in just those respects necessary to explain the difference). Bever claims there is circularity in this formulation: "It is not a literal contradiction to maintain . . . that the essence of language is caused by an organ of the mind. But it does present a picture of language as resulting from a capacity that is mentally isolated in sporadic ways. That is, many aspects of cognition as a whole are reflected in language use and structure; why are the specific exclusions the way they are?" (1982, p. 436). By this route, Bever rejects what he takes to be Chomsky's claim that the essence of language is necessarily caused by the structure of the mind: If there is no independent evidence (independent, that is, of the evidence provided by language itself) for the shape of the mental organ devoted to language, then the claim that the essential structure of language is caused by that mental organ is only a hypothesis, no more certain—although certainly more testable—than the Platonist claim that language is independent of mind.

But once Chomsky's claim has been shown to be hypothetical, one must ask whether the Katz–Bever revelation really changes the empirical problem of explaining language acquisition. Bever argues that one consequence of Platonist assumptions is that it becomes *unnecessary* to hold that language is acquired by a mental organ specifically designed for the task. Fair enough. But it does not follow from this that language acquisition can have a *sufficient* explanation in terms of general learning mechanisms. Even if *language* is caused by the exigencies of some abstract, Platonic reality as Bever suggests, human beings' *knowledge of language* must be psychologically caused. Children must come to know their native tongue. And, as we have been at pains to argue, this knowledge cannot be acquired through unconstrained induction. Exactly what these constraints are and just how they relate to linguistic theory and to general cognition are, we take it, open empirical questions. Indeed, they are the central questions that motivate investigation, and shape our current theories of language and its learning.

ACKNOWLEDGMENTS

This chapter is a revised version of an earlier work (Gleitman & Wanner, 1982), and we thank the Cambridge University Press for allowing us to reprint highly overlapping materials here. The original chapter was constructed as the introduction to a volume of essays from a small group of investigators of child language, and hence organizes the field around these individuals' particular contributions. Although a variety of other sources were cited and discussed, certainly a chapter so constructed will distort credit that is due to many important investigators, by emphasizing particular works and passing too lightly over cognate information contributed by others. Exigencies of time constraints for the present volume prohibited large-scale revision for the current version, which exhibits various technomorphic traces of the prior work. We therefore apologize to contributors to the literature whose work has been inadvertently omitted from this discussion. However, individuals aside, the present chapter does succeed in reviewing our own current vision of the field of language learning and does state our own—to some extent idiosyncratic—beliefs and views about the generalizations to be drawn from currently available data and discussion. We thank The National Foundation for the March of Dimes and the Alfred P. Sloan Foundation, whose continuing support of our work made possible the writing of this paper. And we thank our colleagues, Henry Gleitman, Barbara Landau, and Elissa Newport, whose criticisms of prior drafts materially improved what we have been able to say.

REFERENCES

Armstrong, S. L., Gleitman, L. R., & Gleitman, H. (1983). What some concepts might not be. *Cognition, 13,* 263–308.

Baker, C. L., & McCarthy, J. J. (Eds.). (1981). *The logical problem of language acquisition.* Cambridge, MA: MIT Press.

Bates, E., & MacWhinney, B. (1982). Functionalist approaches to grammar. In E. Wanner & L. R. Gleitman (Eds.), *Language acquisition: State of the art.* New York: Cambridge University Press.

Bellugi, U. (1967). *The acquisition of negation.* Unpublished doctoral dissertation, Harvard University.

Bever, T. G. (1970). The cognitive basis for linguistic structures. In J. Hayes (Ed.), *Cognition and the development of language.* New York: Wiley.

Bever, T. G. (1982). Some implications of the nonspecific bases of language. In E. Wanner & L. R. Gleitman (Eds.), *Language acquisition: State of the art.* New York: Cambridge University Press.

Bickerton, D. (1975). *Dynamics of a creole system.* New York: Cambridge University Press.

Blasdell, R., & Jensen, P. (1970). Stress and word position as determinants of imitation in first language learners. *Journal of Speech and Hearing Research, 13,* 193–202.

Bloch, B. (1941). Phonemic overlapping. *American Speech, 16,* 278–284.

Bloom, L. (1970). *Language development: Form and function in emerging grammars.* Cambridge, MA: MIT Press.

Bloom, L. (1973). *One word at a time.* The Hague: Mouton.

Bloom, L., Lightbown, P., & Hood, L. (1975). Structure and variation in child language. *Monographs of the Society for Research in Child Development, 40* (Serial No. 160).

Bloomfield, L. (1933). *Language.* New York: Henry Holt.

Blount, B. G. (1972). Parental speech and language acquisition: Some Luo and Samoan examples. *Anthropological Linguistics, 14,* 119–30.

Bowerman, M. (1973). Structural relationships in children's utterances: Syntactic or semantic? In T. Moore (Ed.), *Cognitive development and the acquisition of language.* New York: Academic Press.

Bowerman, M. (1982). Reorganizational processes in lexical and syntactic development. In E. Wanner & L. R. Gleitman (Eds.), *Language acquisition: The state of the art.* New York: Cambridge University Press.

Bradley, D. C., Garrett, M. F., & Zurif, E. G. (1979). Syntactic deficits in Broca's aphasia. In D. Caplan, (Ed.), *Biological studies of mental processes.* Cambridge, MA: MIT Press.

Braine, M. D. S. (1976). Children's first word combinations. *Monographs of the Society for Research in Child Development, 41,* (Serial No. 164).

Braine, M. D. S., & Hardy, J. A. (1982). On what case categories there are, why they are, and how they develop: An amalgam of *a priori* considerations, speculation, and evidence from children. In E. Wanner & L. R. Gleitman (Eds.), *Language acquisition: State of the art.* New York: Cambridge University Press.

Bresnan, J. (1978). A realistic transformational grammar. In M. Halle, J. Bresnan, & G. A. Miller (Eds.), *Linguistic theory and psychological reality.* Cambridge, MA: MIT Press.

Bresnan, J. (Ed.). (1982). *The mental representation of grammatical relations.* Cambridge, MA: MIT Press.

Broen, P. A. (1972). The verbal environment of the language learning child. *Monograph of American Speech and Hearing Association, 17.*

Brown, R. (1973). *A first language: The early stages.* Cambridge, MA: Harvard University Press.

Brown, R., & Hanlon, C. (1970). Derivational complexity and order of acquisition in child speech. In J. Hayes (Ed.), *Cognition and the development of language.* New York: Wiley.

Brown, R., & Bellugi, U. (1964). Three processes in the child's acquisition of syntax. *Harvard Educational Review, 34,* 133–151.

Bruner, J. S. (1974/75). From communication to language: A psychological perspective, *Cognition, 3,* 255–287.

Carey, S. (1977). Less may never mean more. In R. Campbell & P. Smith (Eds.), *Recent advances in the psychology of language.* New York: Plenum.

Carey, S. (1982). Semantic development: The state of the art. In E. Wanner & L. R. Gleitman (Eds.), *Language acquisition: The state of the art.* New York: Cambridge University Press.

Carey, S., & Bartlett, E. (1978). Acquiring a single new word. *Papers and reports on child language development.* Department of Linguistics, Stanford University, *15,* 17–29.

Chao, Y-R. (1934). The non-uniqueness of phonemic solutions of phonetic systems. *Bulletin of the Institute of History and Philology, Academia Sinica, 4,* 363–397.

Chomsky, N. (1965). *Aspects of the theory of syntax.* Cambridge, MA: MIT Press.

Chomsky, N. (1972). Some empirical issues in the theory of transformational grammar. In S. Peters (Ed.), *Goals of linguistic theory.* Englewood Cliffs, NJ: Prentice-Hall.

Chomsky, N. (1975). *Reflections on language.* New York: Random House.

Chomsky, N. (1981). *Lectures on government and binding.* Dordrecht: Foris Publications.

Clark, E. V. (1973). What's in a word? On the child's acquisition of semantics in his first language. In T. Moore (Ed.), *Cognitive development and the acquisition of language.* New York: Academic Press.

Clark, E. V. (1982). The young word maker: A case study of innovation in the child's lexicon. In E. Wanner & L. R. Gleitman (Eds.), *Language acquisition: State of the art.* New York: Cambridge University Press.

Clark, E. V., & Clark, H. H. (1978). When nouns surface as verbs. *Language, 55,* 767–811.

Cross, T. G. (1977). Mothers' speech adjustments: The contribution of selected listener variables. In C. E. Snow & C. A. Ferguson (Eds.), *Talking to children.* Cambridge, MA: Cambridge University Press.

Cutting, J., & Rosner, B. (1974). Categories and boundaries in speech and music. *Perception and Psychophysics, 16,* 564–570.

Donaldson, M., & Balfour, G. (1968). Less is more: A study of language comprehension in children. *British Journal of Psychology, 59,* 461–471.

Dorian, N. (1978). The fate of morphological complexity in language death. *Language, 54*(3), 590–609.

Eimas, P., Siqueland, E. R., Jusczyk, P., & Vigorito, J. (1971). Speech perception in infants. *Science, 171,* 303–306.

Ervin, S. (1964). Imitation and structural change in children's language. In E. Lenneberg (Ed.), *New directions in the study of language.* Cambridge, MA: MIT Press.

Feldman, H., Goldin-Meadow, S., & Gleitman, L. (1978). Beyond Herodotus: The creation of language by linguistically deprived deaf children. *In A. Lock (Ed.), Action, symbol, and gesture: The emergence of language.* New York: Academic Press.

Fernald, A. (1982). *Acoustic determinants of infant preference for "motherese."* Unpublished Ph.D. dissertation, University of Oregon.

Fernald, A. (1983). The perceptual and affective salience of mothers' speech to infants. In C. Feagans, C. Garvey, & R. Golinkoff (Eds.), *The origins and growth of communication.* Norwood, NJ: Ablex.

Fernald, A., & Simon, T. (1984). Expanded intonation contours in mothers' speech to newborns. *Developmental Psychology, 20*, 104–113.

Fiengo, R. (1980). *Surface structure: The interface of autonomous components.* Cambridge, MA: Harvard University Press.

Fillmore, C. J. (1968). The case for case. In E. Bach & R. J. Harms (Eds.), *Universals in linguistic theory.* New York: Holt, Rinehart & Winston.

Fodor, J. A. (1975). *The language of thought.* New York: Crowell.

Fodor, J. A. (1983). *The modularity of mind.* Cambridge, MA: MIT Press, Bradford Books.

Fodor, J. A., Bever, T. G., & Garrett, M. F. (1974). *The psychology of language: An introduction to psycholinguistics and generative grammar.* New York: McGraw-Hill.

Fodor, J. A., Garrett, M. F., Walker, E. C., & Parkes, C. H. (1980). Against definitions. *Cognition, 8*, 263–367.

Foss, D. J., & Hakes, D. T. (1978). *Psycholinguistics: An introduction to the psychology of language.* Englewood Cliffs, NJ: Prentice-Hall.

Freyd, P., & Baron, J. (1982). Individual differences in the acquisition of derivational morphology. *Journal of verbal learning and verbal behavior.*

Fromkin, V. A. (1973). *Speech errors as linguistic evidence.* The Hague: Mouton.

Furrow, D., Nelson, K., & Benedict, H. (1979). Mothers' speech to children and syntactic development: Some simple relationships. *Journal of Child Language, 6*, 423–442.

Garrett, M. F. (1975). The analysis of sentence production. In G. H. Bower (Ed.), *The psychology of learning and motivation* (Vol. 9). New York: Academic Press.

Gentner, D. (1978). On relational meaning: The acquisition of verb meaning. *Child Development, 49*, 988–998.

Gentner, D. (1982). Why nouns are learned before verbs: Linguistic relativity vs. natural partitioning. In S. Kuczaj (Ed.), *Language development: Language, culture, and cognition.* Hillsdale, NJ: Lawrence Erlbaum Associates.

Gleitman, H., & Gleitman, L. R. (1979). Language use and language judgment. In C. J. Fillmore, D. Kempler, & W. S-Y. Wang (Eds.), *Individual differences in language ability and language behavior.* New York: Academic Press.

Gleitman, L. R. (1981). Maturational determinants of language growth. *Cognition, 10*, 103–114.

Gleitman, L. R., & Gleitman, H. (1970). *Phrase and paraphrase.* New York: Norton.

Gleitman, L. R., Newport, E. L., & Gleitman, H. (1984). The current status of the Motherese hypothesis. *Journal of Child Language, 11.*

Gleitman, L. R., & Rozin, P. (1977). The structure and acquisition of reading I: Relations between orthographies and the structure of language. In A. Reber & D. Scarborough (Eds.), *Toward a psychology of reading.* Hillsdale, NJ: Lawrence Erlbaum Associates.

Gleitman, L. R., & Wanner, E. (1982). Language acquisition: The state of the state of the art. In E. Wanner & L. R. Gleitman (Eds.), *Language acquisition: The state of the art.* New York: Cambridge University Press.

Goldin-Meadow, S. (1982). The resilience of recursion: A study of a communication system developed without a conventional language model. In E. Wanner & L. R. Gleitman (Eds.), *Language acquisition: The state of the art.* New York: Cambridge University Press.

Greenfield, P., & Smith, J. (1976). *The structure of communication in early language development.* New York: Academic Press.

Gruber, J. (1968). Look and see. *Language, 43*, 937–947.

Hamburger, H., & Wexler, K. (1975). A mathematical theory of learning transformational grammar. *Journal of Mathematical Psychology, 12*, 137–177.

Harris, Z. S. (1951). *Methods in structural linguistics.* Chicago: University of Chicago Press.

Jackendoff, R. (1983). *Semantics and cognition.* Cambridge: MA: MIT Press.

Jakobson, R. (1941). *Kindersprache, Aphasie, und alllgemeine Lautgesetze.* Stockholm: Almqvist & Wiksell.

Johnson, D. E., & Postal, P. (1980). *Arc-pair grammar*. Princeton, NJ: Princeton University Press.

Joshi, A. K. (1983). Processing of sentences with intra-sentential code-switching. In D. Dowty, L. Kartunnen, & A. Zwicky (Eds.), *Syntactic theory and how people parse sentences*. New York: Cambridge University Press.

Jusczyk, P. W. (1980). Auditory versus phonetic coding of speech signals during infancy. *Proceedings of the CNRS Conference*.

Katz, J. J. (1972). *Semantic theory*. New York: Harper & Row.

Katz, J. J. (1981). *Language and other abstract objects*. Totowa, NJ: Rowman & Littlefield.

Kean, M. L. (1979). Agrammatism: A phonological deficit? *Cognition, 7*(1), 69–84.

Keil, F. C. (1979). *Semantic and conceptual development*. Cambridge, MA: Harvard University Press.

Klatt, D. H. (1975). Vowel lengthening is syntactically determined in a connected discourse. *Journal of Phonetics, 3*, 129–140.

Klatt, D. H. (1976). Linguistic uses of segmental duration in English: acoustic and perceptual evidence. *Journal of the Acoustic Society of America, 59*, 1208–1221.

Klima, E., & Bellugi, U. (1966). Syntactic regularities in the speech of children. In J. Lyons & R. Wales (Eds.), *Psycholinguistics papers*. Edinburgh: Edinburgh University Press.

Klima, E., & Bellugi, U. (1979). *The signs of language*. Cambridge, MA: Harvard University Press.

Kuhl, P. K., & Miller, J. D. (1975). Speech perception by the chinchilla, Voiced-voiceless distinction in alveolar plosive consonants. *Science, 190*, 69–72.

Labov, W. (1970). The reading of the -ed suffix. In H. Levin & J. P. Williams (Eds.), *Basic studies on reading*. New York: Basic Books.

Landau, B. (1982). *Language learning in blind children*. Unpublished Ph.D. dissertation, University of Pennsylvania.

Landau, B., & Gleitman, L. R. (1984). *The language of perception in blind children*. Cambridge, MA: Harvard University Press.

Lehiste, I. (1970). *Suprasegmentals*. Cambridge, MA: MIT Press.

Levy. L. S., & Joshi, A. K. (1978). Skeletal structural descriptions. *Information and Control, 5*(39), No. 2.

Levy, Y. (1980). *Gender in children's language: A study of first language acquisition*. Unpublished doctoral dissertation. Hebrew University.

Levy, Y. (1983). The acquisition of Hebrew plurals. The case of the missing gender category. *Journal of Child Language, 10*(1), 107–122.

Liberman, A. M. (1970). The grammars of speech and language. *Cognitive Psychology, 1*, 301–323.

Liberman, A. M., Cooper, F. S., Shankweiler, D. P., & Studdert-Kennedy, M. (1967). Perception of the speech code. *Psychological Review, 74*, 431–461.

Liberman, A. M., & Pisoni, D. B. (1977). Evidence for a special speech-perceiving subsystem in the human. In T. H. Bullock (Ed.), *Recognition of complex acoustic signals*. Berlin: Dahlem Konferenzen.

Locke, J. (1965). *An essay concerning human understanding*. New York: Macmillan. (Originally published 1690)

Maratsos, M. (1979). How to get from words to sentences. In D. Aaronson & R. Reiber (Eds.), *Perspectives in psycholinguistics*. Hillsdale, NJ: Lawrence Erlbaum Associates.

Maratsos, M. (1982). The child's construction of grammatical categories. In E. Wanner & L. R. Gleitman (Eds.), *Language acquisition: State of the art*. New York: Cambridge University Press.

Maratsos, M., & Chalkley, M. A. (1980). The internal language of children's syntax: The ontogenesis and representation of syntactic categories. In K. Nelson (Ed.), *Children's language* (Vol. 2). New York: Gardner Press.

Maratsos, M., Kuczaj, S. A., Fox, D.E., & Chalkley, M. A. (1979). Some empirical findings in the acquisition of transformational relations. In W. A. Collins (Ed.), *Minnesota symposia on child psychology* (Vol. 12). Hillsdale, NJ: Lawrence Erlbaum Associates.

Marin, O., Saffran, E., & Schwartz, M. (1976). Dissociations of language in aphasia: Implications for normal function. *Annals of the New York Academy of Sciences, 280,* 868–884.

Markman, E. M., Horton, M. S., & McLanahan, A. G. (1980). Classes and collections: Principle of organization in the learning of hierarchical relations. *Cognition, 8,* 227–241.

McNeill, D. (1966). The creation of language by children. In J. Lyons & R. Wales (Eds.), *Psycholinguistics papers.* Edinburgh: Edinburgh University Press.

Morgan, J., & Newport, E. L. (1981). The role of constituent structure in the induction of an artificial language. *Journal of Verbal Learning and Verbal Behavior, 20,* 67–85.

Nakatani, L. H., & Dukes, K. D. (1977). Locus of segmental cues for word juncture. *Journal of the Acoustic Society of America, 62*(3), 714–724.

Nakatani, L. H., & Schaffer, J. A. (1978). Hearing "words" without words: Prosodic cues for word perception. *Journal of the Acoustic Society of America, 63*(1), 234–245.

Nelson, K. (1973). Structure and strategy in learning to talk. *Monographs of the Society for Research in Child Development, 38,* 1–2.

Nelson, K. (1974). Concept, word, and sentence: Interrelations in acquisition and development. *Psychological Review, 81,* 267–285.

Newport, E. L. (1977). Motherese: The speech of mothers to young children. In N. J. Castellan, D. B. Pisoni, & G. Potts (Eds.), *Cognitive theory* (Vol. 2). Hillsdale, NJ: Lawrence Erlbaum Associates.

Newport, E. L. (1981). Constraints on structure: Evidence from American sign language and language learning. In W. A. Collins (Ed.), *Aspects of the development of competence: Minnesota symposia on child psychology* (Vol. 14). Hillsdale, NJ: Lawrence Erlbaum Associates.

Newport, E. L. (1982). Task specificity in language learning? Evidence from speech perception and American Sign Language. In E. Wanner & L. R. Gleitman (Eds.), *Language acquisition: The state of the art.* New York: Cambridge University Press.

Newport, E. L., & Ashbrook, E. F. (1977). The emergence of semantic relations in American sign language. *Papers and Reports on Child Language Development* (Dept. of Linguistics, Stanford University), *13,* 16–21.

Newport, E. L., Gleitman, H., & Gleitman, L. R. (1977). Mother, I'd rather do it myself: Some effects and noneffects of maternal speech style. In C. E. Snow & C. A. Ferguson (Eds.), *Talking to children: Language input and acquisition.* Cambridge: Cambridge University Press.

Newport, E. L., & Supalla, T. (1980). The structuring of language: Clues from the acquisition of signed and spoken language. In U. Bellugi & M. Studdert-Kennedy (Eds.), *Signed and spoken language: Biological constraints on linguistic form.* Dahlem Konferenzen. Weinheim/Deerfield Beach, Fl./Basel: Verlag Chemie.

Palermo, D. S. (1973). More about less: A study of language comprehension. *Journal of Verbal Learning and Verbal Behavior, 12,* 211–221.

Perlmutter, D. M. (1980). Relational grammar. In E. Moravcsik & J. Wirth (Eds.), *Syntax and semantics* (Vol. 13). New York: Academic Press.

Phillips, J. (1970). *Formal characteristics of speech which mothers address to their young children.* Unpublished doctoral dissertation, Johns Hopkins University.

Pinker, S. (1979). Formal models of language learning. *Cognition, 7,* 217–283.

Pinker, S. (1982). A theory of the acquisition of lexical interpretive grammars. In J. Bresnan (Ed.), *The mental representation of grammatical relations.* Cambridge, MA: MIT Press.

Pye, C. (1983). Mayan telegraphese. *Language, 59*(3), 583–604.

Quine, W. V. (1960). *Word and object.* Cambridge, MA: MIT Press.

Read, C., & Schreiber, P. (1982). Why short subjects are harder to find than long ones. In E. Wanner & L. R. Gleitman (Eds.), *Language acquisition: State of the art.* New York: Cambridge University Press.

Roeper, T. (1982). The role of universals in the acquisition of gerunds. In E. Wanner & L. R. Gleitman (Eds.), *Language acquisition: State of the art*. New York: Cambridge University Press.

Rosch, E. (1973). On the internal structure of perceptual and semantic categories. In T. Moore (Ed.), *Cognitive development and the acquisition of language*. New York: Academic Press.

Rosch, E. (1975). Cognitive representation of semantic categories. *Journal of Experimental Psychology: General, 104*, 192–233.

Rosch, E., & Mervis, C. B. (1975). Family resemblances: Studies in the internal structure of categories. *Cognitive Psychology, 7*, 573–605.

Rosch, E., Mervis, C. B., Gray, W. D., Johnson, D. M., & Boyes-Braem, P. (1976). Basic objects in natural categories. *Cognitive Psychology, 8*, 382–439.

Rozin, P., & Gleitman, L. R. (1977). The structure and acquisition of reading II: The reading process and the acquisition of the alphabetic principle. In A. Reber & D. Scarborough (Eds.), *Toward a psychology of reading*. Hillsdale, NJ: Lawrence Erlbaum Associates.

Sachs, J., & Devin, J. (1976). Young children's use of appropriate speech styles in social interaction and role-playing. *Journal of Child Language, 3*, 81–98.

Sankoff, G., & Laberge, S. (1973). On the acquisition of native speakers by a language. *Kivung, 6*, 32–47.

Schieffelin, B. B. (1979). Getting it together: An ethnographic approach to the study of the development of communicative competence. In E. Ochs & B. B. Schieffelin (Eds.), *Developmental pragmatics*. New York: Academic Press.

Schlesinger, I. M. (1971). The production of utterances and language acquisition. In D. I. Slobin (Ed.). *The ontogenesis of grammar: A theoretical symposium*. New York: Academic Press.

Searle, J. R. (1975). Indirect speech acts. In P. Cole & J. Morgan (Eds.), *Syntax and semantics: Vol. 3: Speech acts*. New York: Academic Press.

Shatz, M. (1978). Children's comprehension of question-directives. *Journal of Child Language, 5*, 39–46.

Shatz, M. (1982). On mechanisms of language acquisition: Can features of the communicative environment account for development? In E. Wanner & L. R. Gleitman (Eds.), *Language acquisition: State of the art*. New York: Cambridge University Press.

Shatz, M., & Gelman, R. (1973). The development of communication skills: Modifications in the speech of young children as a function of listener. *Monographs of the Society for Research in Child Development, 38*(5), (whole No. 152).

Skinner, B. F. (1957). *Verbal behavior*. New York: Appleton-Century Crofts.

Slobin, D. I. (1966). The acquisition of Russian as a native language. In F. Smith & C. A. Miller (Eds.), *The genesis of language: A psycholinguistic approach*. Cambridge, MA: MIT Press.

Slobin, D. I. (1973). Cognitive prerequisites for the development of grammar. In C. A. Ferguson & D. I. Slobin (Eds.) *Studies of child language development*. New York: Holt, Rinehart & Winston.

Slobin, D. I. (1977). Language change in childhood and in history. In J. Macnamara (Ed.), *Language learning and thought*. New York: Academic Press.

Slobin, D. I. (1982). Universal and particular in the acquisition of language. In E. Wanner & L. R. Gleitman (Eds.), *Language acquisition: State of the art*. New York: Cambridge University Press.

Slobin, D. I., & Bever, T. G. (1982). Children use canonical sentence schemas: A crosslinguistic study of word order and inflections. *Cognition, 12*(3), 229–266.

Snow, C. E. (1977). Mothers' speech research: From input to interaction. In C. E. Snow & C. A. Ferguson (Eds.), *Talking to children: Language input and acquisition*. New York: Cambridge University Press.

Snow, C., Arlman-Rupp, A., Hassing, Y., Jobse, J., Joosten, J., & Vorster, J. (1976). Mothers' speech in three social classes. *Journal of Psycholinguistic Research, 5*, 1–20.

Snow, C. E., & Ferguson, C. A. (Eds.). (1977). *Talking to children*. Cambridge: Cambridge University Press.

Sorenson, J. M., Cooper, W. E., & Paccia, J. M. (1978). Speech timing of grammatical categories. *Cognition, 6*(2), 135–154.

Spelke, E. S. (1982). Perceptual knowledge of objects in infancy. In J. Mehler, M. F. Garrett, & E. C. Walker (Eds.), *Perspectives in mental representation*. Hillsdale, NJ: Lawrence Erlbaum Associates.

Spring, D. R., & Dale, P. S. (1977). Discrimination of linguistic stress in early infancy. *Journal of Speech and Hearing Research, 20*, 224–231.

Streeter, L. A. (1978). Acoustic determinants of phrase boundary perception. *Journal of the Acoustic Society of America, 64*, 1582–92.

Waxman, S., & Gelman, R. *Preschoolers' use of superordinate relations in classification.* Unpublished manuscript, University of Pennsylvania.

Wexler, K. (1982). A principle theory for language acquisition. In E. Wanner & L. R. Gleitman (Eds.), *Language acquisition: State of the art*. New York: Cambridge University Press.

Wexler, K., & Culicover, P. (1980). *Formal principles of language acquisition*. Cambridge, MA: MIT Press.

Wexler, K., & Hamburger, H. (1973). On the insufficiency of surface data for the learning of transformational languages. In K. Hintikka, J. Moravcsik, & P. Suppes (Eds.), *Approaches to natural languages*. Dordrecht: Reidel.

Wittgenstein, L. (1953). *Philosophical investigations*. New York: Macmillan.

Subject Index

Page numbers followed by n indicate footnotes.

definition of, 462
American Journal of Psychology, The, 17
American Psychiatric Association, *Diagnostic and Statistical Manual* of, 552–554
American Sign Language (ASL), acquisition of, 311–312, 322, 325–326, *see also* Language learning
Amphetamines, hyperactivity and, 572–573
Analysis, *see* Data analysis
Analysis of covariance (ANCOVA), 128
Analysis of variance (ANOVA), 72, 73, 123–127
  hierarchical, 127–128
  multivariate extensions of, 128–129
ANCOVA (analysis of covariance), 128
Androgens, masculine gender role and, 428–429
Androgyny, 416–417, *see also* Sex-role development
Anger, empathic, 512
Animism, 216
ANOVA, *see* Analysis of variance
ANS function, perceptual development and, 169–170
Antidepressants, 572
Anxiety
  deviant acts and, 519
  separation, 366, 373–374
  stranger, 365, 370–373
Anxiety hierarchies, 570
Applied research, 595–625
  child day care and, 598–603
  children of divorce and, 603–605
  current trends in, 597–608
  family life changes and, 597–598
  family support programs and, 605–608
  social policy and, 618
    problems with, 618–620
    strategies for change in, 620–622
    work and family life and, 623–624
  social programs and, 608–617
    evaluation research methods of, 610–613
    evaluation results of, 613–616
    policy implications and, 616–617
Artificiality, in experimentation, 58–59
ASL (American Sign Language), acquisition of, 311–312, 322, 325–326, *see also* Language learning
Assertiveness, sex roles and, 418
Assessment, clinical, differential, 582–583
Assessment data, *see also* Data *entries*
  sources of, 97–98

Attention deficit disorders, 557
Attribution theory, moral development and, 521–523
Attrition, longitudinal studies and, 67
Auditory perception
  conditioned head rotation and, 175–176
  old age and, nature and nurture and, 190–191
Autism, infantile, early, 555–556
Autonomic nervous system, perceptual development and, 169–170
Autonomous morality, 498

B

Baldwin, James Mark, 19–20
Behavior
  adaptive role of, 13
  aggressive, 461, *see also* Aggressive behavior
  maladaptive, *see* Psychopathology
  moral reasoning and, 505–506
  prosocial, 461, *see also* Prosocial behavior
  sex-role, *see* Sex-role development
  social, observations of, 98–102
Behavioral reactions, emotional facilitation of, 360
Behavioral studies of perceptual development, 170–184
  auditory perception and conditioned head rotation in, 175–176
  first vision and corneal reflection in, 171–172
  habituation test in, 176–183
  intermodal perception in, 183–184
  preferences and natural reactions in, 172–175
Behavior analysis, mechanistic tradition and, 27–28
Behaviorism, 210, 362
Behavior therapies, 570–571
Berkeley, George, 155
Biology
  aggression and, 464–465
  altruism and, 465–466
  sex-role development and, 423–433, *see also under* Sex-role development
Biquartimin factor rotation, 131
Blindness, language learning and, 315–316
Bloomfield, Leonard, on language learning, 297–304